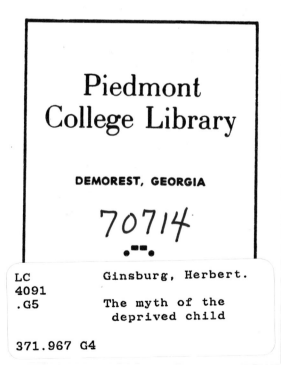

The Myth of
the
Deprived Child

The Myth of
the
Deprived Child

poor children's
intellect
and education

Herbert Ginsburg
Cornell University

Prentice-Hall, Inc., Englewood Cliffs, New Jersey

ISBN: P 0–13–609149–0
      C 0–13–609156–3

Library of Congress Catalog Card Number: 76–166042

Printed in the United States of America

10   9   8   7   6   5   4

Prentice-Hall International, Inc., *London*
Prentice-Hall of Australia, Pty. Ltd., *Sydney*
Prentice-Hall of Canada, Ltd., *Toronto*
Prentice-Hall of India Private Limited, *New Delhi*
Prentice-Hall of Japan, Inc., *Tokyo*

4/4/74 Becker & Tyler 395

To Marlene

The words deprived and disadvantaged may be thought to apply to [poor] children's imagination and their power to create things, and they do not. The tragedy—and for a teacher, the hope and opportunity—is not that children lack imagination, but that it has been repressed and depressed, among other places at school. . . . The power to see the world in a strong, fresh and beautiful way is a possession of all children. And the desire to express that vision is a strong creative and educational force.

KENNETH KOCH

contents

four

Intellectual Abilities   *94*

five

Development   *140*

six

Intellect and the Schools   *190*

References   *240*

Index   *249*

preface

Like many Americans, I belatedly discovered the "crisis in urban education" in the late 1960s. This was a time in the United States when the ghettos were in revolt, when local groups demanded community control of the schools, and when teachers went on strike to protest some of the black community's demands. Black leaders claimed that the schools provide their children with inadequate opportunities to learn. White middle-class parents, feeling that large city public schools are not only inadequate but dangerous, emigrated to the suburbs. Some teachers, believing that ghetto children are unmanageable, demanded (and sometimes got) police protection. Other teachers, alienated by the system, produced a spate of books—for example, Kohl's 36 Children—which inveighed against the schools' oppression and outlined radical solutions.

The crisis in education was not limited to the city's problems, although these naturally received most of the national news coverage. Small town and rural America suffered, too. In Ithaca, New York, a local parents' group formed a "Black Board of Education" to protest the regular school board's policies and practices, especially its alleged failure to provide adequate teaching and guidance for black children. Nearby, in the farm community of Dryden, there were no protests and no overt signs of conflict. But in Dryden many poor rural whites drop out of school, and those who stay in learn little. Most of these children find that education neither enriches their lives nor improves their social and economic position.

Before the crisis in education forced itself into the public consciousness, many educators and psychologists were engaged in attempts to improve poor children's education. Psychologists conducted research on poor children's intellectual abilities and attempted to develop and evaluate new programs of compensatory education. Many teachers experimented with techniques intended to break the cycle of failure associated with poor children's schooling.

Of course these psychological and educational endeavors continue today, and everyone recognizes that it will be a long time before the crisis in education is behind us.

While much of the work on poor children's intellect and education is of great significance, not only for educators and psychologists, but for the public as well, there exist few books which summarize and evaluate recent developments in this area. I try to perform that task in this book. More specifically, my book has several aims.

First, I attempt to describe and evaluate psychological research on poor children's intellect. This is my major endeavor. I devote most of the book to answering the following questions: What is the nature of poor children's mental abilities? How do these abilities develop? Sound answers to these questions are important for a variety of reasons. Perhaps the chief of these is that educational practice is strongly influenced by a psychology of the child. In good measure, teachers teach the way they do because of their beliefs—explicit or implicit—concerning the child's mind and learning. Teachers may think that the young child cannot understand abstractions or that "intelligence" heavily influences school work or that children learn best through concrete activities. These propositions and many others like them obviously have a strong bearing on the teacher's practices in the classroom. It is important then to concentrate on the basic psychological issues—the intellect and learning of the poor child.

My attempt to do this has both positive and negative aspects. On the positive side, I describe what I consider to be the valuable contributions of several researchers. For example, a good portion of Chapter 3 is devoted to a discussion of Labov's work. His studies provide a startling and insightful view of black children's language.

On the negative side, I devote a good amount of space to criticism of research and theories which I consider to be of poor quality. I wish that this task were not necessary, but it is because these studies and theories have been so influential and have even affected educational practice. My criticisms are a reflection of one point of view, namely cognitive theory, which not everyone shares. What this perspective is and what it has to offer will be clear later. For now it is sufficient to emphasize that I am not unbiased, and that my book attempts to promote one point of view and to criticize other approaches. So the first aim of the book is to describe and evaluate attempts to understand poor children's intellect.

The second aim is to analyze and evaluate the psychological assumptions underlying several attempts to improve the quality of poor children's education. In recent years, there have been at least three different approaches to solving the educational crisis. One of these is the compensatory education movement, best exemplified perhaps by Project Head Start. A second is the attempt to improve and make more efficient the methods of traditional education. And a third is the "open classroom," an educational philosophy which has made headway to a considerable extent in Great Britain, and to a lesser extent in the United States. Each of these approaches is based on assumptions concerning poor children's intellectual abilities. I attempt to analyze these assumptions and to determine the extent to which they are accurate and fruitful.

The third aim is to describe the types of work that psychologists can undertake to promote the necessary revolution in education. The situation requires somewhat novel types of psychological-educational research, and I try to describe them and give a few examples. At the same time, we must keep in mind that psychology can give only a limited view of educational problems. Academic failure and success are as much bound up with the city's politics, the community's values, and the teacher's moral sensibility as they are with the child's perception or his motivation. While the psychological point of view can enrich our understanding, we need a larger perspective.

In sum, the book's aims are these: to describe and evaluate psychological research and theory concerning poor children's intellect, to analyze the psychological assumptions underlying several attempts to reform education, and to describe psychology's potential contribution.

To achieve these aims, I have adopted the approach of selective review and analysis. I make no pretense of reviewing the entire literature in any given area. This will be particularly evident in the chapter on IQ testing where I discuss only a few of the literally hundreds of available studies. My strategy is not to be comprehensive, but to concentrate on a few crucial studies and explore the issues in depth. The advantage of this approach is that when used well, it makes possible real analysis and understanding of the issues. The danger is that it can lead to omission of important material and to unwarranted conclusions. The reader will have to decide whether I have succumbed to the dangers.

I have also chosen to supplement the discussion and analysis of the literature with a number of case studies and journalistic reports. The case studies are an unusual form of evidence, if indeed they are given the status of evidence, in cognitive psychology and education. Nevertheless, I believe that they supply valuable information which is not otherwise available. The journalistic reports are also not conventional in a "scientific" book, but again I think they are quite necessary for our overall perspective on the problems of poor children.

The intended audience for this book is anyone with an interest in poor children. I hope that the book will be useful to students, particularly undergraduates, in psychology, education, and related fields. I hope, too, that teachers and educators can read the book with profit; I have tried to keep the psychological jargon to a minimum and to present the material in a clear way.

acknowledgments

Many colleagues, students, and friends (not necessarily mutually exclusive terms) have been kind enough to comment on preliminary versions of the manuscript. Their criticisms have helped me a good deal and have, I hope, improved the quality of this book. Several of these individuals spent long hours in conversation with me about the issues I attempt to discuss: Lorelei Brush, Gregory Lehne, Michael Reigle, Marilyn Samuels, and Robert Speiser. Others were kind enough to provide many helpful comments and even written reviews: Jeffrey Camhi, Terry Dash, Laura Eisenberg, Harry and Susan Fertik, Ezra Heitowit, Dalton Jones, John Kennedy, Jane Knitzer, Edward Mueller, Arden Neisser, Richard Nowagrodski, Sylvia Opper, Joy Osofsky, Halbert Robinson, Lise Wallach, and Mary Wheeler. It goes without saying that they are not responsible for any deficiencies of the book. Hans Furth, Lee Lee, and John Wright prepared extensive reviews of the manuscript prior to publication. I am deeply indebted to them; the reviews were insightful and helpful, and have contributed in no small way to whatever virtues the book may possess.

I owe the greatest debt of gratitude to my wife, Marlene. She contributed in countless ways to the writing of this book. She served as a sensitive critic of each portion as it was written, so that the reader can thank her for the elimination of many defects in style and substance. She also organized the bibliography and references, drew figures, and read many papers and monographs for later inclusion in this book. Most importantly, she provided a compassionate perspective on poor children and their problems in the schools and sustained me through my attempts, difficult as they sometimes were, to come to grips with the real issues. For all these reasons and for many more the book is dedicated to her.

I wish to thank the following publishers and individuals for permission to reprint copyrighted materials in this book:

Certain Language Skills in children. Their development and interrelationships, by M. C. Templin (Minneapolis: University of Minnesota Press, 1957), pp. 88, 89. Reprinted by permission of the University of Minnesota, Copyright © 1957.

"Cognitive development in infants of different age levels and from different environmental backgrounds: an exploratory investigation," by T. D. Wachs, I. C. Uzgiris, and J. McV. Hunt in *Merrill-Palmer Quarterly* (in press, 1971). Reprinted by permission of T. D. Wachs.

"Cognitive elements in maternal behavior," by R. D. Hess and V. Shipman in the *Minnesota Symposia on Child Psychology,* Vol. 1, Edited by John P. Hill (Minneapolis: University of Minnesota Press, 1967), pp. 66, 72, 74. Reprinted by permission of the University of Minnesota, Copyright © 1967.

"Conservation of number in very young children," by B. Rothenberg and R. Courtney, in *Developmental Psychology,* 1969, *1,* p. 497. Reprinted by permission of the American Psychological Association, Copyright © 1969, and B. Rothenberg.

The Disadvantaged Child by M. Deutsch and associates (New York: Basic Books, Inc., 1967), pp. 360–61, 362–64. Reprinted by permission of Basic Books, Inc., Copyright © 1969.

"Early Experience and socialization of cognitive modes in children," by R. D. Hess and V. Shipman, in *Child Development,* 1965, *36,* pp. 877, 878. Reprinted by permission of the Society for Research in Child Development, Copyright © 1965, and R. D. Hess.

"Early intellective training and school performance," by F. H. Palmer. Summary of NIH Grant HD–02253, unpublished manuscript, 1969. Permission to reprint portions of appendix from F. H. Palmer.

"The early training project for disadvantaged children: a report after five years," by R. Klaus and S. Gray, in *Monographs of the Society for Research in Child Development,* 1968, *33,* pp. 1, 8, 15, 16, 20, 21. Reprinted by permission of the Society for Research in Child Development, Inc., Copyright © 1968, and R. Klaus.

Essentials of Psychological Testing, by L. J. Cronbach (New York: Harper and Brothers, 1949, second edition 1960), p. 181. Reprinted by permission of Harper and Row Publishers, Inc., Copyright © 1960.

"Interrelations among learning and performance tasks in disadvantaged children," by H. W. Stevenson, H. M. Williams, and E. Coleman in the *Journal of Educational Psychology* (in press) to be published in June 1971 issue, *62* (No. 3), p. 7. Reprinted by permission of the American Psychological Association, Inc., Copyright © 1971, and H. W. Stevenson.

"Lack of formal schooling, and the acquisition of conservation," by E. Mermelstein and L. S. Shulman in *Child Development,* 1967, *38,* p. 47. Reprinted by permission of the Society for Research in Child Development, Inc., Copyright © 1967, and E. Mermelstein.

The Language of Elementary School Children by W. Loban (Champaign, Illinois: National Council of Teachers of English, 1963), pp. 44, 45,

60. Reprinted by permission of the National Council of Teachers of English, Publishers, Copyright © 1963, and W. Loban.

La Vida by O. Lewis (New York: Random House, 1966), p. xxx, reprinted by permission of Random House, Inc., Copyright © 1966.

"Learning patterns in the disadvantaged," by S. Stodolsky and G. Lesser, in the *Harvard Educational Review,* 1967, 37, p. 572. Reprinted by permission of the Harvard Educational Review and S. Stodolsky, Copyright © 1967 by President and Fellows of Harvard College.

"Mental abilities of children from different social-class and cultural groups," by G. S. Lesser, G. Fifer, and D. H. Clark in *Monographs of the Society for Research in Child Development,* 1965, 30, (4), pp. 60–64. Reprinted by permission of the Society for Research in Child Development, Inc., Copyright © 1965, and G. S. Lesser.

"Mothers as teachers of their own pre-school children: the influence of socioeconomic status and task structure on teaching specificity," by J. E. Brophy in *Child Development,* 1970, 41, p. 89. Reprinted by permission of the Society for Research in Child Development, Inc., Copyright © 1970, and J. E. Brophy.

"Motivational aspects of changes in IQ test performance of culturally deprived nursery school children," by E. Zigler and E. C. Butterfield, in *Child Development,* 1968, 39 (1), p. 7. Reprinted by permission of the Society for Research in Child Development, Inc., Copyright © 1968, and E. Zigler.

"Negro intelligence and selective migration: a Philadelphia test of the Klineberg hypothesis," by E. S. Lee in the *American Sociological Review,* 1951, 16, p. 231. Reprinted by permission of the American Sociological Association, Copyright © 1951, and E. S. Lee.

Problems in Oral English, by W. Loban (Champaign, Illinois: National Council of Teachers of English, 1966), p. 15. Reprinted by permission of the National Council of Teachers of English, Publishers, Copyright © 1966, and W. Loban.

The Psychological Impact of School Experience, by P. Minuchin, B. Biber, E. Shapiro, and H. Zimiles (New York: Basic Books, Inc., 1969), pp. 104, 117, 125, 126. Reprinted by permission of Basic Books, Inc., Copyright © 1969.

The Revision of the Stanford-Binet Scale, by Q. McNemar (Boston: Houghton Mifflin Company, 1942), p. 38. Reprinted by permission of Houghton Mifflin Company, Copyright © 1942.

The School Fix, NYC., USA., by M. Wasserman (New York: Outerbridge and Dienstfrey, 1970), p. 427. Reprinted by permission of Outerbridge and Dienstfrey, Publishers, Copyright © 1970.

"Social class differences in maternal teaching strategies and speech patterns," by H. L. Bee, F. V. Van Egeren, A. P. Streissguth, B. A. Nyman, and M. S. Leckie, in *Developmental Psychology,* 1969, 1, p. 730. Reprinted by permission of the American Psychological Association, Copyright © 1969, and H. L. Bee.

"Social influences on Negro-White intelligence differences," by M. Deutsch and B. Brown in the *Journal of Social Issues*, 1964, *20*, p. 26. Reprinted by permission of the Society for Psychological Study, Copyright © 1964, and M. Deutsch.

"Socio-economic status and intellective performance among Negro preschool boys," by F. H. Palmer, in *Developmental Psychology*, 1970, *3*, pp. 5, 9. Reprinted by permission of the American Psychological Association, Copyright © 1970, and F. H. Palmer.

"The stability of mental test performance between two and eighteen years," by M. P. Honzik, J. W. Macfarlane, and L. Allen in the *Journal of Experimental Education*, 1948, *18*, p. 319. Reprinted by permission of Dembar Educational Research Services, Inc., Copyright © 1948, and M. P. Honzik.

"The standardization of the Wechsler Intelligence Scale for children," by H. Seashore, A. Wesman, and J. Doppelt in the *Journal of Consulting Psychology*, 1950, *14*, p. 108. Reprinted by permission of the American Psychological Association, Inc., Copyright © 1950, and J. E. Doppelt.

"A study of the non-standard English of Negro and Puerto Rican speakers in New York City," by W. Labov, P. Cohen, C. Robins, and J. Lewis. Final Report, U. S. Office of Education Cooperative Research Project No. 3288, New York: Columbia University, 1968. Mimeographed, 2 volumes, pp. 49, 185, 336 in Vol. I, and pp. 36, 69–70, 178, in Vol. II. Reprinted by permission of W. Labov.

Thirty-Six Children by H. Kohl (New York: American Library, Inc., 1967), pp. 24, 35, 54, 55, 109. Reprinted by permission of the World Publishing, an NAL book, Copyright © 1967 by Herbert Kohl.

Wishes, Lies, and Dreams: Teaching Children to Write Poetry, by K. Koch. (New York: Random House, Inc., 1970), p. 46. Reprinted by permission of Random House, Inc., Copyright © 1970.

The Myth of
the
Deprived Child

chapter one

Introduction

In this book I take for granted two simple facts. One is that schools for poor children are not functioning properly, and the second is that poor children often fail in school.

THE SCHOOLS

Here is an account of a visit to one school, perhaps typical of many others.

Rapp Junior High

Driving to the school, I was surprised to find that it was located in a rather pleasant and neat lower-middle-class neighborhood. There were nicely trimmed lawns and frame houses in good repair. This was neither a slum nor a lavish suburb, but an old part of town where people worked hard to keep up property and its value, and to prevent the neighborhood from deteriorating. I found out later that the school's pupils were about 30 percent black. Both blacks and lower-class whites were bussed in from different areas. I also heard that Rapp Junior High was far from the worst school in the city: it was considered about average—not very bad, but not excellent, either.

The building itself was 30 or 40 years old, a plain, box-like structure. The brick walls were a dirty red, apparently with the thickness of a fortress, and were covered at the bottom with crude drawings and graffiti. The courtyard was paved over, windows were smashed, pieces of paper lay about.

I walked through the corridors to check in at the principal's office. A large man in a white shirt and tie, no jacket, stood in the middle of the

hall, arms folded across his chest. He eyed me quietly, even with some sus-
picion, I felt, as he did the children passing through the halls. I was surprised
that even under such surveillance the children—or rather the young men and
women, 12 through 15 years of age—were not scared into silence. Instead
they maintained an atmosphere of constant, low-level violence. They talked
loudly, not quite shouting; they pushed, not quite fighting; they bumped,
not quite brawling. They looked at the adults—the guardian of the corridors
and me—with considerable defiance, and were not about to feign docility.
The battle had certainly escalated since my day when we rebelled by making
faces behind the teachers' backs.

After checking in at the office, I went upstairs to Miss Daley's room,
where a seventh grade math class was due to start at 10:32. Everywhere the
pushing, the shoving, tugging, jabbing, hit and runs of various types were
apparent.

The bell rang and students straggled in, late, but not particularly
apologetic or afraid. They chewed gum. They sat in small groups at moveable desks, blacks mainly at one side, whites on the other, boys together and
girls too. Some of the students began working right away; they seemed to
know what to do without getting the teacher's orders. Other students gos-
siped, kicked now and then, jabbed with a compass. Miss Daley made a
few attempts to maintain discipline—telling one child to stop walking around
the room, another to leave someone else alone—but she did not seem very
concerned with stopping the various conversations or getting everyone to
work. At first I thought she had a relaxed and realistic attitude; later I felt
that she would have liked strict obedience, but had given up on getting it.

The room was quite bare—high ceiling, wood floor, new moveable desks,
a huge slide rule hanging on one wall, a picture of the "universal set" hanging on the other. Some books and papers lay around, but nothing else, no
apparatus to work with, no materials.

Every now and then the school intercom system went on. A voice filled
the room, the teacher spoke to it from wherever she was, lifting her head a
little, but hardly raising her voice. There were not even any buttons to press.

After five or ten minutes, everyone was working, or at least sitting at
a desk on which there was a dittoed worksheet. I found out later that this
was the week's exercise, passed out earlier. It was simply a collection of
problems involving squares and square roots. The students tried to locate
these quantities in a table in their texts. Typically this work was done in
small groups. One student would ask for the square root of, say, 144 and
another would search through the table to find it. From the ongoing conversations, I became convinced that the exercise was merely one of learning
to read the table: many of the students did not know what a square root is;
they were simply reading off numbers from a page, had no idea what the

numbers meant, and were trying to find the trick, the secret, for saying the right words. The teacher walked around the room trying to help anyone who had a problem. To students who had done poorly she gave a little lecture on squares and square roots and on how to use the table, but they did not seem overly concerned with the definitions; they wanted to write down the right number.

The jabbing and talking and walking around increased steadily as the class period went on.

After about 20 minutes, Miss Daley told her class to put away the worksheets and to watch her at the blackboard as she did something new. Everyone was to take out compass, paper, and pencil, and to do as she did.

"Make a straight line. No, it doesn't matter how long it is, just don't let it run off the paper." She did this with chalk on the board. "Mark a point A. No, it doesn't have to be exactly in the middle. Just leave room on both sides. Use the compass to draw an arc. . . ." At each point the students were supposed to imitate. Some made mistakes which were quite stupid. I thought that an 8-year-old could have done most of these things. Many students were once again trying to perform tasks which they did not understand. They were literally drawing lines on paper; their work had nothing to do with geometry.

After making a large number of arcs and lines and points and A's and B's, Miss Daley—and a few of the students—conjured up a right triangle. She interrupted the drawing session to help individual students, to quell disturbances which were becoming more frequent as time went on, to let students go to the bathroom, to let them sharpen their pencils. She seemed to be working very hard now; I thought there was subdued anger in her face, but she was on the whole very patient.

She paced herself well; there were five minutes left, and the triangles were already drawn (more or less), and all that remained was the statement of the Pythagorean theorem. She started lecturing about the hypotenuse and squares and square roots. Now I understood what she was getting at: the arithmetic and geometry *fit together,* and she would demonstrate the connection in the last two minutes, and then the bell would ring and it would be done. Of course, for the majority of students, the connection was about as clear as that between Italian and Spanish when one knows neither. Nevertheless, everything went according to schedule. She wrote the formula on the board in the last two minutes, explained it in a sentence or two, told the students to put away their books and papers, and had to make them wait only a few seconds before the bell rang and they ran—screaming now—into the hall.

A week after my visit to the school, I heard that there were riots in the city. Bands of youths from the junior high schools, including Rapp Junior

High, roamed the streets at night, broke windows, and engaged in racial conflict on a small scale. The schools were shut down for several days and a curfew was imposed.

The Teacher's View

Here are some excerpts of my interview with the teacher.

T (Teacher): Well, the first half of the class isn't too bad. But after that there doesn't seem to be much I can do. I don't give them anything that takes more than 10 to 15 minutes to do. They don't have the attention span and I've gotten them into a real structure. I give them a worksheet the minute they walk in the door. It's usually something they can make an A on. I try hard to make it easy. And they work on that for 10 minutes; then they turn that in and I have a list of things on the board and they do the next one. Then I'll have another worksheet usually on something else altogether. Right now the first worksheet is on division and the next thing is fractions, out of the book.

I (Interviewer): What are they doing in division now?

T: Dividing by two-digit divisors. I've just taken the stuff out of the book and put it on a worksheet; I've found that they work better off worksheets than out of the book. I'll just change a few numbers; I did that for about three days. The next thing, like for today, I gave them six problems and told them if they wanted to make multiplication facts they could, but I didn't put it on paper. Some of them, of course, know that 54 goes into 59 one time. The answer is 11 on the first three problems, so they're real easy and they can do them right in their heads.

I: What do you think of the book, though?

T: I love that book. The only thing that I would like better is if they had put it on worksheet-size pages with room to work the problems so that I could put it on the ditto, every day.

I: Why do you like it? Is it the basic drill aspect of it?

T: The nice thing about it is that what these kids need is drill, drill, drill. They never did learn the basic facts. And I think it's because of progressive math. It wasn't stressed that they should learn what 2 plus 4 was. Instead, every time they go through, it's like proving the theorem that 2 plus 4 is 6. And if you have to prove the thing every time you add up two numbers, you're going to be forever. So they never have learned any of the tables. In this book you don't sit down and write them, either; but they have the problems over and over again. And they look different. That's the good thing. See, they've got little red dots here, and here's a drill here.

I: Do the kids like the book or are they bored, or what?

T: I think they like it pretty much. I kind of ruined it for myself at the beginning of the year. I think they'd like it much better if I had done it differently. But basically I think that they do like it. What happened at the beginning of the year was I had no experience; I tried to take the whole class together, and I did the first two chapters and I decided they were getting nowhere. I decided to let them work on their own. Because the book is simple enough, they can read their own directions and hardly need to ask any questions at all.

I: Do you ever work with any of these different materials that they have available now. Cuisenaire rods for very young kids or Dienes blocks or something?

T: I don't have any of those. I have tried some stuff. I have a series of books that belongs to the math department here that has a lot of different activities in it and often instead of the measuring or one of the 10-minute things I'll do like a 20-minute activity. I've worked with compasses and rulers. They like that. They have projects in this book for geometry, but they're pretty poor. I have a worksheet that I did with all three classes in fact. I have some directions with a drawing—we had practice with this before—and what they were supposed to do was make it bigger. I told them all the directions and they followed them one right after another; they even colored them in.

I: But they don't have learning centers here, like some schools have— math labs where they'll have a lot of stuff.

T: I wish we did. Probably we could have a lot more material up here than we do, but I've been kind of lazy about trying to acquire them and I had no encouragement from the rest of the department; they're pretty . . . stodgy.

I: They want to stay with the textbooks?

T: Yes. Some of the other teachers are young, but they don't seem to want to put any extra effort into it.

I: They want to go through the book?

T: Every morning I run off three or four dittoes and I'm about the only person to use the machine.

I: If you did want to get some of these materials, could you get them easily through the school district, or what?

T: It probably wouldn't be easy; there probably would be a lot of red tape, but I probably could get it if I stuck with it. Special Projects have some of the stuff; I could get some from them. That would probably be easier . . . I inherited this room from a lady who retired last year . . . and she's got *cabinets* of stuff . . . and I haven't even used some of the stuff. Most of it is not related at all to the text. . . . Next year I'll be more secure and I'll have each of the kids work individually on some kind of, as you say, these math learning centers, and come together from time to time as a group or as a small group.

So the teacher is well-meaning; she would like to help the children, and she intends to try out some new approaches. But at the time I spoke with her, her idea of a good lesson was to set the children working at dull drills.

I found out from the teacher that the school uses a tracking system. She told me that there were three groupings: low or "basic"; average or "regular"; and accelerated.

I: When the kids are in one of these tracks, are they in it for all the academic subjects? Or say just for mathematics?

T: They're tracked for each subject separately.

I: Is it common for a kid who's in the regular group for math to be in the accelerated for English?

T: Among the accelerated kids you find very few who are in all accelerated classes so there's quite a bit of variety there. Now most of the kids in the basic classes tend to be basic all the way through. Well, what happens is that the reading skill affects everything including the math. Of course, the social studies and the English are both tracked mostly according to the reading ability. Those two are pretty much overlapped.

Later she was talking about a particular textbook and had this to say:

T: Right now this book has the stigma of being a basic book. I cannot even take drills from the back of the book for my regular class. They see me using this book and say, "We are not a basic class and we will not do those problems." On the other hand, the regular book is a great reinforcer for the basics. If they can see me getting problems out of the regular book, they think they're getting something special.

I: So they know they're basic, too.

T: Oh, yes, everybody knows who they are. One kid just figured it out today.

I: What are the kids in the basic class like?

T: I've got at least three kids who are really poor—the one with the worst skills just freshly arrived from North Carolina. There's a large middle ground, and then I have four or five kids I would like to see in a regular class next year; they're motivated. I don't know why they were put in a basic class except that it is a rule that if they have not finished about level 21 in the elementary school—which is a year behind level—they have to go into basic. They get a letter from their elementary school that says exactly what level they were on when they left.

I: Level on a test, is that it?

T: No, there are 27 levels. There are four or five levels in a class, like in first grade. If they don't pass the 21st level, that means they're still on a fifth grade level.

I: That's on a standard test, is that it? Or teacher's ratings, or what?

T: Well, they work individually and they have a little workbook that they work out of and when they finish with that or when they feel like it they can ask the teacher for a test. She grades the test and if they pass the test they go to the next level. If they don't pass, they do the level again. But supposedly when they finish sixth grade, they will have finished somewhere between 21 and 27 levels.

I: I see. Then depending on where they're at when they leave elementary school they go into a basic class or another.

T: They have an accelerated program in elementary, too, so on the recommendation of the teacher they go into accelerated classes. Some kids are misplaced. They're at that level for no good reason, like the teacher didn't move them. . . . So I have students in here who are very good but they probably couldn't have gone into regular at the beginning of the year because most of them didn't get to addition or fractions.

I: How easy would it be for those to get out of the basic? I mean, are they stuck there for all of junior high school or what can you do?

T: If on two report cards they get A's . . . no, that doesn't work either. What we try to do is move kids around in the first six weeks. Really, a kid who makes A's on two report cards should be moved up, but at that point they're too far behind. The regular classes really build on what they do; and they're going to be a little on the weak side in the first place, so, really, they would just fail.

I: It's really hard to move them out?

T: It's really easy to move them out at the end of the year though.

The Obvious Facts

Nearly everyone agrees that the schools do not function properly, and to a large extent are unsuccessful in coping with the problems of poor children. Rapp Junior High and Miss Daley are perhaps typical in many respects: violence and boredom pervade the schools; the curriculum is dull; the teaching, despite educators' good intentions, is too often unimaginative and sterile; and frequently poor children are locked into a cycle of academic failure from the earliest grades of school. I cite the visit to Rapp Junior High and the interview with Miss Daley only to remind you of these obvious facts.[1]

---

[1] I do not attempt to summarize here the many fine reports on poor children's schools. You should read the original accounts, especially the work of Kozol (1967), Herndon (1968), and Wasserman (1970). Silberman (1970) presents a comprehensive critique of the inadequacies of the current educational system.

POOR CHILDREN'S FAILURE

The second point I take for granted is that poor children, as a group, do quite badly in school. Many studies document this assertion. For example, in 1966 the United States Office of Education undertook a massive investigation of various ethnic and racial groups' educational achievement. James Coleman, a sociologist, and his colleagues collected huge quantities of data from schools throughout the United States (Coleman *et al.*, 1966). The data were in the form of achievement test scores, questionnaire responses, and the like. While some aspects of the report relating to the effects of integration have aroused controversy, one simple fact cannot be challenged: underprivileged children—black, Mexican-American, Puerto Rican, and American Indian—perform quite poorly on almost all measures of academic achievement. Moreover, academic failure increases as the underprivileged child progresses through the school system. Table 1-1 presents some of the Coleman

TABLE 1-1   Number of Grade Levels Behind the Average White
in the Metropolitan Northeast

VERBAL ABILITY

Race and Area	Grade		
	6	9	12
White, nonmetropolitan:			
South	0.7	1.0	1.5
Southwest	.3	.4	.8
North	.2	.4	.9
White, metropolitan:			
Northeast	—	—	—
Midwest	.1	.0	.4
South	.5	.5	.9
Southwest	.5	.6	.7
West	.3	.3	.5
Negro, nonmetropolitan:			
South	2.5	3.9	5.2
Southwest	2.0	3.3	4.7
North	1.9	2.7	4.2
Negro, metropolitan:			
Northeast	1.6	2.4	3.3
Midwest	1.7	2.2	3.3
South	2.0	3.0	4.2
Southwest	1.9	2.9	4.3
West	1.9	2.6	3.9
Mexican American	2.0	2.3	3.5
Puerto Rican	2.7	2.9	3.6
Indian American	1.7	2.1	3.5
Oriental American	.9	1.0	1.6

READING COMPREHENSION

Race and Area	Grade		
	6	9	12
White, nonmetropolitan:			
South	0.5	0.8	1.0
Southwest	.1	.3	.5
North	.2	.3	.5
White, metropolitan:			
Northeast	—	—	—
Midwest	.1	.1	.3
South	.3	.4	.4
Southwest	.4	.7	.4
West	.2	.5	.8
Negro, nonmetropolitan:			
South	2.7	3.7	4.9
Southwest	2.4	3.3	4.5
North	2.2	2.6	3.8
Negro, metropolitan:			
Northeast	1.8	2.6	2.9
Midwest	1.8	2.3	2.8
South	2.1	3.0	3.9
Southwest	2.1	3.0	4.1
West	2.1	3.1	3.8
Mexican American	2.4	2.6	3.3
Puerto Rican	3.1	3.3	3.7
Indian American	2.0	2.3	3.2
Oriental American	1.0	.9	1.6

MATHEMATICS ACHIEVEMENT

Race and Area	Grade		
	6	9	12
White, nonmetropolitan:			
South	0.7	0.9	1.4
Southwest	.3	.3	.8
North	.2	.1	.8
White, metropolitan:			
Northeast	—	—	—
Midwest	.1	.0	.1
South	.4	.6	1.2
Southwest	.6	.7	.6
West	.3	.3	.8
Negro, nonmetropolitan:			
South	2.6	3.7	6.2
Southwest	2.4	3.2	5.6
North	2.2	2.8	5.2
Negro, metropolitan:			
Northeast	2.0	2.8	5.2
Midwest	2.1	2.5	4.7
South	2.4	3.1	5.6
Southwest	2.3	3.0	5.7
West	2.4	3.1	5.3
Mexican American	2.2	2.6	4.1
Puerto Rican	2.8	3.4	4.8
Indian American	2.0	2.4	3.9
Oriental American	1.0	.4	.9

Source: Coleman *et al.*, 1966, pp. 273-75.

report data concerning achievement in verbal skills, reading, and mathematics. The scores in the table refer to the number of grade levels children from other areas fall *behind* the average white child from the metropolitan areas of the Northeast United States. We see, for example, that in the area of mathematics achievement, the average black student in the Northeast metropolitan area is 2.0 years behind the average white student in the sixth grade, and 5.2 years behind in the twelfth grade. Of course, the figures in the Coleman report are averages: there are obviously many black students who receive higher achievement test scores than the typical white, and there are many white students who receive scores lower than blacks. Nevertheless, the group trends are clear: Coleman's research shows that underprivileged children of several races and ethnic groups generally perform poorly in the public schools.

It is hard to know how to react to statistics of this sort. On the one hand, we have learned to distrust them since they can easily be manipulated to prove absurd propositions. Also, the scores on which these statistics are based—standardized tests of achievement—are often poor measures of children's knowledge (I shall try to demonstrate this contention later). On the other hand, there are some considerations which lead us to take the statistics seriously. One is that ordinary observation supports the statistical conclusions. In everyone's city or town, poor children have a difficult time in school. Another reason for accepting the validity of the statistics is that they are so consistent and widespread. For example, as I wrote this, there appeared in the local newspaper (*Ithaca Journal,* 1970) an article describing a New York State Pupil Evaluation Program. All students in Ithaca were given reading and arithmetic achievement tests over a period of several years, and the results showed children in poor, rural neighborhoods (Caroline, Enfield) and in poor urban neighborhoods containing both whites and blacks (Central, St. John) to be less competent than children in the middle-class suburban areas (Cayuga Heights, Belle Sherman). These social-class differences in achievement occur despite the fact that the Ithaca school system, which has the reputation of high quality, has tried in various ways to eliminate them.

The statistical data, as well as the evidence of our senses, should convince us that there exists a widespread problem with respect to the education of the poor. But test scores are merely an abstract summary of performance on examinations. By their very nature the scores cannot capture most of what it means for a poor child to do badly in school. Academic failure is not just getting low grades on tests. For the child, it often means frustration, guilt, and despair. It means the waste of many years in a painful situation. While psychologists have had little to say about experiences like these, we must not forget them.

We should not forget too that there are many different kinds of "poor children." (I use that phrase because it is relatively simple and direct, especially in comparison with terms such as "lower-socioeconomic status" or "culturally deprived.") The category includes Puerto Ricans, urban blacks, rural southern whites, and so on. While these groups share a common poverty and oppression, and usually achieve little success in the current social system, they clearly differ from one another in important ways. Further, it is obvious that people *within* the groups—no matter how narrowly we define them—differ from one another, too. I cannot continually keep reminding the reader of these obvious facts; I hope I remember them myself and make the necessary distinctions where I should.

THE ISSUES

Our starting point, then, is that the current situation is unacceptable. It is obvious that drastic reforms must be effected. But what these should entail is not at all clear.

Approaches to Education

Some writers have emphasized various forms of compensatory education as a solution to the educational crisis. Their thesis is that on entrance to school poor children are intellectually deficient and that this handicap must be removed before any measure of academic success is possible. A second proposal, not necessarily exclusive of the first, is that the educational crisis can be solved, or at least ameliorated, by improving traditional forms of education. In this view, the educational system should be made far more efficient than it is today, but its fundamental nature need not be challenged. A third proposal, which is now receiving considerable attention, is that changes in the very foundations of education are necessary for significant improvement to occur. In this view, we need a new spirit of freedom in the schools; we need an openness to change; and we need a redefinition of the aims and techniques of education.

Each of these proposed solutions is based on a psychology of the poor child. The compensatory education movement assumes that his intellectual abilities are deficient. For example, Klaus and Gray's (1968) Early Training Project (discussed at greater length in Chapter 4) proposes that the poor child at the age of 4 or 5 years is characterized by inadequate speech and that this may hamper his later work in school. As a result, Klaus and Gray's nursery school offers instruction in the elementary uses of language. The Project also assumes that the poor child's perception is deficient and that this too may diminish the chances for later academic success. To remedy this deficiency, the Klaus and Gray program offers instruction in perception in which an attempt is made to get children to see the differences among elementary stimuli.

The traditional education view is based on several psychological assumptions. For example, suppose a school attempts to improve the reading scores of poor children by introducing a new "phonics" approach (a method which attempts to get children to learn the sounds of the letters). The teacher introduces to the classroom a new primer, gives lessons in sounding, and judges the success of her efforts by the students' performance on certain standardized achievement tests. This approach assumes, among other things, that children's learning needs to be controlled and motivated by an adult, that a large group of children can be interested in reading at the same time, and that the children can learn at roughly the same pace.

Proponents of the third approach to educational reform, that of the "open classroom," propose a view of the child which is different from that held by advocates of compensatory education and of traditional schools. On the one hand, the open classroom assumes that poor children are not intellectually deficient; on the other it assumes that they are naturally motivated to learn and can in good measure control the process of learning themselves. For example, Herbert Kohl (1967), whose work is discussed in Chapter 3, developed an open classroom based on the belief that his elementary school students in Harlem could read and write interesting literature when they were given a large amount of freedom to do so.

Which set of psychological assumptions is correct, or at least closest to the truth? Is the poor child intellectually deficient or normal? Can he learn in a self-directed way or does he require instruction? In general the question is this: What is the nature of poor children's intellect and how does it develop? That is the question we must attempt to answer in this book.

Unfortunately psychology does not speak with a clear voice on these issues. Just as there are several approaches to poor children's education, so there have been several theories of poor children's intellectual development. Consider now an outline of the major positions and of the controversies which surround them.

Poor Children's Intellect

Many psychologists believe—mistakenly, I think—that the poor child's intellect is deficient, although they disagree to some extent on the precise nature of the deficiency.

The *nativists* have traditionally asserted that poor children are characterized by inadequate "intelligence" as measured by the IQ test. Intelligence refers to a basic mental capacity which is at the root of the child's learning, his thinking, and his problem-solving. Intelligence is the fundamental intellectual ability, the basic power of the mind. Superior intelligence permits the child to cope with the environment and to profit from experience. Deficient intelligence hinders both adaptation and learning.

The *empiricists* generally place less emphasis on general intelligence and tend to stress the role of specific intellectual abilities. For example, many empiricists propose that poor children employ an impoverished mode of speech which in turn degrades thought. In this view, the poor child uses a "restricted code"—a language which is simple and terse, containing few abstractions. Lower-class speech is emotional, not intellectual; it is authoritarian, not reasonable; it is concrete, not abstract. Speech of this type is not a good vehicle for complex thinking, for logical reasoning, for considered judgments. Deficient speech produces deficient thought: the poor child's language produces an intellect which is overly concrete and illogical and which bases its judgments on emotion rather than reason. It should therefore come as no surprise that the poor child, burdened as he is with a restricted language and a deficient intellect, cannot succeed in academic endeavor.

At first the nativist and empiricist positions seem quite reasonable, either alone or in combination. Yet closer examination reveals serious flaws in each argument.

There is a great deal of confusion regarding the notion of intelligence as it is usually employed by the nativists. Try to define what "intelligence" is. When people do this, they generally succeed in producing two or three definitions which are at odds with one another or which at least seem to refer to different things. For example, is intelligence the ability to engage in abstract reasoning or to profit from experience? Is it the ability to adapt to the environment or to use verbal and symbolic skills? Confusion over the meaning of intelligence is not limited to the lay public. David Wechsler, a leading worker in the area of intelligence testing and the originator of the Wechsler Intelligence Scale, writes as follows:

> Some psychologists have come to doubt whether these laborious analyses have contributed anything fundamental to our understanding of intelligence while others have come to the equally disturbing conclusion that the term intelligence, as now employed, is so ambiguous that it ought to be discarded altogether. Psychology seems now to find itself in the paradoxical position of devising and advocating tests for measuring intelligence and then disclaiming responsibility for them by asserting "nobody knows what the word really means" (Quoted in Tuddenham, 1962, pp. 470–71).

This confusion is obviously quite damaging to the nativist position. How can intelligence be so fundamental, so basic, when after years of research "nobody knows what the word really means"? How can a presumably scientific psychology employ so ephemeral a concept as that of intelligence to explain poor children's academic failure? And if poor children's IQ is relatively low, what does that fact mean?

The empiricist view also suffers from serious deficiencies. For one thing, the research evidence is full of contradictions. Some studies seem to support the empiricist view. They show that poor children's intellectual performance on a variety of measures is inadequate to some degree. But other research efforts support a different conclusion. They show that poor children's language and thought are generally no different from middle-class children's abilities in these areas. Moreover, one can make the argument that the empiricist position suffers from the limits of a middle-class perspective. For example, some empiricists ask whether poor children are capable of the kind of speech that the middle class happens to consider congenial. The empiricists generally do not attempt to determine whether poor children use a language which is both distinctive and well suited to their own environment.

These considerations raise many questions. Chief among them is whether poor children's intellect is really deficient. If not deficient, is it at least different from that of middle-class children?

In Chapters 2, 3, and 4, I attempt to deal with many of these issues—with the nature of poor children's cognition, their intelligence, language, and thought. I try to probe the nativist and empiricist positions, to identify defects in their reasoning, and to evaluate both the evidence which supports their arguments and the evidence which contradicts them.

My conclusion, which I call the *developmental view,* is that in many fundamental ways poor children's cognition is quite similar to that of middle-class children. There are *cognitive universals,* modes of language and thought shared by all children (except the retarded and severely emotionally disturbed) regardless of culture or upbringing. At the same time, there do exist social-class differences in cognition. Yet the differences are relatively superficial, and one must not make the mistake of calling them deficiencies or considering them analogous to mental retardation.

Development

If for the sake of argument we grant the conventional wisdom that poor children's intellect is deficient, we must next consider how this deficiency comes about. What causes low intelligence, or restricted speech, or inadequate reason?

In the nativist view, differences in intelligence are largely innate. Heredity determines the ultimate level of intelligence, so that the environment can exert but little influence on intellectual functioning. Intelligence is fixed at birth, or at least early in life; and if the child has a low IQ there is little that anyone can do to change it. Even special training or remedial education cannot materially improve the child's intelligence.

Here is where the empiricist view differs most strongly from the nativist. The empiricists assert that the poor child grows up in an environment which is "deprived" in a variety of ways. The home may contain few toys, books, or other forms of stimulation.[2] More importantly, the social environment is also impoverished. The mother talks little to the child and often communicates through facial expression or intonation, rather than through speech. When she does talk, it is in the "restricted code," described earlier, which is inadequate for both communication and thought. All this is not without effect on the poor child. During the formative years (birth to 5) the deprived environment retards his speech and thought, producing a massive intellectual deficiency from which he cannot easily recover.

Again I think that the nativist and empiricist views are in error. In the case of the nativist position, it now seems clear that the environment exerts strong effects on intellectual growth, particularly early in life. An extreme form of nativism is simply incorrect. This is not to deny, of course, that biological factors are influential too. For example, certain kinds of mental retardation are clearly due to genetic factors, and no amount of education or training can remove the deficit. Chapter 2 reviews the evidence concerning the nativist position.

The empiricist position is defective in a variety of ways. First, is it really the case that poor children's environment is deprived? Once again I must raise the possibility that a middle-class perspective prevents researchers in the empiricist tradition from appreciating the richness of the lower-class environment. Certainly a slum is not a pleasant place to live in, and certainly the middle class does not approve of much that occurs there. But this does not necessarily imply that the slum is not a stimulating environment in its own way. Like other environments, it contains sounds and shapes and it presents obstacles to surmount. In some respects, living in the slum requires a sharper intellect than that required to survive in middle-class suburbs.

Second, there is almost no research evidence showing that poor children's environment is deprived. The empiricists generally assume the deprivation but do not bother to study it in any detail.

Third, the empiricists' arguments concerning the effects of deprivation may be quite irrelevant if—as I believe to be the case—poor children's intellect is not fundamentally deficient. If this is so, then the empiricists not only give the wrong answer, they also ask the wrong question. The real issue is not why poor children are deficient, but why they develop as well as they do.

This is the question which the developmental view seeks to answer. The fact seems to be that poor children develop an adequate intellectual life. As I pointed out earlier, certain features of cognition are universal. All children learn certain aspects of language, and, at the same time, poor children's cognition is in some respects distinctive. For example, they may speak a dialect which the middle class finds difficult to understand.

---

[2] Other empiricists have claimed that the lower-class home contains *too much* stimulation and that this produces the same deficiencies as a deprived environment. Presumably, the lower-class home contains too much noise and general chaos.

Why do the cognitive universals develop and why are there social-class differences? According to the developmental view both these features are the inevitable results of biological adaptation to the environment. By virtue of their humanity, poor children are active organisms. Like everyone else, they organize their own learning, they are curious about the world, they practice what needs to be learned, they work out a reasonable adjustment to the environment. Poor children take an active role in devising solutions to the reality which confronts them.

In some ways, these solutions must be the same as those developed by other children. In the early years, all children encounter adult languages which, despite cultural differences, are similar in basic grammatical form. As a result of their biological nature, all children, again regardless of culture, develop languages which share a remarkable similarity in grammatical form.

At the same time, poor children live in a unique environment. They hear a distinctive dialect; they must solve problems that middle-class children cannot even imagine; they suffer special kinds of oppression; they often live in despair. These are all distinctive conditions with which the poor, but not some others, must cope and for which they develop special accommodations, unique ways of behaving and thinking. The result of all this is that poor children must in some respects be different from middle-class children. Chapter 5 reviews the empiricist and developmental views on these matters.

Frameworks for Education

After proposing a theory of poor children's intellect and its development, I shall attempt to apply it to problems of education. At the outset, I should emphasize that psychological theories do not and cannot provide comprehensive and detailed solutions to the educational crisis. For one thing, education is to a large extent a question of values, and psychology cannot settle issues of this type. For another, education must be concerned with details of teaching and curricula, and these are not the traditional or proper subject matter for psychology. Nevertheless, psychological theory can offer a framework for educational practices. It can provide a perspective on poor children and the ways in which they learn, and this perspective can serve as a rational basis for reform in education.

Chapter 6 attempts to apply what was presented earlier in the book to the three major approaches to educating poor children. I attempt to determine whether the assumptions underlying each educational approach make sense in terms of what we know about poor children's intellect and its development.

I argue that the psychological theory forming the basis for compensatory education is incorrect. Poor children are not intellectually deficient or poorly motivated to learn. Therefore, education need not concentrate on removing these nonexistent deficiencies. Moreover, there is little reason to suppose that early compensatory education can have long-range effects. Why should a child's nursery school experience affect his performance in school 5 years later?

Similarly, traditional education approaches are based on several faulty assumptions. One is that the child's knowledge is a simple quantitative trait, like height, and that this knowledge can best be measured by standardized testing procedures. Traditional approaches are based to a large extent on illusions concerning what children learn. A second faulty assumption is that knowledge is most effectively acquired through systematic instruction. There may be some cases where this is true, but most often it is not. Genuine intellectual work in many areas—writing, mathematics, science—often proceeds best on a relatively self-directed and intrinsically motivated basis.

The psychological assumptions underlying the open classroom seem generally consonant with what we know about children's intellect and their development. The open school assumes that the child is an active learner, that he strives to make sense out of his world, and that he is a natural intellectual. Developmental theory agrees with these propositions and presents a good deal of evidence supporting them. Yet the open school is still in an experimental, formative stage of development. It holds out the promise of hope, but there is still much to be done.

The Psychologist's Role

How can the psychologist help to promote the necessary reforms in education? In the past decade or so, many psychologists have begun to feel that their discipline has come of age and has something to contribute to problems of education. The question now is not *whether* psychology can be "relevant" but *how* it should be relevant. In Chapter 6, I outline three approaches to this problem, two "basic" and one "applied." One approach is entirely obvious and yet bears some emphasis. The approach involves basic research into child psychology. While this approach is clearly necessary, I attempt to show how it can be made more relevant to teachers than it usually is. Second, we need basic research into educational problems. An example is the psychology of reading and of mathematics. Unfortunately, not enough of this type of work has yet been undertaken. Third, we need applied research into educational issues. We need to "evaluate" educational experiments. Much of this type of work has, of course, been conducted by educational psychologists. Yet we need more applied research, and not only that, we need to infuse it with a new spirit of openness. Evaluational research should focus on much more than the standard test.

These then are the major issues and the basic theoretical positions. Let us now explore them in some depth.

chapter two

The IQ

The IQ test has traditionally played an important role in research on poor children's intellect and in the measurement of academic potential and achievement. This chapter attempts to provide an understanding of the IQ test and of the research which uses it to study poor children. We begin with a description of the Stanford-Binet, a typical IQ test, so that the reader will be familiar with its content and method of administration.

ADMINISTERING THE TEST

Several years ago, I gave IQ tests and other examinations to 4-year-old children in local Head Start programs. My work was a small part of a study by the Educational Testing Service, which was under contract with the Federal Government to conduct an "evaluation" of Head Start programs around the country. I will try, below, to present a picture of the typical administration of the IQ test in this program.

I arrived at the Head Start Center and went immediately to see the head teacher, who had been informed in advance of the purpose of my visit. I gave her a list of children I wished to see and asked for a quiet place in which to do the testing. Usually I was shown to an empty classroom, and before seeing the children spent some time preparing the test materials and reviewing the test manual. I found this essential since the Stanford-Binet IQ test, like other individually administered tests, is not easy to give: the examiner must memorize a long series of test items, as well as the answers to them, and must be thoroughly familiar with the concrete materials—such as blocks or puzzles—that constitute some of the test items. The examiner must keep track of the right and wrong answers, must decide which questions to ask and when to ask them, and at the same time must maintain rapport with the child.

Usually I went to get the child myself. I felt this was better than his simply being deposited at my doorstep. I would go into the classroom, find out from the teacher who the child was, and then ask him if he would like to "play some games with me." Children show different reactions to a request such as this, which almost all examiners use in some form. Young children, in nursery school or kindergarten, often appear quite apprehensive when a strange adult—who is sometimes called "doctor"—puts the question to them. It is, after all, an absurd situation: strange adults do not often seek the company of children for games or anything else; the request must be threatening or at least unsettling. Other young children are quite thrilled about the prospect of a game, particularly if they previously have been subjects for experiments or tests. The children know that the test may be fun, or at least not painful, and that there may be rewards—candy, trinkets, etc. In fact, children at university nursery schools, who often serve in experiments, are sometimes so jaded by their experiences that before agreeing to participate, they negotiate the reward with the experimenter. I once heard the daughter of a well-known psychologist ask the potential experimenter: "How many reinforcements am I going to get today?"

I find that older children are generally somewhat suspicious of individual tests—that is, examinations given to one child at a time—since they are apart from the natural order of things. They are not given to all children, but only to those few who, for some reason, are in trouble of one kind or another. The school psychologist gives an individual IQ test if a student is suspected of retardation, if he is a severe behavior problem—in short, only if the situation is drastic. A child usually knows this in his own way. He can sense when matters are serious, and when something out of the ordinary is about to occur, especially when he himself is involved. So the older child is wary, suspicious, frightened. The examiner's attempt to be friendly means nothing. The child knows that he is not there to play games, and he is used to adult dishonesty.

On the way to the testing room, and once we were in it, I usually engaged the child in conversation about his brothers and sisters, his favorite games, and his best friends. The aim was to find some topic about which the child, 4 years of age, might talk with pleasure and animation, some device by which we would establish rapport so that the real work could begin. I seldom succeeded, however. Usually the conversation was only empty ritual.

P (Psychologist): How many brothers and sisters do you have?
C (Child): Two.
P: Are they older than you or younger?
C: Older.
P: How old?

C: One is 7 and the other is 9½.
P: Do they play with you a lot?
C: Sometimes.
P: What games do you like to play best?
C: I don't know.
P: Oh, I'll bet you like some games best of all.
C: Sometimes we watch "Captain Kangaroo."
P: That's a good program. . . .

Eventually the test had to be started. "Today, we're going to play some games." I opened the testing kit. The Stanford-Binet materials are conveniently packed in a special briefcase, with compartments for the examiner's manual, the blocks, the puzzle pieces, and so on. There is a wide array of test problems, graded in terms of difficulty for various age levels. The standard procedure is to begin with tests of moderate difficulty—the child should be able to pass some but not all. At the outset, the examiner can only guess what these tests may be. If the child is 5 years of age, the examiner first tries out several 5-year test items. If the child passes these too easily, the examiner then gives him harder items, 6- or 7-year tests. If the 5-year tests are too hard, the examiner then selects items from the 3- or 4-year-old levels.

I began with 4-year-old test items. The first item at this age level is "picture vocabulary." The child is shown a series of pictures on 2 by 4 inch cards—e.g., cup, book, jacket, etc.—and he is asked, "What's this? What do you call it?" In the examiner's manual, some examples of correct and incorrect responses are given. For example, when shown a picture of a coat, the child may answer "coat" or "jacket," but he is wrong if he says "suit" or "shirt" or "overcoat." If the 4-year-old gives the correct answers to at least 14 pictures (from a total of 18), then he is considered to have passed the test "item." In examining a 4-year-old, I usually worked briskly, not wasting any time, to avoid boring the child or stretching out the test beyond his endurance. This meant that in giving picture vocabulary, I had only a few minutes to present each card, score the child's response, turn to the next card, score the response again, and finally add up all of the successes and failures to see if the child passed the item. If he watched at all—and most children did—the child saw me flip through the pages of the picture vocabulary booklet, make little marks on the examination form, occasionally look at the examiner's manual, keep an eye on him, put the picture vocabulary booklet back in the briefcase, and finally emerge with a new booklet or set of toys.

At the 4-year-old level, the second item is "naming objects from memory." I took from the briefcase several small toys. I asked the child what each was called and accepted whatever name he gave, even if wrong. Then I placed three of the objects—for example, lion, ball, block—in a row and said, "Now shut your eyes tight so that you can't see them." I placed a screen, also part of the standard test equipment, in front of the objects just in case the child did not close his eyes. Then I covered one of the three toys with a small box. "Open your eyes. Look! Which one did I hide?" The child must say the name of the hidden object, and not just point to it. I repeated the procedure twice, each time, of course, with different objects. The child must succeed on at least two of the three problems to pass the hidden-object test.

The examination ranges through a variety of tests. There are analogies ("Father is a man; sister is a . . ."), similarities and differences ("See these things that are just alike? Here's one that is *not* like the others. Put your finger on the one that is not like the others."), definitions, copying geometric figures, memory tasks, number concepts, memory for stories, comprehension, interpretation of proverbs, and so on. In each case, the examiner must present the questions exactly in the manner set forth in the manual. Since no deviation is permitted, the examiner usually memorizes the questions or reads them from the manual. If the child fails to understand, the examiner may sometimes repeat a question, but in general should not rephrase it or give additional help. If the child wants to know whether his answer was right or wrong, the examiner cannot tell him. Administration of the test must be standard; if it is not, then one child's score is not comparable to another's. The Stanford-Binet was one of the earliest and most successful IQ tests. It is usually seen as a standard against which other IQ tests must prove themselves. As a result many IQ tests are highly similar to the Stanford-Binet and to one another. Most of the points I raise in this chapter apply to the great majority of IQ tests.

Standard testing can lead to absurdities. I remember many children who were nonresponsive, refusing to work at the test. They got most answers wrong, but I was sure that they knew much more than the test showed. I remember other children who had difficulty with one particular item. For various reasons I felt they simply did not understand what I wanted them to do; if they did understand, then they could solve the problem. Many examiners are, of course, aware of these difficulties. If they feel that the child is not trying, they discount the score and perhaps give the test again another time. But the canons of standardized testing prevent them from modifying the testing procedure itself: this must be done in one way, and in one way only.

After giving two items, I still had a long way to go. At each age level (2, 2.5, 3, 3.5, 4, 4.5, 5, 6, 7 . . . 14, average adult, superior adult I, superior adult II, superior adult III) there are six problems, each of which may contain several parts, as in the case of picture vocabulary or hidden objects. Some problems are repeated at several age levels. For example, the same vocabulary test is given at years 6, 8, 10, 12, 14 and adult. To pass at the 6-year level, the child must get at least six correct; to pass at the 10-year level, he must be able to define 11 of the words, and so on. In testing a child I had to work in two directions. First, I needed to determine the level at which he failed all the tests. For example, suppose my 4-year-old passed 4 of the 6 tests at the 4-year level. Then I had to give him the 4.5 year tests, then the 5, then the 6, until he failed all 6 items at a certain age level. Once this was established, I worked in the other direction. I went back to the 3.5-year level, then the 3-year level, etc., until he passed all six of the tests at a given level. Once this was determined, the examination was over. For a young child, it can be lengthy and taxing; the same holds true for the examiner.

So now the child has been tested. He has passed some problems and failed others. He has defined eight words correctly (at least by the examiner's criteria), he has given the proper analogies, he has failed to locate the hidden object, and so on. The examiner escorts him from the room, assuring the child that he did quite well. After the child is gone, the examiner determines his IQ. While the computation of the IQ score involves certain statistical complexities, the basic rationale is quite simple. If a 4-year-old passes most of the items at the 4-year level and below, and in addition succeeds at some tests from higher levels, his score will be above 100, which is the average. If he fails many items at the 4-year level and below, then the score will be below 100. The test is constructed in such a way that a certain percentage of children at a given age level get scores below 80, a certain percentage below 90, and so on.

As the day went on, my administration of the test changed in subtle ways. While following the standard procedures, I tended to rush with the last few children. Perhaps I sometimes did not encourage them enough, or did not give them sufficient time to respond. The children, too, got more tired as the day went on; maybe they did not try as hard, either. In any event, I completed the testing and said goodbye to the teacher. Neither she nor the children would ever know what the "evaluation" revealed.

This, then, is an example of the IQ test. We can now turn to a consideration of social-class differences. Are poor children less "intelligent" than middle-class children?

THE FACTS OF SOCIAL-CLASS DIFFERENCE

It is a fact that after infancy, poor children as a group have a lower IQ than middle-class children.

Consider first the lack of social-class differences in infancy. Bayley (1965) has conducted the most comprehensive and careful study in this area. She administered the Bayley Scales of Mental and Motor Development —an infant IQ test—to 1,409 infants, from 1 to 15 months of age. The subjects were carefully selected so as to be representative, in terms of social class and race, of all infants in the United States. Bayley found that in the first 15 months of life, the average scores of infants from different social classes are essentially the same.

This is not true, however, of older children. Investigators have repeatedly shown that poor children receive lower scores on IQ tests than do middle- or upper-class children. Table 2-1 presents McNemar's (1942) data

TABLE 2-1   Mean Stanford-Binet IQs of 2,757 Children
Classified According to Paternal Occupation

		Chronological Age of Child			
	Father's Occupation	*2.5–5.5*	*6–9*	*10–14*	*15–18*
I.	Professional	114.8	114.9	117.5	116.4
II.	Semiprofessional and Managerial	112.4	107.3	112.2	116.7
III.	Clerical, Skilled Trades, and Retail Business	108.8	104.9	107.4	109.6
IV.	Rural Owners	97.8	94.6	92.4	94.3
V.	Semiskilled, Minor Clerical, and Minor Business	104.3	104.6	103.4	106.7
VI.	Slightly Skilled	97.2	100.0	100.6	96.2
VII.	Day Labor, Urban, and Rural	93.8	96.0	97.2	97.6

Source: McNemar, 1942, p. 38.

on the Stanford-Binet intelligence test. The table shows that shortly after infancy there are significant social-class differences in IQ. At ages 2 through 5.5, for example, the average IQ for children of professional parents (doctors, lawyers, etc.) is 114.8, whereas the average IQ for children whose fathers perform day labor is 93.8. At ages 15 through 18, a similar difference is found: the averages are 116.4 and 97.6, with the poor children receiving the lower score.

The same pattern exists in the case of race differences. Bayley found that black infants (again from 1 to 15 months) receive essentially the same scores on the Scales of Mental Development as do white children. In the case of the Motor Development Scales, black infants score higher than whites at months 3, 4, 5, 7, 9, and 12. At the other months, the average scores for the two groups are about the same.

As black children grow older, however, their average IQ decreases. Deutsch and Brown (1964) studied the IQs of a large number of first and fifth graders in New York City. The investigators found that white children, combined across all social classes, have an average IQ of 103.88, whereas black children, again from all social-class groups, have an average IQ of 94.32.

How can we evaluate this racial difference? First, we must be clear on what an average difference means. Table 2-2 presents data concerning class

TABLE 2-2   Frequency Distribution of Lower- and Middle-Class Children's Scores
on the Performance Scale of the Wechsler IQ Test

	Number of Children	
Performance IQ	Professional	Lower Class
150–154	—	—
145–149	1	—
140–144	1	—
135–139	—	—
130–134	3	—
125–129	16	4
120–124	13	3
115–119	22	7
110–114	31	7
105–109	21	12
100–104	20	17
95–99	18	15
90–94	15	27
85–89	8	10
80–84	1	5
75–79	4	8
70–74	1	3
65–69	1	4
60–64	—	—
TOTAL		
Number	176	122
Mean	107.8	96.9
SD	13.4	13.7

Source: Seashore, Wesman, and Doppelt, 1950, p. 108.

differences on the Wechsler IQ test. We see from the table that children of professional parents received an average IQ of 107.8 and that children of lower-class parents (domestic, protective, and other service workers) had an average of 96.9. The table clearly shows that not all of the poor children had scores lower than those obtained by the middle-class children. There were many poor children—50/122 or 41 percent—with scores above 100 (the national average); and there were many poor children who did better than middle-class children. The spread of scores was large in both cases. All of this is to say that one must interpret average differences carefully. The average is an abstraction which describes one characteristic of a *group*; the statistic does not describe all the group's *individuals*, whose scores depart from the average in various amounts.

Second, we must consider the possibility that in Deutsch and Brown's study the racial difference is only apparent: it may be the spurious result of blacks' disproportionate membership in the lower class. The argument is as follows: We know that a higher proportion of Negroes than whites is poor.

We know, too, that poor people receive lower IQs than do others. In view of these facts, is it not possible that blacks receive a lower IQ than whites simply because the former are poorer than the latter, and not for any other reason? By this argument, there should be no IQ differences between poor blacks and poor whites, between middle-class whites and middle-class blacks, and so on. Deutsch and Brown investigated this possibility, and Table 2-3 pre-

TABLE 2-3   Race and Class Differences in IQ Scores

Group	Mean IQ
SES I	
White	97.24
Negro	91.24
SES II	
White	105.59
Negro	94.87
SES III	
White	114.92
Negro	102.57

Source: Deutsch and Brown, 1964, p. 26.

sents their data. The results show that poor blacks (SES I) receive lower IQ scores than do poor whites, and the same difference is found in the case of the other social classes as well. It would appear then that while social class contributes to IQ differences, so does race: we conclude this because blacks at each social-class level receive lower IQ scores than do whites.

At this point, some people find it easy to accept the conclusion that the difference between the races must be the result of genetic factors. If social class cannot explain the results, then the cause of blacks' lower IQ scores must lie in the biology of race; blacks must inherit a relatively weak intelligence. In a later section of this chapter, we will deal with the problem of inheritance of the IQ. For now, I wish only to call attention to some of the problem's complexities. It is not so easy to demonstrate that genetic factors are responsible for racial difference in IQ. There are many reasons. To prove that genetic factors alone account for the racial difference, one must show that blacks are fully equivalent to whites (at the same social-class level) in all respects except for genetic inheritance. If both groups are the same, then the IQ difference must in some way be due to the genes; if not, then other factors may account for the observed difference between the races.

The second possibility seems most plausible. It is clear that blacks and whites at a given social-class level undergo vastly different experiences. Blacks are generally subjected to discrimination, exclusion, oppression, economic exploitation—in short, to the various manifestations of a racism which most whites do not encounter and of which they are often not aware. The truth of this should no longer be in doubt, and it needs no documentation here. It should also be quite obvious that many blacks now participate in a culture which is in a variety of ways different from that of whites at any social-class level: the language is different, the art is different, the consciousness of political reality is different. No one with the slightest awareness of American history or the current political situation can believe that blacks and whites—at any social-class level—are fully equivalent except for genetic inheritance. It follows that genetic factors alone do not necessarily account for racial differences in IQ. If not genetics, what is the cause of the racial differences in IQ? We shall see later in this chapter that our understanding of these causes is quite limited; I think myself that motivational factors—not genetics and not "intelligence"—may be crucial.

In summary, the evidence shows that after infancy poor children receive lower IQ scores than middle-class children, that blacks have lower IQ scores than whites, and that poor black children have the lowest IQ scores of all. At the outset, we can dispose of the argument that racial differences in IQ are solely genetic in origin: this is highly unlikely, since at any social-class level, blacks are different from whites in many ways besides biological endowment. But regardless of the causes of the racial difference, what does it mean for blacks and for the poor in general to get relatively low IQ scores? What is the "intelligence" that the IQ test measures?

FOUR MYTHS CONCERNING THE IQ TEST

Consider four myths concerning the IQ test and the "intelligence" that it presumably measures. (These myths apply to the Stanford-Binet as well as most other IQ tests.)

The first myth is that the IQ test measures an intelligence which is a unitary mental ability. In this view, there exists a cohesive mental power or entity called "intelligence" which dominates the intellectual life. Intelligence is a single, unitary mental skill; it is one fundamental ability. According to this theory, individuals differ in the extent to which they possess the entity or ability of intelligence, and the IQ score reflects this difference. As in the case of height, some people have more of it than others. But we shall see that this view is incorrect. There is not one intelligence, but many; and because of this it is not clear what the IQ score reflects.

The second myth is that differences in IQ scores reflect fundamental differences in intellect. The usual assumption is that differences in IQ reflect those abilities which are at the heart of the intellectual life; in addition, it is assumed that what the test fails to measure is not very important. If people did not believe this, why would there be such a fuss about racial differences in IQ? Again, the proposition is in error. Many of the skills which the test measures are dull, pedestrian, and unimaginative. The test focuses on relatively minor differences among children and ignores some basic similarities.

The third myth is that the IQ test measures intellectual competence. The common view is that an individual's IQ reflects the best he can do in the intellectual sphere. The IQ represents the upper limit on his mental capabilities. While this may be true for some people, it is not for all. In the case of poor children especially, the IQ test may not measure intellectual competence; it may not give a true picture of what poor children are capable of. I will show that because of low motivation, poor children's performance on the IQ test does not indicate the full extent of their competence.

The fourth myth is that the IQ test measures an innate ability which is relatively unaffected by experience. In this view, the child's level of intelligence is set at birth and later experiences have relatively little effect on the IQ. Except in rare and unusual cases, intelligence cannot be raised or lowered: the genes endow the child with a certain amount of the fundamental power of the mind, and little if anything can be done to change the situation. Again this view is incorrect. The level of IQ is not determined at birth; it can fluctuate and change. Moreover, the theory of innate intelligence is not even a very interesting myth. For reasons I shall discuss, it does not seem possible at this point in time to resolve the nature-nurture issue in a sensible way.

We shall now consider each myth in turn. In doing this, I shall interpret the IQ test from the standpoint of modern cognitive theory (particularly Piaget's). To my knowledge, this has seldom been done. Psychology is a fragmented discipline. Work on the IQ test (the Binet and others) has been carried out quite independently of research and theory on cognitive development, that is, the growth of intellect in children. IQ testers have evidently felt that cognitive theory is not relevant to their concerns, and theorists of cognition have reciprocated the sentiment. The result is that the IQ test stands in splendid isolation from the rest of psychology (or vice versa, depending on your point of view), particularly the theory of cognition. In the following pages I shall try to narrow the gap between cognitive theory and the IQ test.

One Intelligence or Many?

Does the IQ test measure one mental entity or many? To answer this question, let us begin by looking at several IQ test questions.

A COGNITIVE ANALYSIS

At the 2-year level, one problem involves "delayed response." The examiner first shows the child a small toy cat. Then he places three small boxes, about two inches apart, in a row before the child. The examiner says, "Look, I'm going to hide the kitty and then see if you can find it again." As the child watches, the cat is placed under the middle box, where the child can no longer see it. The examiner places a screen in front of the boxes for ten seconds, removes it and says, "Now find the kitty." After the child makes his choice, the examiner repeats the procedure twice, hiding the cat under the left box and then the right.

Suppose that you take this test, and that when the screen is removed you immediately choose the box under which the cat is hidden. The question then is, what mental operations must you have performed to solve the problem? First, you must perceive the cat through all its displacements in space. When you first see the cat, it is far away and faces you head-on. Then the examiner picks the cat up and moves it forward so that it is closer and you now see it from the side. Yet despite these changes in the stimulus, you continue to see the object as the same cat. It seems to be the same size, even though it was initially far away and later close. It seems to have the same shape, even though at one point you saw it head-on, and at another point the examiner's hand covered it, and at another point you saw it from the side. Each of these accomplishments requires considerable perceptual activity; and if you cannot perform this activity, you cannot solve the task.

The examiner puts the cat under one of the boxes. Then he places a screen in front of the entire array, and after ten seconds says, "Now find the kitty." At this point, you must understand the instructions. You must "know" what the sentence means. The understanding of language is again an enormously complex act, involving several components. You must comprehend the individual words. The sound "kitty" reaching your ears is different from any other "kitty" you have ever heard: the examiner's intonation, pronunciation, volume level, and the like, are completely unique. Yet you perceive this string of sounds as the same as each other "kitty" you have heard. Moreover, when you hear "kitty" in the absence of the actual object, you know what this sound refers to. Perhaps the sound evokes a visual image of the absent object or perhaps it does not; in either event, you know what the speaker is talking about. The act of comprehension is further complicated by the fact that most words have several meanings. My dictionary says that *find* means, "To come upon, either by chance or as a result of search and effort; discover; to gain; attain to; arrive at. To perceive; feel. To gain the use of. To provide; supply. A finding; something found." If you have several meanings for "find," you must, therefore, pick out the right one. How do you do this? Probably you take account of context. You must know what is going on in the world and infer from that information which meaning of "find" makes sense in these circumstances. You must also know what is going on in the sentence. For example, if the word preceding "find" is "a," then you will give "find" its noun meaning.

But to understand a sentence, one must comprehend more than individual words (as the last example already suggests). One must take syntax into account. Although the individual words are the same, "Dog bites man" is quite different from "Man bites dog." Similarly, to understand "Now find the kitty" you must recognize that "find" is an imperative, that "you" is implied, and that the kitty is the object of the finding.

Suppose now that you have seen the cat placed under the box and that you have understood the instructions. What must you do next? You must in some way "remember" where the cat is. Consider what this entails. You must store within you for at least ten seconds the information that the cat was put in such and such a location, or some equivalent of that proposition. For example, you may construct and keep in your mind's eye for ten seconds a visual image of the location of the correct box. Or you may point your hand in the direction of the correct box and resolve simply to reach straight ahead when the ten seconds are over. In either event, something that happend in the past controls what you do now. Moreover, your current action seems to be predicated on a basic assumption concerning the nature of objects: they continue to exist even though you cannot see them. This assumption makes the task possible in the first place: you would not bother to remember the object's location if you did not believe that when invisible, it still exists.

So simple an act as finding a hidden cat involves a number of complex activities: perception, comprehension, memory. We have seen that each of these words is simply a blanket description for an intricate set of psychological processes. Looking closely at one test item on the Stanford-Binet, we see immediately that the notion of "intelligence" is misleading: there is no mysterious "entity" that can solve a problem like finding a hidden object; the problem must be solved by a series of discrete and determinate psychological processes. "Intelligence" does not find the cat; complex acts of perception, comprehension, and memory do the job.

Consider next several problems typically given to older children. At the 12-year level, the first test is vocabulary. This test is given at several other age levels as well. The examiner says: "I want to find out how many words you know. Listen, and when I say a word, you tell me what it means. What is a . . . ?" The child defines the word as best he can, and if his definition agrees with that in the scoring manual, he is considered correct. We have seen above (in the case of comprehending instructions) that understanding a single, spoken word involves auditory perception and the association of a pattern of arbitrary sounds with a meaning. In defining a word, you must employ at least one additional set of processes. You must put into language certain aspects of your own reaction to the word, that is, its meaning. Suppose the word "orange" elicits in you a visual image of the fruit, memories of eating an orange, feelings of pleasure, associations to other fruits, and even the words, spoken only to yourself, "That is an orange." Some of these reactions are relevant to a definition of "orange" and some are not. For example, your idiosyncratic reactions—that you like oranges or that they remind you of golf balls—are not proper aspects of the definition; whereas other reactions, like your image of the color, are quite relevant. The problem then is to sort through all your associations in order to emphasize those that are in some way central. But this is not all. Some of the associations may be nonverbal, and yet you must put them into words. Moreover, you must organize the selected ideas into a coherent form that is communicative to another person. You must, in short, translate personal knowledge, in all its complexity and incoherence, into a social response.

We have seen then that defining a word involves several complexities: perceiving the word, reacting internally (meaning), organizing and sorting through the internal reactions, and putting the product into words. Note that success at word definition depends considerably on experience. You cannot define any word unless you have heard it or read it before or unless it is obviously derived from words you know, and you will find definition easier if you have had some experience with the objects, actions, or concepts named. Note that again several skills are involved in the performance of this task; "intelligence" does not solve this problem either.

Another task is to "Repeat five digits reversed." The examiner recites a string of five random digits—e.g., 9, 3, 6, 2, 7—and asks the child to "say the numbers backward." To do this well, several mental acts seem to be necessary. First, you need to perceive each number properly: you must detect that "three" is different from "two." Second, you need to hold the entire sequence, in its proper order, in memory. You must remember 9,3,6,2,7 and not 9,6,2,3,7. To do this, some people may use visual imagery, picturing the sequence to themselves. Other people may retain in memory the sounds of the numbers—"nine, three . . ."—in sequence. Other people may "chunk" the digits to make memory easier. They may remember the number 93,627 or perhaps the numbers 9, 36, 27, and further remember that all are multiples of 9. Whatever the device, the sequence must be stored. Third, the remembered sequence must be reversed. If you have a visual image of 9,3,6,2,7, you may then read it off from right to left. If you have stored the number 93,627, you must retrieve it, examine it, and reverse the digits.

I think that by now the basic point has been amply demonstrated: there is no such thing as a unitary intelligence which allows one to solve problems on the IQ test (or anywhere else). Several discrete and determinate psychological processes are necessary for success at the IQ test. There is not one intelligence; there are many intellectual activities.

It is interesting to note that Alfred Binet, who devised the first successful intelligence test, as well as the rationale on which almost all subsequent IQ tests are based, was in full agreement with this proposition. Binet knew quite well that the test did not measure "intelligence"—some unitary and monolithic psychological entity. Consider, for example, his discussion of a very simple problem on the original form of the test, namely the comparison of two lines of unequal length:

> As we enter the field of what may properly be called psychological experimentation, we shall find it difficult to define which mental functions are being exercised because they are very numerous. Here the child must understand that it is a question of comparison, that the comparison is between two lines that are shown to him; he must understand the meaning of the words "Show me the longer." He must be capable of comparing, that is, of bringing together a conception and image and of turning his mind in the direction of searching for a difference. We often have illusions as to the simplicity of psychical processes, because we judge them in relation to others, still more complex. In fact, here is a test which will seem to show but little mentality in those who are able to execute it; nevertheless, when analyzed, it reveals a great complexity (Binet and Simon, 1916, pp. 52–53).

Thus, to judge the difference between two lines, one does not draw on some mythological entity called intelligence. Instead, one engages in a series of very specific mental operations: attending, listening, interpreting, comparing, abstracting, and so on. The same is true of the other test items. So the intelligence test, in Binet's view, is not a test of a single faculty of intelligence; it is rather a test which elicits different mental operations. These operations are only a part of human intellectual functioning or "intelligence."

RESEARCH STUDIES

There are many research studies bearing on the issues which we have just considered. Shortly after Binet published his test, psychologists divided sharply on the question of whether the IQ is a measure of a single, unitary intelligence, or whether instead the test measures a collection of diverse mental abilities. Like many controversies involving the IQ, the argument was both prolonged and bitter. On the one side, many English psychologists led by Spearman proclaimed that the IQ measured unitary mental ability, general ability, general intelligence, which they labeled the "g factor." On the other side, many American psychologists led by Thurstone proclaimed that the test measured several abilities or "multiple factors." (Tuddenham, 1962, presents an interesting historical account of the controversy.)

It is very hard to give a brief and simple explanation of the origins or nature of the dispute. The main reason is that the argument centered around an obscure statistical technique called "factor analysis." Both sides to the controversy had available essentially the same evidence—scores on IQ tests and related measures—but differed on the statistical procedures necessary to interpret the data. Using Spearman's methods one obtained a g factor, and using Thurstone's one arrived at multiple factors.

It would appear that the multiple factor theorists have won the battle. While some disagreement persists, most workers in the area of factor analysis seem to accept the idea that the IQ test measures several factors. Consider one study in this tradition.

Jones (1949) performed a factor analysis of Stanford-Binet items at several age levels. He found that Binet items typically given to 7-year-olds may be described in terms of three clear factors. The "verbal factor" is the strongest and underlies such items as vocabulary (defining words). A second factor at the 7-year level is called "reasoning." It underlies such items as comprehension, an example of which is, "What should you do if you found on the streets of a city an injured dog?" (Jones does not maintain that the item measures "reasoning" alone; several factors may contribute to one item. In this case, the verbal factor is involved, too.) A third factor is "memory." It may be illustrated by an item on which the examiner tells the child a story and then asks him certain questions about it.

At the 13-year level, several additional factors appear. For example, in addition to verbal, reasoning, and memory factors, there emerges a "visualization" factor. This may be illustrated by the following item: "Suppose you are going north, then turn left, then turn right, then turn left again; in what direction are you going now?" Jones argues that success on such items depends in part on an ability to visualize oneself moving sequentially in various directions.

Three general points emerge from Jones's study. First, the intelligence test, at least after the age of 7, is heavily loaded with a verbal factor. Almost all interpretations of the test agree on this. Our informal "cognitive analysis" was no exception. We saw that many items involved definition of words, comprehension of language, and the like. Second, Jones concluded that intelligence is not a single, unitary trait. Several factors, or different mental abilities, underlie the test at each of the age levels investigated. As we pointed out earlier, intelligence does not solve a problem; some combination of memory, reasoning, verbal ability, and other factors does. Third, I do not think that Jone's approach, based on multiple factor theory, takes us very far. While it is useful to know that "intelligence" involves more than one factor, the labels for these factors—reasoning, verbal ability, and so on—are still quite vague. We need a more precise description of the mental operations which underlie performance on the test.

THE IQ SCORE AND POOR CHILDREN

We have seen, then, that several mental operations are required for successful performance on each item of the IQ test. In view of this, what does the IQ score mean?

The chief implication is that the IQ score is merely a smokescreen concealing a complex series of events. First, when presented with a test problem, the child performs a set of mental operations. Second, these result in performance on a test item, that is, an answer to the question. Third, the examiner derives the IQ score from the total of such performances over several test items. His central operation is simply to add up the number of correct responses: the more of these, the higher the IQ. The IQ score is, therefore, simply a gross summary, a composite of the child's test performance. The IQ tells us little about the events which preceded it in the series. While the score is based on test item performance, and while test item performance is based on mental operations, the IQ tells us almost nothing about the mental operations which produced it. In other words, even though several intellectual activities are required to produce success on the test, the IQ provides almost no information about what these are. The IQ simply tells us how successful a child was; it does not reveal what made him successful.[1]

What does all this mean for interpreting social-class differences in IQ? The major implication is that these do not involve differences in unitary intelligence. To be sure, middle-class children answer more test items correctly than do lower-class children, but that does not mean that the former have more of that mysterious entity "intelligence" than do the latter, since the test does not measure unitary intelligence. In fact, the meaning of the observed IQ difference is not at all clear, because the IQ hides what lies behind it.

So there exists a social-class difference in IQ; this does not necessarily indicate a difference in unitary intelligence; what the difference does indicate is not clear.

Does the IQ Reflect
Fundamental Intellectual Activities?

Suppose that I am correct in arguing that the IQ test does not measure a unitary entity of intelligence, that instead many skills go into performance on the test. Suppose further that I am correct in proposing that the IQ score does not give a clear indication of what these skills are, that it is a composite which obscures what goes into it. Despite all this, one might maintain that the test is still quite important. One might contend that IQ differences

[1] Some IQ tests have attempted to provide a more detailed view of the mental operations which produce the IQ score. For example, the WISC gives a verbal and a nonverbal IQ score. But attempts like this are often not very successful when fine detail is involved. Cronbach (1960) maintains that although fairly successful in distinguishing between verbal and nonverbal factors, the WISC cannot do much more than this with any degree of accuracy. Therefore, I think that my general point holds with regard to the majority of IQ tests: they can give little detailed information concerning the intellectual skills which produce the final scores.

reflect variations in fundamental aspects of intellectual functioning, even if we cannot specify with precision what they are.

The basic question then is whether IQ differences reflect fundamental differences in intellectual ability. Of course, the answer to this question is determined by one's definition of "fundamental intellectual ability." Many such definitions are possible, depending on one's point of view. From the outset, I wish to rule out only one definition, namely that a skill is fundamental if it is measured by the IQ test. This is completely circular and gets us nowhere.

CREATIVITY

Perhaps we can approach the problem by asking what type of skills go into performance on the test and what type are not represented. Recall the type of items represented at the older age levels: vocabulary, repeating digits backwards, definitions. These problems do not seem to call forth very exciting or creative mental abilities. For example, repeating digits backwards seems to be a test of persistence and brute strength; it is more like doing push-ups than like writing a poem. Getzels and Jackson (1962) have studied this issue in a systematic way. They administered a number of creativity tests and an IQ test (either the Stanford-Binet or the Hemnon Nelson) to a large number of students in a private school (grades 6 to 12). One of the creativity tests was "unusual uses." In it, the child is given the name of a common object, such as "table," and is asked to find as many unusual uses for it as possible. If he says that a table is to eat on, his creativity is considered minute. If he says that a table can be used to plug a rectangular hole in a dike, then he gets a higher creativity score. The findings are simple to describe: IQ scores have a low correlation with the tests of creativity. This means that a high IQ does not guarantee a high score on a creativity test, nor does a low IQ go along with low creativity. For example, the IQ and unusual uses tests correlated 0.19 for boys and 0.15 for girls. Knowing a child's IQ score is of almost no value in predicting his creativity score: if the former is high, the latter might be either high or low, and so on. Therefore, if we believe that creativity is fundamental, the IQ test falls short in measuring this aspect of intellect.[2]

VERBAL SKILLS

Examination also shows that the IQ test places a strong emphasis on verbal skills. Our informal cognitive analysis showed this; so did the factor analysis of Jones. What kind of verbal skills are these? They seem to be relatively passive ones. To do well on the test, one must understand instructions;

[2] I should point out a weakness in my argument. Not everyone agrees that Getzels and Jackson's tests in fact measure creativity.

one must be able to produce conventional definitions of various words. The IQ test does not seem to emphasize the creative uses of language. It does not have an item requiring the composition of a story or even a well-formed sentence.

Suppose we grant that the IQ test emphasizes rather conventional verbal skills, at least at the older age levels. What does this mean? How fundamental is the test? The answer will depend on one's perspective. On the one hand, we all need at least some conventional verbal skills. This is particularly important in traditional schools (which seem, in an important sense to be discussed below, to be constructed along the lines of an IQ test). From this point of view, the IQ test measures something quite fundamental and important. On the other hand, one might argue that the test fails to stress the creative and unconventional verbal skills. Also, its emphasis on verbal abilities results in a lack of concentration on the nonverbal aspects of intelligence; and several psychological theories, especially Piaget's (discussed in chapter 4), stress that these are quite pervasive. From this point of view then, the IQ test measures extremely limited aspects of intellectual functioning. Perhaps the name of the test should be *The Binet Test of Conventional Verbal Skill and Other Assorted Intellectual Abilities Which the IQ Score Obscures.*

COMMONALITIES IN INTELLECTUAL FUNCTIONING

I wish to argue now that differences in IQ scores obscure many commonalities in children's abilities and that those commonalities are quite crucial to intellectual functioning.

First consider a concrete example. Suppose two 12-year-old children, each well motivated, take the IQ test, receiving scores of 90 and 110. What does this mean? How does the child receiving the score of 110 differ from the child whose IQ is 90? Again, we must look at the details of the examination. Both children took the vocabulary test: one child (whose score was 110) defined 15 words correctly, and the second child (scoring 90) defined 13 words correctly. The two mistakes cost the second child some points and contributed to pushing his score below the average. These hypothetical children also took an item called "verbal absurdities." This consists of five problems of the following type: The examiner says, "Listen to this. A policeman hurried to catch a criminal, pulled out his gun, and after smoking a cigar, placed the handcuffs on him. What is foolish about what I just said?" (The absurdity, of course, is that policemen on duty do not smoke cigars.) To receive credit for the verbal absurdity item, the child must resolve at least four such questions, the total being five. In our example, one child (whose IQ is 110) answered all five correctly, and the other child only three of the five.

Suppose that a similar situation exists with respect to other test items. One child does slightly better on several questions in precisely the same manner. This relatively minor difference in pattern of response is sufficient to give one child a score of 110 and the other a score of 90. What does the difference of 20 IQ points mean? I think its significance is not very great. The difference does *not* mean that one child possesses an array of intellectual skills which the other child completely lacks. Recall that both children solved at least some vocabulary problems and at least some verbal absurdity problems. This means that both children possess mental operations (whatever they are) sufficient for those problems. Each child knows how to define a word, and each child knows how to identify an absurdity. The basic psychological function of definition is not lacking in the child with an IQ of 90; what is lacking is the ability to define a *particular* word, such as "regret."

So a difference in IQ score does not reflect important ways in which the children are the same. The fact that one child's IQ is 90 and the other's is 110 seems to indicate that the two differ in fundamental ways. But this is misleading. The children differ in the number of words they can define; but they both can define words. This is a minor quantitative difference, not a major qualitative one.

What is more important, the general ability to define, or the ability to define a particular word? On the one hand circumstances may punish a child for not knowing a particular word such as "regret." For example, he may not be able to understand what someone using that word says to him. Thus, the ability to define particular words may have practical consequences of some importance. But on the other hand we should not overlook the fact that both children possess the basic cognitive skills which are involved in the definition of any word. Both children can define. Whether one of them can define "regret" is entirely the result of the vagaries of experience; he may or may not have heard that word before. But he could learn it because he has the intellect which is sufficient for learning it. If he has learned to define other words, why could he not learn "regret," too?

In summary, my argument is that a difference in IQ scores may obscure some commonalities in intellectual functioning. The difference may show that one child can do a few things slightly better than a second child, but it does not demonstrate that the second child completely lacks the fundamental intellectual skills possessed by the first child. The first child may be able to remember seven things and the second child five, and this may sometimes benefit the first child; but both can remember, and that is the crucial fact to keep in mind. The IQ test focuses on differences, not similarities. Yet many similarities are quite crucial.

This argument has important implications for the interpretation of social-class differences. An IQ difference of 10 or 20 points—the typical difference between middle- and lower-class children—is usually taken to mean that the social classes differ in an important way. We have already seen that they do not differ in unitary intelligence and that they may differ mainly in conventional verbal skills and other noncreative mental abilities. Now we must recognize that the IQ difference is misleading. It fails to inform us that the children are in many ways the same. *The numerical difference falsely implies a general difference in intellect; it fails to reveal that lower- and middle-class children share many of the same intellectual skills.* In this sense, then, the IQ test does not reveal much that is important about intelligence.

MORE ON COMMONALITIES

I wish to argue further that *by necessity* differences in IQ scores cannot reflect some crucial aspects of intellect. The argument is simple. The first point is that the IQ test feeds on differences. If properly constructed, the IQ test *must* discover differences among children within an age level and among age levels. Within an age level, there must be an average—100—and there must be higher and lower scores. Similarly, the average 10-year-old must do better than the average 9-year-old. Another way of putting this is to say that at the very heart of the IQ test are the assumptions that within an age level some children are smarter than other children, and that older children are in general smarter than younger ones.

The second point is that such assumptions guarantee that similarities among children will be overlooked. If one must obtain a spread of IQ scores within and among age levels, one cannot use test items on which children fail to differ. Yet there are some ways in which 10-year-olds (except the re-tarded or emotionally disturbed) do not differ among themselves and in which they do not differ from 9-year-olds. Obviously, if the aim is to locate differences, the test cannot measure these identical skills. Are they important? The answer is definitely yes. Piaget's theory, which we shall discuss in Chapter 4, is largely concerned with skills of this type. He focuses on *cognitive universals*—ways in which *all* children after a certain age are alike. And as we shall see these universals are the foundations of the mind.

So the IQ test, by definition, must concentrate on measuring the mental abilities on which children differ. These abilities, however, are not the only abilities which children possess, and it is folly to think that they represent the *entirety* of intelligence. Children possess many mental operations in common. While differences in IQ scores cannot reflect these, they are no less a part of intelligence than the skills the test does measure.

THE IMPORTANCE OF THE TEST AND SOCIAL CLASS

The IQ test focuses on verbal skills and on other intellectual abilities which are relatively noncreative. IQ differences imply that children of the same age are characterized by general and pervasive differences in intelligence. But this is not true. Children receiving different scores on the test nevertheless possess many of the same skills. Moreover, the basic principles governing construction of the test guarantee that IQ differences cannot reflect some important similarities among children.

In view of this, it seems fair to conclude that the IQ test is of limited significance. It should not be the only or major method for obtaining information about social-class differences in intellectual functioning.

Does the IQ Test Measure Competence?

The third myth is that the IQ test measures the child's intellectual competence—the best he can do. For example, Terman and Merrill (1960), authors of the Stanford-Binet, give in the testing manual the following advice to prospective examiners:

> It is customary to emphasize three conditions which are essential to securing valid test results: (1) standard procedures must be followed; (2) the subject's best efforts must be enlisted by the establishment and maintenance of adequate rapport. . . . If an examiner has failed to elicit the subject's best efforts, the only certain thing is that the resulting score will be too low to some unknown degree (p. 46).

It is usually assumed, however, that it should not be especially difficult to get subjects to work hard at the test; the problem of inadequate motivation should not often arise.

While this question is central to IQ testing, there has been surprisingly little research into the examiner's ability to establish rapport and into children's propensities to work hard at the test. The small amount of available research leads to the conclusion, I think, that the standard methods of administering the test fail to arouse adequate motivation in many children. Further, I shall argue that this failure is an inevitable outcome of the logic of standard testing: it is not possible to motivate all children if the examiner tests them in a standard way.

THE EFFECTS OF MOTIVATION

Zigler and Butterfield (1968) studied the intelligence test performance of poor 4-year-olds, both white and black. The hypothesis was that one cause of poor children's low IQs might be inadequate motivation. For example, the poor child may be "fearful and wary" of strange adults (the tester, for example) and this negative reaction may lead him to respond "I don't know" to the test items in order to terminate the session as quickly as possible. Also, failure may produce fear and anxiety which then further depress the poor child's score. It is possible to imagine many motivational factors which could adversely affect the performance of young, poor children in a strange situation.

To investigate these possibilities, Zigler and Butterfield first administered the Stanford-Binet to two classrooms of poor nursery school children. Three weeks later, the test was administered again in the standard fashion to 16 of the 40 children. The remaining 24 children, however, were tested in a way that was designed to maximize their motivation. This included giving an easy·item first, giving an easy item whenever the child failed two consecutive items, and giving "gentle encouragement." In general, the aim of this "optimal" testing procedure was to give the child a feeling of success, to prevent too many failures, and to lead him to perceive the adult as nonthreatening. If fear and similar factors depress the poor child's IQ under standard testing conditions, then the optimal testing method should alleviate these motivational difficulties and produce better performance. Some of Zigler and Butterfield's results are shown in Table 2-4. They reveal that the

TABLE 2-4   Mean IQs under Standard and Optimal Test Conditions

	Standard	Standard
Nursery one (N=13)	79.31	84.69
Nursery two (N=3)	88.30	93.00
	Standard	Optimal
Nursery one (N=16)	80.13	91.94
Nursery two (N=8)	95.34	103.38

Source: Zigler and Butterfield, 1968, p. 7.

optimal testing condition produces a significant increase in IQ scores. Further, this increase is significantly larger than the one produced by repeated testing under standard conditions. The results support Zigler and Butterfield's contention that motivational factors deflate the poor child's IQ under standard testing conditions and that special testing procedures can increase the IQ.

Zigler and Butterfield's hypothesis, while provoking, requires further exploration. We need to know whether motivational factors affect IQ test performance at older age levels as well. Also, we need to explore the effects of other ways of administering IQ tests. Zigler and Butterfield's optimal condition was, after all, not very different from the standard procedure. In fact, it is remarkable that the rather weak "optimal" condition resulted in relatively large IQ gains. Could we develop still more effective procedures for administering tests to poor children? Finally, we need to determine more precisely the nature of the motivational conditions which lower IQ scores. Since Zigler and Butterfield did not obtain direct measurements of fearfulness and wariness, it is possible that other motivational factors can account for the results.

Hertzig, Birch, Thomas, and Mendez (1968) have performed about the only study which obtains direct measures of motivational factors operating during test taking. The subjects were 116 3-year-old middle-class children, and 60 3-year-old working-class children of Puerto Rican descent, living in New York. The middle-class children came from predominantly native-born, professional families; and the Puerto Rican children generally came from Spanish speaking families, where the fathers were either unskilled or semi-skilled workers. The middle-class children were given the Stanford-Binet intelligence test in the standard way. The Puerto Rican children were tested by a Puerto Rican examiner, who gave the test in Spanish when necessary. As each child was tested, an observer sitting in the side of the room wrote a detailed description of the child's behavior. Here is an example of a behavioral record of a child's performance on an item which required the stringing of beads: "She nodded her head yes as she watched E [the examiner] string. She then shook her head no when the string was offered to her. She moved a little closer to the table and shook her head no when asked to string again. She pulled on her skirt and looked at E" (p. 10).

As can be seen from the example, the observer attempted to describe the basic features of the child's behavior in an objective way. It is difficult, however, to evaluate the soundness of the descriptions since Hertzig *et al.* did not compare them with records made by a second, independent observer.

After the testing session, the behavioral records were coded in several ways. One category was *work* vs. *not work*. The former was scored when the child attempted to do what the examiner asked (whether or not the result was successful). The latter was scored when the child failed to work at the task. A second category was *substitution* or irrelevant behavior. This was scored when the child responded to questions by making an irrelevant verbal response such as, "I want a drink," or an irrelevant behavioral response such as playing with toys. A third category was *passive nonwork*. This applied when the child's response to a question was simply sitting still or staring straight ahead. Other categories were also used.

The investigators first compared the behavioral records of the middle-class children as a whole with those of the Puerto Rican children as a whole. They found that, in comparison with middle-class children, Puerto Rican children showed: (1) fewer work responses (72 percent vs. 64 percent respectively); (2) fewer work responses immediately after an initial nonwork response (53 percent vs. 42 percent); (3) fewer work responses to verbal test items (82 percent vs. 66 percent); (4) an equal proportion of work responses to nonverbal test items (86 percent vs. 85 percent); (5) fewer spontaneous verbal remarks (74 vs. 20); (6) more task irrelevant remarks (28 percent vs. 64 percent); (7) more passive nonwork responses (31 percent vs. 46 percent). The average Puerto Rican IQ was 95.6, and the average middle-class IQ 122.4.

In general, the middle-class children were friendly, interested in the test situation, followed instructions, and worked persistently. The Puerto Rican children were also friendly, but were easily distracted, were somewhat less verbal, did not follow instructions well, and did not focus attention on the task.

In a second analysis, Hertzig *et al.* compared the behavioral records of middle-class and Puerto Rican children who were specially selected so as to be equivalent in IQ scores. In both groups, the IQs ranged from 90 to 110 (although the investigators fail to reveal the averages for each group). Even under these conditions, the results were the same as those found in the first analysis: the Puerto Rican children showed fewer work responses, were less task oriented, and so forth.

A third analysis showed that middle-class children with IQs in the range of 90 to 110 behaved in essentially the same ways as middle-class children with higher IQs. A fourth analysis compared Puerto Rican children with IQs above and below 90. Those with lower IQs showed (1) fewer work responses; (2) fewer work responses to verbal test items; (3) fewer verbal responses; and (4) more irrelevant verbal responses.

In summary, the study shows that Puerto Rican children are in general less task oriented than middle-class children, even when IQs are equivalent; low IQ (below 90) Puerto Rican children show this tendency to a greater extent than do average IQ (90–110) Puerto Ricans; both average IQ (90–110) and upper level IQ (110 and above) middle-class children are relatively well motivated to take the test.

There are at least two interpretations which might account for the Puerto Ricans' generally lower level of motivation. One is that the poor motivation is a result of a real inability to do well in the testing situation. That is, the children do not try because they know they cannot do well. This interpretation might hold for some of the low IQ Puerto Rican children, but it seems inadequate for those receiving higher scores. The Puerto Rican children with IQs in the range 90–110 were less motivated than middle-class children in the same range, even though both groups achieved the same degree of success.

A second interpretation asserts that Puerto Rican children's behavior in the testing situation is a reflection of a general cultural orientation. Hertzig *et al.* observed that Puerto Rican families are sociable and relaxed, do not pressure the children, and do not try persistently to "educate" their children with toys and by other means. The investigators feel that the Puerto Rican children come from a "person-oriented" rather than a "problem-oriented" culture. The result is relatively low motivation for a task like the intelligence test. Of course, the writers do not assert that Puerto Rican culture is *deficient* when compared with middle-class culture. Rather, the two groups are characterized by different life styles, by different modes of adaptation to the environment. Who is to say the problem-orientation of the middle-class culture is better than the person-orientation of the Puerto Rican culture?

Several features of the Hertzig *et al.* study should be emphasized. First, it shows that, for at least one group, the IQ test may not be a good measure of intellectual competence. If Puerto Rican children do not expend effort at the IQ test, then it is very hard to evaluate their "intelligence." On the one hand, it is p ssible that were the Puerto Rican children to try harder, their IQ scores would be precisely as low as they are now. On the other hand, it is possible that increased effort would raise their IQs. At the very least, the Hertzig *et al.* study calls into question the validity of the IQ score as a measure of intellectual competence. It raises significant doubts as to whether, in Terman and Merrill's words, the test elicits the "subject's best efforts," and consequently whether the score reflects his highest intellectual abilities. One cannot properly evaluate competence when motivation is low.

Second, the Hertzig *et al.* study suggests a fruitful area and technique for research. We need to explore the motivational factors affecting the test performance of children in various age, ethnic, racial, and social-class groups. For example, to what extent do motivational factors depress the IQs of the poor, rural white children? This kind of research should employ the techniques of direct observation. We need to know what actually happens during the administration of an IQ or achievement test and the best way to find out is to watch; it would not seem to make too much sense to measure motivation by giving another test which the child might also not be motivated to take.

COMPETENCE AND THE STANDARD TESTS

I would argue that if the aim is to measure intellectual competence, then standardized testing is a poor approach, leading inevitably to the kinds of results obtained by Hertzig *et al.* The essence of standard testing is the attempt to give the test in the same way to all subjects. The rationale is that if the stimulus conditions—that is, the testing procedures—are the same, then any variations in response (the subjects' scores) must be due to characteristics of the subjects, and not to differences in the way the tests were administered. On the other hand, according to this rationale, if the test were given in a distinctive way to each subject, then the variation in IQ scores might be simply the result of different methods of testing, and not the result of real differences among the subjects. In devising the first IQ test, Binet was particularly anxious to avoid this last possibility. In his day, physicians, each using a different method of examination, frequently could not agree among themselves on a diagnosis of retardation, and the result was chaos. To eliminate this, Binet felt, it was necessary to have all examiners conduct the test in essentially the same way.

These arguments may seem powerful, but I think they are wrong.

Standard test theory would make sense if all subjects were motivated to take the test, or could easily be motivated to do so. If this were the case, then it is clearly an advantage to have all examiners give the test in the same way; this will assure agreement among different testers and will permit the inference that differences in performance are the result of variations in subjects' characteristics, not methods of testing.

But it would appear that all children are not well motivated to take the test and that ordinary methods of establishing rapport are not effective. This is the message of the Zigler and Butterfield and Hertzig *et al.* studies. It is also the message of common sense. All children are not the same; they differ in motivation and in their response to attempts to motivate them. If you interact with children, particularly young ones, you will soon find that it is difficult to get them to work at a problem in which you happen to be interested, but in which they are not. For example, two of my children became interested in printing at about the age of 5. The twins would spend long periods of time making letters, copying words from books, and so forth. I was particularly interested in this, since I had just conducted a study of children's printing. When I wanted to make some observations on the twins's work with letters, I would sometimes get paper and pencil, and ask them to make some letters for me. There were several responses. They might do the work I was interested in. Or they might refuse, quite adamantly. If the latter were the case, there was little I could do to interest them in printing. A half hour later, however, when for one reason or another I could no longer make the observations, one or both of the children might be hard at work making letters. It became abundantly clear to me that the motivation for doing a task, involving letters or anything else, stems from the child; there is not too much the adult can do to create interest or manipulate motivation. Of course, adults in positions of power may force the child into doing a task. Under these conditions, the child will do something because he has no choice in the matter. (John Holt, 1964, describes such occurrences as the foundation of traditional education.) But most frequently the child's behavior is not what it might be if he were properly motivated, and the main result is merely that the adult has fooled himself into thinking that the child has done well.

I take it as axiomatic then that when unmotivated, children do not perform well at many tasks and that it is not easy for an adult to create or elicit the motivation. Anyone who accepts this proposition, particularly as it applies to the IQ test, must reject the basic rationale for standard tests. If it is difficult to obtain adequate motivation, one should not give tests in the same way to all children. The examiner must go to extraordinary lengths to tap the competence of some children; the standard procedure, since it does not "reach" them, yields data of little value.

Another way of putting my argument is to say that there was a basic contradiction in Binet's logic. On the one hand, Binet wanted to establish standard conditions for testing so that examiners would agree on a diagnosis. On the other hand, he recognized that rapport must be established in order to tap competence. Binet thought that his test satisfied both conditions. But this is often impossible to do. Achieving one goal guarantees not reaching the other. If one standardizes testing conditions, one cannot achieve rapport with all subjects; if one achieves rapport, one cannot have standard testing conditions. Which is preferable, to motivate the child when attempts at rapport fail or to maintain standard testing conditions?

SUMMARY

Research shows that the IQ test does not seem to measure intellectual competence in at least some groups of poor children. Further, one can argue that the use of standard testing procedures guarantees this result. All this makes data concerning social-class differences in IQ even more suspect than we thought earlier. Before, we saw that the test does not measure unitary intelligence and fails to measure much of what is important. Now we see that poor children may not even be well motivated to take the test, so that it does not measure their intellectual competence.

What Does the IQ Test Measure?

It is now possible to give a comprehensive picture of what the IQ test measures. If a child is well motivated to take the test, then his final score is the result of an array of mental operations—reasoning, comprehension, perception, and, above all, verbal skills. Many of these operations seem rather pedestrian and do not involve a great deal of creativity. While mental operations like these must contribute to the final score, one cannot determine from the IQ precisely which mental operations were employed.

If a child is poorly motivated to take the test, then the meaning of the IQ score is even more ambiguous. The child may well possess intellectual operations of superior quality and efficiency; he simply does not apply them to the test. One cannot determine from the IQ score which mental operations were used, and whether they were the most advanced available.

Moreover, differences in IQ scores obscure the fact that almost all children possess many mental skills of considerable importance. These are the "cognitive universals"—skills which characterize all children at a particular developmental level and which, therefore, are slighted by a test whose aim is to find differences among children.

Given these considerations, suppose that we know that a 10-year-old child's IQ is 90. How can we interpret this? I think that it means very little; it is fundamentally ambiguous. We do not know the extent of the child's motivation to take the test. Consequently, the score may or may not be too low; it may or may not reflect his competence. In addition, that score may have been achieved by a variety of mental processes, and we cannot tell precisely which were involved. We can guess perhaps that the child used verbal skills of the definition type, some sort of reasoning processes, and so on, but we cannot give a detailed description. We know further that the test fails to reflect many interesting and creative mental skills.

Suppose now that you are told that the score of 90 is the average IQ for lower-class 12-year-olds and that middle-class children score 110 on the average. What can you conclude? Very little. There is the possibility that lower-class children are not as well motivated to take the test as middle-class children. If this is the case, then the IQ difference may be illusory. Even if the lower-class children are well motivated, the IQ difference does not mean a great deal. It means that lower-class children perform slightly less well, as a group, on a set of tasks demanding for their solution a particular array of mental skills. These skills are largely verbal, not very creative, and not necessarily of great importance. Moreover, lower- and middle-class children possess many of the same skills, and the difference in IQ does not reflect these. This, I think, is the meaning of social-class differences in IQ.

HEREDITY AND ENVIRONMENT

In 1969 Arthur Jensen published in the *Harvard Educational Review* an article describing social-class and racial differences in IQ, and proposing that they are largely genetic in origin. There immediately ensued a bitter controversy in both professional journals and the public press. The *Harvard Review* published a large number of rebuttals by prominent psychologists and geneticists; *The New York Times* entered the fray, and so did *Life,* the *New Republic,* and many others. Segregationists seized on Jensen's work to justify their policies; radical students at the University of California forced Jensen —so the press reported—to hold his classes in secret.

To me, the central question is not whether Jensen's genetic argument is right or wrong (although I think it is wrong). The issue is rather: Why did everyone get so upset? Why do psychologists and laymen take the IQ test so seriously that they care whether Jensen is correct? If one accepts the interpretation of the IQ test that I have offered above, he will find the Jensen controversy, and in fact the entire question of the relative influence of heredity and environment on IQ, of little interest. But since the nature-nurture issue has been of historical importance, we should examine it. At the same time we must remember that the question is not how heredity and environment influence *intelligence*. The question is rather, how heredity and environment contribute to the particular intellectual skills which the IQ test measures.

The literature on the nature-nurture controversy is so voluminous that we cannot hope to cover it all here. We will review a few representative studies on *IQ stability, family resemblance,* and *regional differences.*

Stability

Soon after the IQ test was invented, there developed a school of thought which held that heredity determines an individual's level of intelligence; the IQ is fixed at birth and remains constant thereafter.

To investigate this issue, several psychologists performed "longitudinal studies"—that is, studies of the same children over a long period of time—of IQ development. The most thorough investigation of the issue has again been performed by Bayley (1949). She began the research with 61 one-month-old infants and studied those children who stayed in the geographic area (about half the original sample) for 28 years. During the first year, Bayley tested the infants monthly with the California First Year Mental Scale, an infant "intelligence" test. Later she tested them, although not as frequently, with such tests as the California Preschool Scale and the Stanford-Binet.

The major technique of analysis was the correlation coefficient. This statistic describes the extent to which two sets of scores, usually from the same individuals, are related. Suppose that children take the IQ test at two different times. If their scores are almost the same on both occasions, then the correlation coefficient will be high and positive, approaching +1.00. If their scores are unrelated, so that knowledge of one score does not help in predicting the other, then the correlation is low, approaching zero. If the scores reverse their order, so that persons scoring high the first time score low the second time and vice versa, then the correlation is high and negative, approaching −1.00.

Bayley correlated individuals' test scores at various ages; Table 2-5

TABLE 2-5   Correlations between IQs at Various Age Levels

Average of Months	Average of Months			Average of Years		
	7, 8, 9	13, 14, 15	27, 30, 36	5, 6, 7	11, 12, 13	17, 18
1, 2, 3	.42	.10	.09	.13	.02	.05
7, 8, 9		.67	.22	.02	.16	.20
13, 14, 15			.54	.30	.19	.23
27, 30, 36				.70	.53	.54
Average of Years						
5, 6, 7					.85	.86
11, 12, 13						.96

Source: Bayley, 1949, p. 181.

presents the correlations. They show (1) that within the period of infancy, the scores at various ages do not correlate highly with one another. For example, the average IQ score during months 1, 2, and 3 correlates only .42 with the corresponding score during months 7, 8, and 9, and correlates only .10 with the average IQ score at months 13, 14, and 15. (2) Infant test scores during the first year of life are nearly useless for predicting scores at later ages. For example, the correlation between the average score at months 7, 8, and 9 and the average score at years 11, 12, and 13 is a negligible .16 (3) Infant test scores during the second year of life (months 13, 14, and 15) are moderately correlated with scores during the third year of life (months 27, 30, and 36), but are poorly correlated with scores after that point. Scores during the period from about the third year of life to years 5, 6, and 7 are fairly stable, showing a correlation of .70. (4) After the age of about 5, the scores are highly stable. For example, the correlation between the average scores at years 5, 6, and 7 and the corresponding score at years 17 and 18 is .86.

A study by Honzik, MacFarlane, and Allen (1948) comes to similar conclusions concerning IQ constancy: IQ scores fluctuate a great deal early in life and become increasingly stable as the child grows older. In addition to presenting correlations among scores at various ages, the writers offer clinical data on individual children. Figure 2-1 shows the IQ data for one child (case number 567). Her IQ scores obviously change a great deal from age 2 to age 18. The investigators report that early in the child's life there was a great deal of sickness in the family and that she was shy and withdrawing. After the age of 10, however, she developed a number of interests, including music and sports, and became more sociable as well. While data of this sort are not conclusive, they suggest that environmental influences and the child's emotional life affect intelligence test performance in obvious ways.

In sum, the IQ is not constant throughout the life span. Environmental events and emotional experiences can affect the level of "intelligence." The IQ test is not a measure of native intellectual capacity, fixed at birth.

Family Resemblance

Several studies have investigated the relations among the IQs of parents, children, siblings, and twins. Table 2-6 reports typical findings. The correlation between the IQs of parents and their children is approximately .50. This means that children and their parents have moderately similar IQs. But this relationship can be interpreted in several ways. On the one hand, perhaps hereditary similarity between parents and their children accounts for the moderate correlation in IQ. On the other hand, it may be that parents of different IQ levels provide their children with different environments, with the result that the children's IQs are correspondingly different.

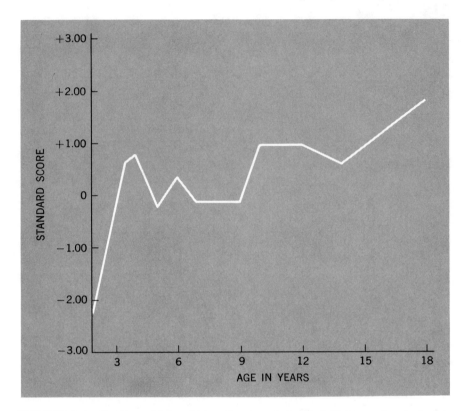

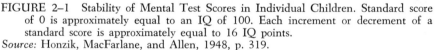

FIGURE 2–1   Stability of Mental Test Scores in Individual Children. Standard score
of 0 is approximately equal to an IQ of 100. Each increment or decrement of a
standard score is approximately equal to 16 IQ points.
Source: Honzik, MacFarlane, and Allen, 1948, p. 319.

TABLE 2-6   Correlations between IQs of Various Groups

Parent-child	.49 *
Siblings	.49 *
Fraternal twins	.63 **
Identical twins	.88 **
Identical twins reared apart	.77 **

* Reported in Conrad and Jones, 1940.
** Reported in Newman, Freeman, and Holzinger, 1937.

The correlation between siblings in the same family is also about .50.
This is once more ambiguous. The moderate similarity in IQ could be due
either to similarities in environment or heredity.

Of more interest than the preceding are studies of twins. Fraternal twins result from the insemination of two different ova. Dizygotic (two egg) twins are therefore no more alike in genetic endowment than are ordinary siblings. Identical twins derive from the splitting of one fertilized ovum. Monozygotic (one egg) twins are therefore genetically identical. One would expect, then, that if heredity plays a large role in the determination of intelligence, identical twins' IQs should be more similar than fraternal twins'. This is indeed what is found. The correlation for identical twins is about .90 and that for fraternal twins is about .65. At first, the results would seem to offer clear support for the nativist position: identical heredity seems to produce extremely similar intelligence. Nevertheless some opposing arguments may be offered. It is possible that identical twins are treated more alike than are fraternal twins: this greater similarity of environment then accounts for the high correlation between identical twins' IQs. Although the matter has not been thoroughly studied, the hypothesis seems plausible. Identical twins, who usually look alike and who are of course always of the same sex, may elicit from parents and others highly similar reactions. I know that many people could not tell my twins apart and often had a strong compulsion to emphasize their similarities and treat them the same way. People called them "twinny," and friends bought them identical clothes. On the other hand, fraternal twins, who often do not look alike and who are not necessarily of the same sex, may therefore elicit different reactions. So heredity may affect intelligence, but only in an indirect way. It determines the degree of physical similarity of twins. The greater the similarity, the more equally the environment (parent, teachers, other children) treats the twins. The more equal the treatment, the greater the similarity in IQ. By this hypothesis, the environment, and not genetic endowment, is the most immediate cause of IQ similarities in identical twins.

Finally, consider a study of identical twins who have been reared apart. Newman, Freeman, and Holzinger (1937) obtained IQ scores from 19 pairs of identical twins who were separated from one another early in life (mostly during the first year) because of the death of their parents or other misfortunes, and who were raised in different homes. These regrettable circumstances constitute an experiment of nature: twins identical in heredity are subjected to apparently different environments. If heredity is the chief determinant of IQ, then the correlation between twins' IQ scores should be extremely high. If it is not, then the correlation should be lower.

The study showed that the correlation between the IQs of twins reared apart is .77. At first, this result seems quite favorable to the nativist position. Additional data, however, suggest that an environmentalist interpretation has some power. First it seems to be the case that welfare agencies attempt to place children in foster homes similar to their own. Each separated twin was not randomly assigned to one of a wide variety of foster homes. Therefore, the similarity of IQs may result from similar environments. Second, when the environments of the separated twins did differ, the IQs generally varied accordingly. For example, when one twin had greater educational opportunities than the other, the former's IQ tended to be higher. We see then that even in the case of identical twins reared apart, it is not easy to obtain conclusive evidence on the nature-nurture issue.

Regional Differences and Migration

We turn now to several studies involving black children. First, it seems to be the case that the general living conditions and cultural milieu affect the IQ. Black children in the South receive lower IQ scores than their peers in the North. Baughman and Dahlstrom (1968) report that Negro children in a poor, small Southern town receive a mean IQ of 84.6, while Deutsch and Brown (1964) show that the average IQ of lower-class black children in New York is 91.2.

Several investigators have focused on blacks' migration from South to North. The hypothesis, originally proposed by Otto Klineberg, is that general living conditions improve when Negroes move from South to North, and that this improvement is reflected in an increase in the average IQ. A well-controlled study by Lee (1951) gives typical results. He compared the IQ scores of Negro children who migrated to Philadelphia from the South with those of black children who were born in Philadelphia. Table 2-7 shows some of the results. They indicate that Philadelphia born children consistently receive average IQ scores in the low and middle 90s. There is no general improvement in their scores from the first to the ninth grade. By contrast, migrants who arrive in Philadelphia in time for the first grade begin with lower IQ scores (86.5), but these steadily improve until they reach about the same level as those of Philadelphia born children. Migrants who arrive in Philadelphia at later ages improve in IQ, but not as much. In sum, migration improves the IQ; the earlier the migration, the greater the improvement.

Lee's study is usually taken to demonstrate the effects of environment on IQ. No doubt, the improvement in general living conditions, in school opportunities, and so forth, contributed to the IQ increase. But the study does not rule out possible effects of heredity. Conceivably, it is the more intelligent parents, the parents of better genetic stock, who migrate, and the improved environment then enables the children to attain the IQ limits set by heredity.

Some General Comments

I think that the dispute over environmental and genetic influences on the IQ is a hopeless muddle and must remain so. The nature-nurture issue is too ambiguous and vague. There are several reasons for saying this.

TABLE 2-7 Mean IQ Scores of Migrants and Philadelphia Born Negro Children

Group	N	\multicolumn{5}{c}{Grade in which test was taken}				
		1	2	4	6	9
Philadelphia-born who attended kindergarten	212					
Mean		96.7	95.9	97.2	97.5	96.6
Philadelphia-born who did not attend kindergarten	424					
Mean		92.1	93.4	94.7	94.0	93.7
Southern-born entering Philadelphia school system in grades						
1A	182					
Mean		86.5	89.3	91.8	93.3	92.8
1B–2B	109					
Mean			86.7	88.6	90.9	90.5
3A–4B	199					
Mean				86.3	87.2	89.4
5A–6B	221					
Mean					88.2	90.2
7A–9A	219					
Mean						87.4

Source: Lee, 1951, p. 231.

First, the notion of environment includes such diverse categories as injury to the fetus during pregnancy, nutritional deficiencies during childhood, parental child-rearing practices, cultural milieu, and school experiences. Each of these categories is in turn complex and poorly understood. There are many kinds of fetal injuries and it is not clear how each affects intellectual growth. Psychologists have just begun to conceptualize the myriad of events that constitute child-rearing practices, and the same may be said of the cultural milieu and school experiences. Consider too that each of these categories may interact with the others in elaborate ways. A birth injury may influence not only the child's intellect, but the parents' and teachers' treatment of him, which in turn may affect the child's behavior toward them, and so on, until there results an apparently impenetrable maze of events. To ask about the effects of environment—let alone its interaction with heredity—is to pose a huge question. In fact the question is so enormous that it seems fruitless to raise it in the first place. It is bad scientific strategy to attempt to solve problems at so global and vague a level of analysis.

Second, the situation is similarly complex in the case of hereditary factors. There must always be interaction between heredity and environment. At the most obvious level, if there is no environment, then an organism cannot develop at all. Similarly, if there are no genes, then there is no basis for any development, regardless of how benevolent the environment may be. It is therefore impossible to find a pure case of genetic influence even for relatively simple phenotypes (observable characteristics) such as eye-color.

Also, heredity does not always operate in simple ways. A phenotype may be due to effects of a single gene, dominant or recessive. But inheritance may be multi-factor or *polygenic*, as well. A characteristic may be influenced by pairs of genes. The effects of these may summate in a simple way, or there may be an interaction between the genes, or *epistasis*, such that one gene's effects may be contingent on another's. It is almost certain that more than one gene is involved in "intelligence" and that these interact in complex ways. In view of all this, it seems naïve to assume there is a simple answer, or even the possibility of achieving a complicated answer, to the question of genetic effects on the IQ.

A third reason for considering the nature-nurture controversy an impossible muddle is that intelligence too is complex. The IQ is not a simple phenotype or trait, as is eye-color or height. As we have seen, the IQ, while a single score, is in reality a reflection of many intellectual operations and of motivational factors as well. This means that the problem of tracing the influence of environment (in all its complexity) and of heredity (in all its complexity) on intelligence becomes even further complicated. We need to know how these factors affect the intellectual and motivational skills which contribute to the IQ. For example, how do certain child-rearing practices affect spatial reasoning? Unfortunately, questions such as these are almost unanswerable since one does not usually know which intellectual or motivational factors contribute to the IQ score. As we showed earlier, a given score can be achieved in a variety of ways.

In sum, "environment" refers to many different kinds of influences; heredity operates in extraordinarily complex ways; and "intelligence" is not one thing but many. Given all these complexities, a sensible answer to the nature-nurture issue seems beyond our grasp (that is to say, the question is non-sensible). All we can offer are cliches: the environment influences the IQ, so does heredity, and yes, Virginia, there is an interaction between the two.

THE IQ AND SUCCESS IN SCHOOL

I have tried to demonstrate that the IQ test measures several intellectual skills, some not very interesting; that its scores are affected by the child's motivation; and that the nature-nurture question is hardly worth asking. If you accept these propositions, then at this point you might conclude that social-class differences in IQ are uninteresting and ask why we do not go on to another topic. While it should be obvious by now that I do not find the IQ test particularly instructive, I wish to consider one further question before concluding the chapter.

It is possible to argue that one cannot dismiss the IQ test as unimportant, since it is a predictor of school success and failure. If a child does well on the test, the chances are that he will perform ably in school; if he has a low IQ, he will do poorly in school. For these reasons, the IQ is an important and valuable test, even if all my criticisms of it are true.

To deal with this issue, we must first consider the facts—the empirical relations between IQ and school success. A common finding is that the intelligence test correlates fairly highly with standard tests of academic achievement. Cronbach (1960) reports data from a typical study, in which Stanford-Binet scores in grade nine were correlated with achievement tests one year later. Table 2-8 shows that all of the correlations are fairly high, and that their average is in the .50s.

TABLE 2-8   Correlations of Stanford-Binet
with Certain Achievement Tests

With reading comprehension	.73
With reading speed	.43
With English usage	.59
With history	.59
With biology	.54
With geometry	.48

Source: Cronbach, 1960, p. 181.

Note that the correlations, while statistically significant—that is to say, it is highly unlikely that they are spurious—are not perfect. Knowledge of the child's IQ does not permit unerring prediction of his school performance. Nevertheless, knowing the correlations allows better prediction than not knowing them.

Why does the IQ test correlate moderately well with school grades? The usual assumption is that the correlation exists because "basic intelligence" is required for successful academic work. But we have already seen that there is no such thing as basic intelligence and of course the IQ test does not measure it. But if it is not useful to employ the concept of intelligence, what then forms the basis for children's work in school?

Unfortunately, this matter is poorly understood. There are available few studies of the cognition involved in school work. In the absence of useful research into this area, I wish to offer a few speculations into the relation between IQ and academic achievement.

First consider several propositions concerning intellectual activity in school.

1. Some intellectual skills are involved in school work even though we may not know what they are.

2. The intellectual skills must vary to some extent in different subject areas and at different ages. To do mathematics seems to require mental processes that are different from those required to write a poem.

3. The diversity of intellectual skills is limited by the fact that most traditional schools place heavy emphasis on verbal and reading abilities. Most schools are places to read.

4. The extent to which significant intellectual activity is required for success in school is vastly over-rated. Even in "good" middle-class schools education does not always require a high degree of intellectual endeavor. (I suspect that more students than professors will agree with this speculation.) John Holt (1964) describes the lack of genuine intellectual activity in prep schools. He shows that students can often achieve good grades by outwitting the teacher at various game-like activities. What is learned is not a deep understanding of algebra; it is rather how to make the teacher think that one knows algebra.

If this analysis is correct, then it is easy to see why the IQ test has some ability to predict academic achievement. Like the schools, the IQ test:

1. involves some intellectual activity,

2. requires several mental skills, different ones at different ages,

3. emphasizes verbal skills,

4. is vastly overrated.

Some of these points may be illustrated by the correlations in Table 2-8. The three highest correlations (with reading comprehension, English, and history) involve achievement tests that seem to emphasize verbal skills. This is certainly true of reading comprehension and English usage. History, as usually taught in schools, also seems to involve a great deal of reading and other language skills. While verbal skills are quite important, they cannot account for everything. The three lowest correlations (reading speed, biology, and geometry) involve achievement tests that seem in part to require skills of a somewhat different nature. The reading test introduces an element of speed; the biology test may tap scientific reasoning; and the geometry test may measure spatial or mathematical thought. Since the IQ test emphasizes verbal skills, it correlates less highly with tests in these areas.

The IQ test is a decent predictor of school success for another reason: both activities require a certain kind of motivation. Recall the Hertzig study, which showed that Puerto Rican children's motivational style tended to depress their IQ scores. When taking the test these children were less "task oriented" than middle-class children. It seems reasonable to assume that such a motivational style is also required for school work. As Binet put the matter, ". . . the scholastic aptitude admits of other things than intelligence; to succeed in his studies, one must have qualities which depend especially on attention, will, and character; for example, a certain docility, regularity of habits, and especially continuity of effort" (Binet and Simon, 1916, p. 254). Binet did not seem to realize that the IQ test requires these qualities too, and that is another reason why it predicts school performance fairly well.

There seems to be yet another reason for the correlation between IQ and academic achievement. Rosenthal and Jacobson (1968) have shown that teachers' expectancies can affect pupils' performance. These investigators conducted an experiment in which teachers were told that certain disadvantaged students would show "dramatic intellectual growth." These predictions were allegedly made on the basis of a test of "academic blooming"; in fact the experimenters selected the children randomly and lied to the teachers. Subsequent tests revealed that the potential bloomers bloomed. For example, their IQ scores were higher than those of other children whom the teachers did not expect to show dramatic intellectual growth. It would appear, then, that teachers' expectancies can influence children's academic performance. This should not be regarded as a mysterious phenomenon. Expectancies affect the way a teacher treats the child; expecting him to do poorly, she may ignore him or fail to look behind a poorly formulated response to find the glimmer of understanding that it betrays.

We may speculate that a similar phenomenon occurs in the case of IQ tests and academic achievement. Knowledge of the child's IQ may produce in the teacher expectancies concerning the child's potential for academic achievement and these may affect his actual performance. If the teacher believes, for example, that the IQ test measures innate intelligence, then she might easily come to the conclusion that low IQ children cannot do mathematics or other subjects. As a result of this belief she might unintentionally contribute to the children's poor academic performance. If she believes the outcome is predetermined, she will not try as hard.[3] The same may be said of the students.

In sum, the IQ test does predict school performance fairly well. One reason is that the IQ test measures intellectual skills which are important for success in our schools as currently constituted. Another reason is that the test measures motivational skills appropriate for academic work. Third, IQ scores may influence teachers' expectancies which in turn may produce a certain level of performance in the child.

For all these reasons, then, the IQ test is a useful predictor of academic achievement, and I do not deny that this is so. Binet's original aim in devising the test—to identify children who would not do well in school—has been largely achieved. I argue only for placing the test in proper perspective. It

[3] After this was written, I came across a study by Rist (1970) showing that the teacher's knowledge of the child's social class may affect the way she treats him. If the child is poor, the teacher may not think him capable of academic success and her belief may in fact help to fulfill this prophecy.

does not measure innate intelligence. It fails to tap many important intellectual skills. It is an index of motivation as well as intellect. The correlation between IQ and academic achievement does not necessarily stem from the fact that success in school requires fundamental intellectual skills. Rather, both academic achievement and IQ test performance may be based on rather dull intellectual skills and on a somewhat docile motivational style. In brief, the correlation between IQ and academic achievement does not indicate that either one is valid, accurate, or real; rather, both suffer from similar deficiencies and biases.

SUMMARY AND CONCLUSIONS

After a brief description of the IQ test, we began the chapter by presenting the facts of social-class and racial differences in "intelligence." Research has repeatedly shown that poor children have a lower IQ than middle-class children, and that blacks score more poorly on the test than whites. A major question then arose: What is the "intelligence" that the IQ test measures?

First, we saw that the test measures several mental operations, not a unitary intelligence. It is hard to interpret a given score: since it may be achieved in a variety of ways, the examiner does not know precisely what intellectual activities it reflects.

Second, we saw that verbal skills predominate and that the test does not stress creativity. An IQ difference of 10 or 20 points is of no great significance; it does not necessarily signify a difference in the availability of important intellectual operations. Moreover, the IQ test, by its very nature, focuses on differences among children, and it ignores intellectual similarities, many of which are quite fundamental.

Third, the test may not measure intellectual competence. Several studies suggest that lower-class children may be poorly motivated to take the IQ test. Puerto Rican children, for example, seem to have a relaxed attitude toward the test: they are not as "task oriented" as middle-class, white children. The result is a lower IQ than the Puerto Ricans might achieve if they were more highly motivated. A situation like this makes the IQ test even more difficult to interpret. It may not reflect the child's competence, the best he can do. Further, I argued that the failure to measure competence in some children is an inevitable result of standard testing.

Fourth, examination of the nature-nurture issue shows that the IQ is not fixed early in life, and that environmental events and emotional experiences can effect drastic changes in an individual's IQ. Identical twins reared apart have very similar IQs. This seems to show a strong genetic influence on the IQ. But the finding is somewhat ambiguous; the twins' environments may have been similar too. There are regional differences in IQ scores, and migration to another region can change the IQ. It seems unlikely that we can achieve a satisfactory answer to the nature-nurture question. The issue is too ambiguous, ambitious, and complex.

IQ scores are moderately accurate predictors of academic achievement. The reason for this is not necessarily that the IQ test measures "intelligence" or profound intellectual abilities. One reason may be that both school and the IQ test emphasize verbal skills, mental drudgery, and a certain docility of character. Another reason is that on the basis of IQ scores, teachers may develop expectancies concerning students' performance and may act in ways unintentionally calculated to bring reality in line with prophecy.

What can we conclude from all this? I wish to make several general points. First, social-class differences in IQ should not be taken too seriously. The numerical difference is relatively small—10 or 20 points—and does not necessarily indicate fundamental intellectual differences between middle-class and lower-class children, or between blacks and whites.

At most, the IQ test may indicate that poor children possess to a lesser degree than do middle-class children certain intellectual and motivational skills which current schools approve and reward.

Second, the IQ test fails to teach us much of a positive nature about the intellect of poor children. It indicates that they are slightly deficient in skills that middle-class children possess and current schools favor. But what are the unique capabilities of the poor? What intellectual skills have they developed to cope with their environment? The IQ test is not designed to discover the answer to such questions.

Third, the relatively high correlation between IQ and academic achievement is not immutable. The correlation shows that poor children's skills are not well matched with the demands of schools *as currently constituted*. But drastic reform of the schools could change the situation. If schools nurtured, encouraged, and utilized the skills which poor children possess, then the IQ might be irrelevant for predicting academic achievement.

So the IQ tells us little. Let us now turn to more informative research.

chapter three

Language We have seen that the IQ test tells us little about the intellectual functioning of poor children. We need to abandon the vague notion of "intelligence" and instead examine closely the many activities which comprise the intellectual life. In this chapter, we shall begin that examination by investigating the nature of poor children's language.

THE CONVENTIONAL WISDOM

There seem to be two major views of poor children's language. One view, which is both extremely popular and, I think, seriously incorrect, holds in essence that a deprived environment retards children's speech, that this inferior speech leads to deficient thought, and that deficient speech and thought result in school failure. Many writers on poor children hold this view—for example, Bereiter and Englemann (1966)—and claim that there is a great deal of evidence to support it. Very often, these writers cite the early work of Basil Bernstein, a British sociologist, and model their theories on his approach. While in recent years Bernstein has changed his mind about several crucial issues (see, for example, Bernstein, 1970), many of his American disciples have not; it is still the early Bernstein who influences their thought. For this reason, and with apologies to the later incarnation of the British sociologist, we must review Bernstein's early contribution.

Bernstein's Theory

Bernstein (1961) proposes that, in England at least, middle- and lower-class parents employ different child rearing techniques which result in different patterns of language and thought. Consider first the middle class.

THE MIDDLE CLASS

In Bernstein's view, middle-class life is oriented around the values of order, rationality, stability, and the control of emotion. A middle-class parent impresses on his child the need to plan for long-range goals, such as financial security, which are believed to be ultimately far more valuable and satisfying than the immediate gratification of current needs. Consequently, the child must learn to exert control over his desires and to orient his behavior toward distant ends.

The parent teaches that the unbridled expression of emotion, particularly hostility, may create stress, damage interpersonal relations, and in general make life chaotic. The child is therefore encouraged to verbalize emotions, to control them, and to try to understand why he feels as he does. In disciplining the child, middle-class parents tend to use verbal rather than physical punishment, to take pains to elaborate on the rationale for a prohibition, and to try to explore the child's motivation.

In Bernstein's view, middle-class child rearing depends heavily on verbal exchange. The parents use language to express goals, to discipline the child, to explain the value system, and the like. The accomplishment of these purposes requires a verbal system that is complex and that can carry subtle shades of meaning. Middle-class language must be able to describe feelings and intentions, to elaborate the reasoning underlying decisions, and to postulate hypothetical events in the future. Bernstein calls this kind of language an *elaborated code.*

The middle-class child is exposed to this code and to these child-rearing practices from the earliest days of infancy until late adolescence. This has several effects. On the one hand, he acquires middle-class culture and values. He accepts the norms of order and stability, and the pre-eminence of distant, rational goals over momentary desires. He avoids the direct expression of emotion and attempts to rationalize his own intentions and those of others. His moral code consists not only of prohibitions and goals, but also of a rationale for them.

On the other hand, the middle-class child acquires a distinctive style of language and thought. The parents' language influences the ways in which he thinks. Their speech is subtle and contains many words of relation, such as "although" and "bigger." To comprehend what his parents say, the child must learn to think in relational terms. Similarly, the parents use words to indicate abstract categories such as "justice," and this forces the child to think in conceptual terms. Further, the child must learn to use the elaborated code if he is to communicate with the parents. To talk with them, he must acquire linguistic means for expressing relations, for describing abstract concepts, and for rationalizing his intentions. He must be able to discuss why he wants to do certain things, what his feelings are, and how he thinks he should proceed. All this requires the elaborated code. In addition, the middle-class child learns to use the elaborated code as a vehicle for thought. The child possessing this kind of language can think and reason more easily since it embodies abstractions and other intellectual subtleties. With the code, his thought can be fluid and complex; without it, thinking is made feeble.

In sum, the middle-class child learns to comprehend the abstractions of the elaborated code, to use it for communication, and to employ it in reasoning. His speech and, consequently, his thought are suited for complex intellectual activity.

THE LOWER-CLASS

In Bernstein's view, lower-class socialization and its results are almost antithetical to those characterizing the middle class. Lower-class parents do not present to the child an ordered and rational system of living. Their lives are strongly affected by chance events, such as the sudden availability of a new job, and are not constrained by careful and thoughtful plans for the future. Such plans, if they exist at all, are fragile and easily abandoned. Thus, the parents do not promulgate a stable and well-delineated set of goals to which the child may aspire.

Parental discipline often takes arbitrary forms. Lower-class parents simply tell a child what he must or must not do—for example, "Shut up" or "Get that"—and fail to elaborate on the rationale for a prohibition, or on the motivations of the participants. The parents express themselves in emotional, direct, and often volatile ways. Their language is a *restricted code* which is ill suited for the expression of subtle shades of meaning or the elaboration of thought. Consequently, the child is not faced with the problem of comprehending a complex chain of reasoning involving relations and abstract categories.

The lower-class child tends toward the direct expression of emotion and the immediate satisfaction of current desire. He lacks both long-range plans and the ability to delay gratification so that future ends may be realized. Since he is oriented to the present, current frustrations or gratifications seem absolute; he cannot evaluate them in terms of a wider time perspective. The lower-class child does not try to discover the reasons for decisions or to present a rationale for his own behavior. Rather than appeal to reasoned principles, he accepts authority or tries to invoke it himself.

The lower-class child acquires a language that is in many respects deficient. His restricted code contains the following features:

1. Short, simple sentences which are often incomplete and syntactically weak.

2. Simple and repetitive use of conjunctions such as "so," "then," "and," "because."

3. Few subordinate clauses.

4. Limited and repetitive use of adjectives and adverbs.

5. Statements which confuse reasons and conclusions so as to produce a categoric statement.

In Bernstein's view, the lower-class child is generally limited to language of this kind; he has great difficulty with the elaborated code. By contrast, the middle-class child is capable of both forms of speech. He employs the restricted code particularly for communicating with peers, and the elaborated code with adults.

The restricted code has several disadvantages. It cannot precisely communicate complex ideas or relationships. Since its sentence structure is simple and makes little use of conjunctions, the restricted code cannot express logical relationships in other than a crude way. For example, logical implication requires conjunctions such as "if" and "then," as well as an initial subordinate clause (the "if" clause); since the restricted code is deficient in both of these grammatical features, it cannot deal properly with logical implication. Also, the simplicity of the restricted code limits the planning functions of language. Since the code is concrete, it cannot embody the hypothetical complexities of the future.

The restricted code is inadequate for presenting a rationale for one's behavior or a justification for a decision. The language relies instead on categoric remarks whose essence is the confusion of reasons with conclusions. This illogical approach can be used to justify or rationalize very little; in fact, the attempt at rationality is soon abandoned in favor of the appeal to authority. In making decisions or justifying them, the lower-class child generally relies less on logical reasoning than on personal relationships.

The poor child's language is a poor vehicle for thought. It employs a large number of idiomatic, traditional phrases which are concrete, descriptive, and simple. This limits the generality and abstraction of thought and forces it into stereotyped channels, preventing the child from verbalizing his unique relationship with the environment. The restricted code orients the child toward a primitive understanding of causal relations and toward concepts which are descriptive rather than analytic. This low level of conceptual functioning then inhibits the child's ability to learn from the environment. And in school his curiosity is limited and focused only on events which can be understood in a simple way.

We will summarize the restricted code in Bernstein's own words:

> [There is] a relatively low level of conceptualization, an orientation to a low order of causality, a disinterest in processes, a preference to be

aroused by, and respond to, that which is immediately given . . . this partly conditions the intensity and extent of curiosity. . . . These logical considerations affect what is learned and how it is learned, and so affect future learning. . . . There will be a tendency to accept and respond to an authority that inheres in the form of social relationships, rather than in reasoned or logical principles (1961, pp. 302–3).

To highlight the contrasts between the elaborated and restricted codes, we will consider a hypothetical example, described by Hess and Shipman (1965, p. 572), which nicely illustrates Bernstein's theory. Suppose that a child is playing noisily in the kitchen with pots and pans when the telephone rings. The lower-class mother orders him to "shut up" or "be quiet," whereas the middle-class mother says, "Would you keep quiet a minute? I want to talk on the telephone." When the restricted code ("Shut up") is used, the message is simple and does not require much reflection or thought. The child need only perform a simple response, namely putting down the pots and pans. In the case of middle-class speech, on the other hand, the child is forced to attend to a rather complex message. He is asked to consider the desires of another person (the mother's desire to talk) and to organize his behavior according to a time dimension ("Would you keep quiet *a minute?*"). Moreover, the mother's speech takes a more complex syntactic form than the restricted code of the lower class ("Shut up"). To understand, the middle-class child must develop a verbal facility that the lower-class child lacks. Also, the middle-class mother's speech expresses an implicit logical relationship ("Do not make noise so that I can talk") which stimulates the thought of her child. By contrast, both the logical relation and its consequent stimulation are absent from the restricted code of the lower class. As a result of such experiences, repeated daily over a period of years, lower-class children develop a style of language and of thought which is deficient and which ultimately decreases their chances of academic success.

Educational Practice

This kind of theory—of which Bernstein's view is only one example—provides the underpinnings for a great deal of educational practice. Psychological theories are not irrelevant abstractions: teachers base much of what they do on informal psychological theories of what children are like; and the work of curriculum developers often stems from an explicit and deliberate application of psychological ideas (see, for example, Brottman, 1968). Consider an example of the latter.

Bereiter and Englemann (1966), accepting Bernstein's general view of lower-class children's language deficiency, have attempted to develop special programs of remedial education. These writers begin by describing poor children's language.

> From what is known about verbal communication in lower-class homes, it would appear that the cognitive uses of language are severely restricted. . . . What is lacking . . . is the use of language to explain, to describe, to instruct, to inquire, to hypothesize, to analyze, to compare, to deduce, and to test. And these are the uses that are necessary for academic success (p. 31).
>
> The speech of the severely deprived children seems to consist not of distinct words, as does the speech of middle-class children of the same age, but rather of whole phrases or sentences that function like giant words . . . these "giant word" units cannot be taken apart by the child and re-combined. . . . Instead of saying, "I ain't got no juice," he says "Uai-ga-no-ju" (p. 34).

To correct these deficiencies, Bereiter and Englemann devised an "academically oriented" preschool program. This involved teaching 3- and 4-year old children a number of academic skills, including language. Language training began with "pattern drill" in "identity statements." Bereiter and Englemann's instructions to the teacher are as follows:

1. Adopt a stereotyped procedure.
   a. Present an object and give the appropriate identity statement. "This is a ball."
   b. Follow the statement with a *yes-no* question. "Is this a ball?"
   c. Answer the question. "Yes, this is a ball."
   d. Repeat the question and encourage children to answer it.
   e. Introduce *what* questions after the children have begun to respond adequately to the *yes-no* questions (p. 140).

The writers go on to describe in great detail how to advance from the singular identity statement to the plural, and from that to the "not statement."

There has been a great deal of controversy about the Bereiter and Englemann program. Some critics believe that Bereiter and Englemann's methods are too harsh, or that they are not sufficiently effective, or that they could focus on more important aspects of language. Yet the controversy should not obscure the fact that many pre-school programs accept Bereiter and Englemann's fundamental assumption: poor children suffer from a serious language deficit and require some form of compensatory education to overcome it. For example, *Sesame Street,* a popular television program designed especially for poor children, places heavy emphasis on labeling objects, on introducing new vocabulary, and the like.

So the fact is simply this: with Bernstein, many workers in compensatory education believe that poor children's language is deficient and that it adversely affects their thought and chances of academic success. As a result of this belief, educators have developed, on a massive scale, programs of language remediation for poor children. Literally millions of dollars are spent to correct poor children's language deficiency. This is the conventional wisdom. And it is the thesis of this chapter that the conventional wisdom is deficient, not poor children's language. We turn now to studies of the basic question: is poor children's language deficient?

NORMATIVE RESEARCH ON LANGUAGE

Templin's Study

Templin's (1957) report is one of the major studies of social-class differences in language. Her subjects were 480 children, half boys and half girls, from 3 to 8 years of age. All were white and monolingual. Seventy percent of the children were lower class, their fathers being day laborers, semi-skilled workers, etc. Thirty percent were middle class, as defined by paternal occupations of the professional or skilled trade variety. The IQs of the children were rather high. In the case of 7-year-olds, for example, the average middle-class IQ was 117.1, and the lower-class IQ was 102.6. Templin reports that these figures are typical for the Minneapolis-St. Paul area, where the study was conducted. Nevertheless, the lower-class IQ is higher than that reported in other studies.

Each child, tested individually, was given a battery of tests involving articulation, sound discrimination, sentence structure, and vocabulary. In the case of sentence structure, the child was allowed to look at and play with a number of picture books and toys. The adult examiner recorded verbatim the child's first 50 verbalizations. Unfortunately, Templin does not describe the procedure with sufficient precision. We do not know to what extent the adult questioned the child, interacted with him, prompted him, and so forth.

Templin's general aim was to establish age norms for certain aspects of speech, and to describe lower- and middle-class children's performance relative to these norms. The data are extensive, and we shall report only several typical findings. One of the analyses deals with types of sentence construction.

Templin categorizes sentences in several ways, although she does not present data concerning the reliability of scoring. *Functionally complete but structurally incomplete* includes remarks which are not complete sentences in themselves, but which clearly answer the preceding remark or are appropriate to the context. A hypothetical example is as follows: A child, asked whether a toy goes up here or down there, answers "down there." A *simple sentence without phrase* is illustrated by "He goes." An example of a *simple sentence with phrase* is "He runs with great speed." An illustration of a *complex sentence* (one main clause, one subordinate clause) is "She watches the movie while he gets the popcorn." A *compound sentence* is "He pays the clerk and she gives him the popcorn." An *elaborated sentence* is illustrated by "He ate the cat who bit the dog who lived in Jack's house" (several subordinate clauses). An *incomplete sentence* is fragmentary, omitting subjects or verbs, etc.

In general, the results, given in Table 3-1, show few differences between the social-class groups. For example, consider 5-year-olds. Both lower-class and

TABLE 3-1   Mean Percentage of Remarks in Various Sentence Categories for Middle- and Lower-Class Children of Several Ages

	Middle Class							
Type of Sentence				*Ages*				
	3	3.5	4	4.5	5	6	7	8
Functionally complete but structurally incomplete	26.0	20.2	18.4	11.6	16.1	12.0	9.1	7.0
Simple without phrase	36.4	39.2	38.6	40.2	32.2	36.0	29.5	30.4
Simple with phrase	15.3	21.5	19.3	18.3	17.6	17.4	22.2	18.0
Compound and complex	4.2	5.3	6.0	8.0	8.8	10.4	12.7	19.0
Elaborated	4.7	4.9	6.0	9.0	8.4	13.1	14.0	16.0
Incomplete	13.3	8.6	11.4	12.0	15.8	9.9	12.3	8.8
	Lower Class							
Type of Sentence				*Ages*				
	3	3.5	4	4.5	5	6	7	8
Functionally complete but structurally incomplete	27.7	24.1	20.9	21.8	16.5	8.5	8.6	10.0
Simple without phrase	33.2	37.7	35.9	34.7	52.1	37.4	34.4	30.6
Simple with phrase	12.5	13.5	17.3	15.1	15.7	21.9	23.2	22.8
Compound and complex	2.2	2.9	6.7	5.3	8.6	9.9	9.9	12.6
Elaborated	2.3	2.1	6.8	6.6	7.6	10.9	12.5	11.2
Incomplete	17.1	15.1	10.6	12.0	10.6	7.6	7.7	9.8

Source: Templin, 1957, pp. 88-89.

middle-class children show approximately equal percentages of *functionally complete but structurally incomplete* remarks, *simple with phrase* remarks, *compound and complex* sentences, and *elaborated* sentences. The middle-class children show slightly more *incomplete* sentences than do the lower-class children. The only large difference occurs in the case of *Simple without phrase* sentences. About half of the lower-class children's sentences and about a third of the middle-class children's sentences are of this type. A reasonable summary statement of the data is that class differences are quite small, if not negligible, and that lower-class children may have more of a tendency to produce simpler sentences than do middle-class children.

Another of Templin's analyses concerned possible class differences in subordinate clauses, which are assumed to be a sophisticated form of speech. Subordinate constructions were classified as *noun clauses* (*What is needed is rigor*"), *adjective clauses* ("We all live in a submarine *which is yellow*"), and *adverb clauses* ("I sink *when I float*"). Middle-class children used an average of .9 adjective clauses, 2.7 noun clauses, and 4.1 adverbial clauses. Lower-class children produced a mean of .8 adjective clauses, 2.0 noun clauses, and 2.7 adverbial clauses. All of these social-class differences are small, and none is statistically significant.

In general, we may say that Templin's study often shows the virtual absence of social-class differences in the production of sentences of various types. When differences occur, they are usually small and most often favor middle-class children.

What does Templin's study mean for theories of poor children's language? On the one hand, one might argue that Templin's work fails to confirm the usual conception of language deficit in the poor. For example, Bernstein maintains that the restricted code of the lower class is unable to produce subordinate clauses. Yet Templin found a lack of significant differences between the social classes in the production of adjective, noun, and adverbial clauses. In general, her work fails to support the hypothesis of a large gap between middle- and lower-class speech.

On the other hand, one might argue that there are certain limitations in Templin's study which severely reduce its significance. The major difficulty, perhaps, is that Templin's lower-class children did not appear to be extremely impoverished. They were generally members of the stable working class and lived in a city which apparently does not suffer from the squalid conditions of a Harlem or a rural Southern town. Further, the lower-class subjects' IQs were in the average range, close to 100, and this is not typical of poor children. As a result of all this, one might argue that Templin's study is not a fair test of the issue in question.

Loban's Studies

Fortunately, there is available a longitudinal study by Loban (1963) which provides data on the speech of children poorer than Templin's sample. Loban's subjects were 338 children, both white and black, from the Oakland,

California area. They were selected to be representative of the larger population, especially in terms of social class. The Oakland area probably contains more real urban poverty than Minneapolis, the location for Templin's study.

Once a year, beginning in kindergarten and ending in grade six, the experimenter interviewed each child individually and recorded his speech. The interview took a fairly standard form. The experimenter first attempted to put the child at ease by asking him questions about his friends, games, and the like. Then he showed the child a series of six pictures and asked him to describe them, elaborate on them, and so on. The children's speech during the interview formed the basis for the study. Like Templin, Loban analyzed the speech sample in terms of grammatical constructions, vocabulary, and so forth. Like Templin, too, he fails to give information concerning the reliability of the scoring procedures.

Loban presents data concerning three groups of children: (1) the entire sample of 338 kindergarten children (237 children were still in the school by grade six); (2) 30 subjects who were exceptionally proficient in language ability; and (3) 24 subjects who were especially poor in language ability. The extreme groups, high and low, were chosen on the basis of a standard vocabulary test and teachers' ratings on language ability. Both sources of evidence, teachers' ratings and vocabulary scores, were weighted equally. The extremely proficient group contains mainly middle-class children, and the extremely poor group contains mainly lower-class children. Unfortunately, Loban does not provide data concerning the exact numbers of middle- and lower-class children or of black and white children in each group. Further, he sometimes falls into the error of using the high and low proficiency groups for social-class comparisons. This method obviously exaggerates the difference between the social classes, since it ignores the large number of lower- and middle-class children who are moderately proficient in language. Loban's methods of selecting subjects, therefore, biases the class comparisons from the outset. Aware of this bias, we will review Loban's data concerning the high and low subgroups for information concerning class differences in speech.

One analysis concerns the percentage of certain sentence constructions in the high and low proficiency groups. In Table 3-2 are presented data concerning five constructions. (1) is a simple sentence such as "Mary eats" or "The fat robin with the sharp bill sits"; (2) is a simple sentence with a direct object, such as "Mary eats strawberries" or "The fat robin eats skinny worms"; (3) is a sentence with a subject, linking verb, and its complement, such as "Blue strawberries without stems are unusual"; (4) is a sentence such as "Here is Mary" or "There are four houses on the street"; and (5) is an incomplete sentence. The table shows that the only large difference between the classes involves incomplete sentences. Particularly in the early years of school, low-proficiency children produce more incomplete sentences than the high-proficiency group (this agrees with Templin's results). There is a slight difference, favoring the high group, in the case of sentence type 3. Data not shown in Table 3-2 reveal that almost no one in either group used

TABLE 3-2   Percentage of Certain Constructions in High and Low Groups

Grade	Construction				
	1	*2*	*3*	*4*	*5*
High Group					
K	24	27	11	3	34
1	21	37	16	3	24
2	21	34	17	7	21
3	20	38	17	5	19
4	27	36	17	5	13
5	28	35	18	3	13
6	28	39	15	2	14
Low Group					
K	23	26	6	0	45
1	25	26	7	0	42
2	25	31	10	4	30
3	24	33	10	2	31
4	27	36	11	2	23
5	28	34	12	4	22
6	28	36	12	2	18

Source: Loban, 1963, pp. 44-45.

passive constructions ("The ball *was hit*"), indirect objects ("She gave *the boy* some bread"), or outer complements ("We elected him *president*").

A second analysis of sentence constructions dealt with adjective, noun, and adverb subordinate clauses. These are assumed to be more complex than the constructions described in Table 3-2 and may, therefore, be a better test of group differences. Figure 3-1 shows that the high-proficiency group consistently produces more subordinate clauses of each type than does the low-proficiency group. This result is at variance with Templin's finding that lower- and middle-class children do not differ in the production of these constructions.

Loban's data concerning subordination are hard to interpret on at least two grounds. One, already mentioned, is that his method of selecting subjects biases the results. If he had compared *all* of the middle-class children (not just those rated highly proficient in language) with *all* of the lower-class children (not just those rated minimally proficient in language), the differences in subordination might be considerably reduced.

A second difficulty is that the data do not adequately deal with poor

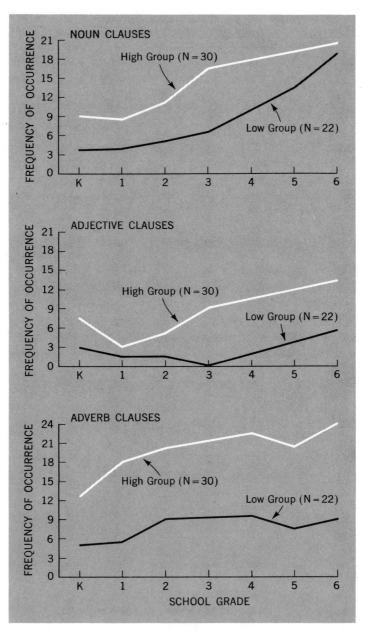

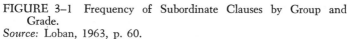

FIGURE 3–1 Frequency of Subordinate Clauses by Group and
Grade.
Source: Loban, 1963, p. 60.

children's *competence* in language. For example, Loban reports that the low-proficiency (lower class) group produces fewer subordinate clauses than the high-proficiency group. But what does this performance mean? Does it mean that poor children lack competence in this area? Not necessarily. After all, they did produce *some* subordinate clauses, and this in itself might be taken to indicate competence. But suppose now that some children in the lower proficiency group produced no subordinate clauses at all. (It is impossible to tell from Loban's group data what individual subjects did, but this is a reasonable hypothesis; there must have been at least one such child.) Do these children lack competence in this area? Not necessarily. Perhaps they comprehend constructions of this type but do not choose to produce them.

Let me state the criticism in more general terms. Loban has used only one method—analysis of speech in response to pictures and questions—to study children's speech. This method gives information on language *performance* in certain circumstances; it tells us something about how children ordinarily use language in response to an adult in school. This performance may not, however, indicate the full extent of the child's competence with language. Perhaps the child understands constructions he does not ordinarily use. Perhaps outside of school and with his peers he uses language more freely. To investigate the child's competence in language, one must use a variety of methods, and Loban has not done this. As Chomsky puts the matter:

> . . . if anything far-reaching and real is to be discovered about the actual grammar of the child, then rather devious kinds of observations of his performance, his abilities, and his comprehension in many different kinds of circumstances will have to be obtained . . . (1964, p. 36).

Unfortunately, Loban's data are far from "devious" or comprehensive. My overall conclusion about his study is this: Loban's results, biased as they are in favor of making social-class distinctions, reveal few differences among middle- and lower-class children's speech. When differences are found, their meaning in terms of linguistic competence is unclear.

How does this reflect on Bernstein's view? Perhaps the most cautious interpretation is this: Loban's data, like Templin's, fail to give support to the hypothesis that certain classes of American children exhibit certain language deficits which Bernstein describes. This leaves open the possibility that Bernstein's theory is useful for English children or for classes of American children which Loban did not study.

In another study, Loban (1966) focuses not on grammatical complexity, but on ways in which lower-class speech deviates from *Standard English* (as spoken in the United States). Standard English is the dialect which is most socially acceptable in the country at large. The mass media—radio, television—use the dialect in an attempt to communicate to all regions of the country. Well-educated people generally attempt to speak Standard English, and so do politicians, religious leaders, and businessmen. It is the language of the mainstream, of the establishment. In American literature and films, the "success" of the upwardly mobile is often seen to involve the abandonment of ethnic dialect and the adoption of Standard English.

Loban studied deviations from Standard English in four sub-samples of children chosen from the larger group of 338 subjects in his extensive longitudinal study. Responses to the semi-standard interviews again form the raw data for the analysis. The groups were: white (high proficiency in language), white (low proficiency), Negro (low proficiency), and a group randomly selected from the entire sample. The white (high proficiency) group is mainly middle class; the white (low proficiency) is mainly lower class; and the Negro group involves lower-class children whose parents had recently migrated from the South. My earlier criticism applies once again: Loban's method of selecting subjects biases the results from the outset.

The main finding was that lower-class black children speak a dialect which is different from the more or less Standard English used by both the lower- and middle-class white. In Negro speech, the chief departures from the Standard English involve verbs, and to a lesser degree, pronouns and nouns. Figure 3-2 presents data concerning omission of auxiliary verbs. Some examples of this are: "He running away"; "How you know he isn't here?"; "He been here." The graph shows that the randomly selected group and the lower- and middle-class white groups seldom use this type of construction. The black children use it most at the age of about 5 and increasingly less often thereafter. Even in grade nine, however, there remains some racial difference in use of the construction.

Loban also found that black speech was characterized by the following features: (1) Lack of agreement of subject and verb, third person singular (excluding all forms of the verb *to be*). Examples are, "He *say* he is going home," "One girl *have* a basket." (2) Lack of agreement of subject and verb while using forms of the verb *to be,* for example, "I *is* going outside." (3) Omission of the verb *to be:* "He happy," "That girl my friend." (4) Nonstandard use of verb forms. Some illustrations are: "He *don't be* there much" and "She *bes* my friend." (5) Nonstandard use of pronouns: "*Her* went to town," "*They* eyes are blue." (6) Nonstandard use of noun forms: "I see two *mans.*" (7) Double negatives: "We don't have *no* books at our house" and "There wasn't *nobody* coming to visit him."

Loban's study simply describes a few features of lower-class Negro dialect. His data do not deal with a number of important questions. Even if blacks typically speak in a distinctive dialect, to what extent can they use Standard English? To what extent do they understand Standard English? How different is Negro dialect from Standard English in terms of underlying grammatical structure? Is there any sense in which black dialect is deficient?

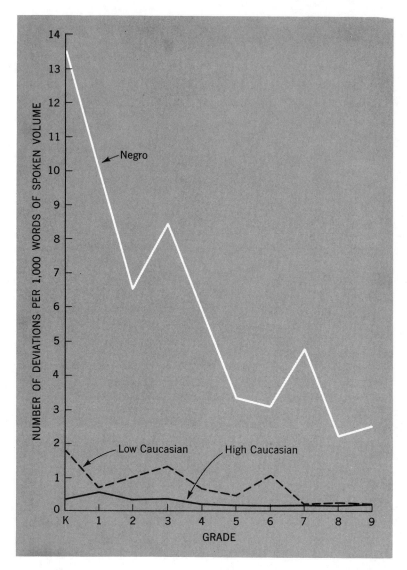

FIGURE 3–2   Omission of Auxiliary Verbs.
Source: Loban, 1966, p. 15.

Conclusion

We have now reviewed several normative studies of poor children's speech. We have seen that in general these studies show few social-class differences in language complexity. The performance differences that do exist may or may not mirror differences in competence. Loban's work also describes some dialect differences between whites and blacks. These, of course, exist, but their meaning is not clear. In general, normative language studies give little support to several of Bernstein's hypotheses (for example, those regarding subordinate clauses).

We turn now to some recent studies which give deeper insight into poor children's speech.

FURTHER STUDIES OF LANGUAGE

Robinson's Work

Robinson (1965) has done an interesting but incomplete study comparing poor children's ordinary language performance with their competence. His hypothesis is that the "restricted code" is a better description of poor children's performance than of their competence. According to this view, members of the lower class may possess the basic competence for the elaborated code, but for several reasons may not use it, especially with peers. For example, lower-class boys in particular may view the elaborated code as overly "fancy," effeminate, and in general as too closely associated with school and the values it represents. In interaction with peers, they feel that they must uphold the values of the group, and this requires use of the "tough" restricted code, even though the elaborated code is fully available.

To test this hypothesis, Robinson developed a very simple experiment. His subjects were lower- and middle-class English children, 12 and 13 years of age. (Here again we are faced with the problem of comparability of subjects. Is the English lower class comparable to the American?) He asked them to write two letters, one formal and the other informal. In the first case the children were asked to write to a close friend a letter containing the latest news and gossip. Part of the instructions were:

> All that is important is that you write *naturally* to him in the way you would if this were a real letter. This is not an English exercise of any sort, so just be yourself. If you'd normally write differently from how you write in English lessons, carry on and do so (p. 245).

In the case of the formal letter, the children were told to imagine that an official of the school system had available some money to give students for a trip. Only a limited number of students could go, and they were to be selected on the basis of letters to the school official. These letters had to describe the student's reasons for wanting to make the trip.

Robinson's intention, which the experimental manipulations seem to accomplish, is to place the children in one situation which demands the informal speech of the restricted code, and another which seems to require the formal code.

The children's letters were analyzed on a large number of linguistic variables, including many that Bernstein had suggested, such as the use of subordinate clauses. Unfortunately, Robinson's report presents very few of the data, so that we shall have to rely on his general comments for an understanding of the results. As he puts it, "the 'formal' letter imposed constraints on the subjects. Under these conditions, virtually no social class differences appeared" (p. 250). "However, most of the significant differences in the 'informal' letters were of the type Bernstein would have predicted" (p. 248).

In short, when a formal situation made it necessary for the children to use the elaborated code, they could do so; the necessary competence is available. When the children did not need to use the code, they often did not bother with it and instead reverted to other modes of speech. Thus, the performance of poor children—at least those in England—does not necessarily mirror their competence. Cazden (in Williams, 1970, p. 93) discusses several similar studies.

Labov's Work

But what about poor American children? What is the nature of their linguistic competence? William Labov, a linguist, has performed a number of extremely creative studies on poor black children's language, and it is to his work that we turn now.

Labov and his colleagues (Labov, Cohen, Robins, and Lewis, 1968) focus on several major problems, the first of which is the relation between Negro speech and Standard English. It is possible to conceive of Standard English as the "proper" way of talking. One can then determine the extent to which Negro speech deviates from the norm or is in "error." Labov feels that such an approach fails to provide an accurate characterization of Negro speech. The notion of "error" obscures the richness and complexity of Negro speech as well as its unique features. Labov takes a different approach. He assumes that Negro language is a coherent system with its own structure and lawfulness. The researcher's task is then to describe and understand the system *as it is*. He must determine the syntactic and phonological rules which underlie the speech of Negro children and not just count the number of deviations from an assumed norm. Once he has begun to understand Negro speech as a coherent system, the researcher can then attempt to compare it with the Standard English of the middle class. Are the two forms of speech similar in terms of underlying structure, or does one employ a set of rules radically different from those of the other?

Labov's second question refers to the functions of speech. He notes that the research literature gives little attention to the ways in which language is used, to the attitudes people have about it, or to the social factors which influence speech. Most modern investigations focus on the linguistic structure underlying speech and ignore the functions and determinants of language. It is obvious, of course, that language may be used for several purposes: among others, for communicating information, for talking to oneself, and for conveying attitudes and social values. As an illustration of the last function, consider this example. The teenager, when playing with friends, tends to slur his speech, to use slang, and to make a point of flaunting taboo words. He does this to convey an attitude of toughness and to proclaim solidarity with the group. It is also obvious that the style of speech shifts according to the setting. The teenager speaks in one way on the street corner and in another at school. No doubt social factors—the relation between speaker and listener, for example—control much of this process. While we know in a general way that all this must be true, we have little detailed information on either the functions or determinants of speech. These issues have particular relevance in the case of Negro children. Teachers find that in school these children talk little and seem to employ an impoverished language. Yet, on the streets the same children seem to have no difficulty in finding something to say. What functions does this informal language serve? What inhibits speech in school?

Third, Labov is interested in determining how the use of nonstandard English affects the acquisition of reading skills. In his view, there are at least two potential sources of difficulty. One is *structural conflict* between Negro speech and the Standard English employed in texts. For example, Negro speakers tend to drop the final *ed* from words in the past tense, for example, "He walk home" instead of "He walked home." When the child is asked to read this sentence from a book, he may have difficulty, since the pronunciation the teacher wants does not often appear in his own speech. Do structural conflicts like this form a major obstacle in learning how to read? A second source of difficulty is *functional conflict*. For the lower-class child, particularly boys, the speech of the school room may be viewed as effeminate, strange, and in general undesirable, so that there results a conflict between learning to read and maintaining one's own identity and culture. The problem, then, is not that the Negro child cannot speak Standard English and use it in reading; rather he has reasons for not wanting to. Are conflicts like these largely responsible for the functional illiteracy of the lower-class Negro child?

STRUCTURAL ASPECTS OF SPEECH

To deal with questions of this sort, Labov has performed a comprehensive research study in Harlem. The major group of subjects was composed of Negro boys from 10 to 17 years of age in a lower-class area. These subjects were members of several different organizations. Some of them attended summer day camps run by the city; others were members of peer groups or gangs in the neighborhood. Almost 200 boys were involved. In addition, data were obtained from middle- and lower-class Negro adults, from younger boys in the neighborhood, from adolescent girls, and from several other groups. Several methods were used to obtain the data, including interviews with individuals and group interviews.

The *individual interviews* were intended to elicit a great deal of speech in a variety of styles. It was hoped that these data would provide information on the speaker's phonological usage, the system underlying his speech, his values, and the nature of the peer group. The investigators found that interviews between 10-year-olds and adults (white or black) conducted in a classroom were unsuccessful. Under these circumstances, the teacher-student relationship dominated, so that the child's speech was inhibited and unnatural. Modifications of the interview format or topics did not help. Consequently, the interview was conducted outside of school, in a relatively flexible way, and was tape recorded by an adult quite familiar with the culture of the streets. The interviewer used informal speech and attempted to phrase the question in language familiar to the boys. For example, the interviewer said: "We'd like to dig how hip folks are around here. We know folks here in Harlem have a hipper way of doing things than folks in other parts of the country. . . . Is one cat the leader? Who? . . . Is he the slickest, the biggest, or the best with his hands?" (Labov *et al.,* 1968, I, 49).

One of the major aims of the interview was to elicit speech in several styles, particularly casual speech heavily loaded with the vernacular. Even outside of school, however, the general social definition of the interview— that it is a rather formal occasion for which proper speech is appropriate —interferes with this aim. To combat this tendency, several techniques were used. One was for the interviewer to use taboo words. Another was to ask very personal questions about fighting or the danger of death. These seemed to involve the youths deeply and elicit spontaneous speech. (Another technique was the group interview, to be discussed below.) The researchers were quite sensitive to possible impediments to obtaining useful samples of data. With their detailed knowledge of the subjects' way of life, they were able to see that certain research techniques would be uncomfortable for the subjects or would elicit only a very stilted and uncharacteristic performance. Indeed, Labov emphasizes that the methods of research must stem from a deep understanding of both the subjects and their language. We may point out, and we shall return to this issue later, that most psychological research on poor children's cognition has been deficient in this respect. How else can one characterize investigations into poor children's cognition which rely exclusively on standard tests or on data obtained in the unfriendly school setting?

The *group sessions* were the most important source of data, since the setting was informal and the influence of adults was kept at a minimum. The sessions had to be held at Columbia University in order to obtain an adequate tape recording of the group interaction. While this may have tended to inhibit speech, the investigators designed the setting so as to provide as much informality and freedom from adult control as possible. For example, one part of the sessions involved a card game while the staff engaged itself in "testing" the recording equipment for 20 to 30 minutes. Presumably the subjects did not see this as a formal interview session and paid little attention to their speech. Another part of the group session involved the interviewer's asking several questions relating to the gang's recent activities such as fights with other gangs. These topics presumably are important to the subjects and elicit spontaneous speech of various sorts. In general, the peer group members were in charge of the session and determined its sequence. Fighting and other forms of disruptive behavior were allowed. The group interaction seemed to resemble what is typically found on the streets.

The data from both types of interview are tape recordings which were later transcribed. Labov and his associates analyzed the transcripts in terms of phonological and syntactic structure, and in terms of function. Consider first an example of syntactic analysis.

Labov notes that Negro speech often omits the copula (e.g., *is, are*) as in the following sentences, which are taken from the data:

1. "Means he a faggot or sumpin like that."
2. "You crazy."
3. "They not caught."

In sentence 1, the copula *is* is deleted before a noun phrase (faggot). In sentence 2, *are* is not present before a predicate adjective (crazy), and in sentence 3, the copula *were* is omitted before the negative (not).

One way to approach these sentences is to classify them as "errors"; Negro speech is then an imperfect and inferior form of Standard English. Labov, however, takes a different position. Assuming that lawful rules govern Negro speech, he sets as his task the discovery of the linguistic structures underlying use of the copula. Also, he asks how the rules governing use of the copula relate to other rules in Negro speech and to rules in Standard English.

Pursuing this strategy, Labov begins by asking whether the copula is completely absent from Negro speech. Even cursory examination of the transcripts shows that many forms of the copula do appear, as in these sentences:

4. "I was small."
5. "If we wasn't playing now, it wouldn't happen."

Thus, *was* and *wasn't* are used to indicate past tense. The present tense in its negative form is indicated by *ain't*, as in sentence 6:

6. "It ain't no cat can't get in no coop."

Similarly, the abbreviated *am* of the present tense of the copula is often used as in sentence 7:

7. "I'm tired, Jeanette."

The copula also appears as the infinitive *be:*

8. "You got to be good, Rednall."

These examples, and many others which we have not cited, show that Negro speakers frequently use the copula. Labov's data further show that blacks make frequent use of both contraction and deletion (that is, completely omitting the copula); whites never delete and instead show a greater amount of contraction; and that the style of speech (careful vs. casual) has no great effect on the use of the copula.

So, Negro speakers can use the full form of the copula. How then can we explain its absence in sentences 1, 2, and 3? One possibility is that the copula is omitted in a random way. Sometimes it appears, sometimes it does not, and there is no pattern to this. Another possibility, which Labov favors, is that the copula exists in the deep structure of Negro speech and that systematic rules control the appearance or nonappearance of the copula at the surface level of speech (what is actually said). What is the nature of these rules? Part of Labov's solution is as follows:

> One general principle holds without exception: *wherever SE* [Standard English] *can contract, NNE* [Negro speech] *can delete* is *and* are, *and vice-versa; wherever SE cannot contract, NNE cannot delete* is *and* are, *and vice-versa* (Labov, *et al.,* 1968, I, 185).

Let us now explore some of the details in this solution. In Standard English, one rule is that the copula cannot be contracted when it is in the final position of the sentence. Thus sentence 9 is an impossible utterance.

9. "He's as nice as he says he's."

The contraction *he's* (for *he is*) is quite natural at the beginning of the sentence, but is clearly never used at the end. Since Standard English cannot contract at the end, Negro speech cannot delete the copula in the final position. Thus Labov's records show no instances of sentences like this:

10. "He's as nice as he says he."

Rules like the one concerning final position explain why Negro speech does *not* delete the copula under certain circumstances. But when *is* the copula deleted? The data show that an unexpected rule is quite important: the copula is more often deleted in Negro speech and contracted in white speech after a pronoun (such as *he*) than after a noun phrase (such as *the bear*). In both careful and casual speech, the pattern is similar. The black adolescents and pre-adolescents, and to a lesser extent the black adults, delete *is* far less frequently after a noun phrase subject than after a pronoun subject. The same tendency is observed for contraction in the case of the whites. While more pronounced for casual speech, the pattern holds for careful speech as well. Thus, both groups—white and black—respond to the same set of syntactic constraints; both groups are sensitive to the grammatical form of the subject and tend to respond in one way if it is a noun phrase and in another way if it is a pronoun. The difference between whites and blacks lies in the nature of the response. Whites contract more after the pronoun than the noun phrase; blacks delete more.

You might argue that this result is some sort of oddity—a fluke. But Labov's data show a similar pattern for the words *following* the copula. For example, if these words are a noun phrase, there is much less deletion for blacks and contraction for whites than if the following word is a verb ending in *-ing*.

Labov goes on to explore in great detail the rules which govern the contraction and deletion of the copula. We shall not pursue his analyses further, since the complex details are of interest mainly to linguists. We shall, however, make a few general points.

First, it is clear that there are many ways in which Standard English and Negro English are the same. As we have seen in the case of the copula, both forms of speech are responsive to similar constraints, such as grammatical forms preceding or following the copula. There are, of course, some differences, for example the tendency for Negro speech to delete the copula to a greater extent than Standard English. But on the whole, the similarities far outweigh the differences, especially if one considers not merely the spoken utterance, but the underlying structure. As Labov puts it, "of the sum total of rules of English grammar and phonology, whatever that might be, we have no doubt that the overwhelming majority will be the same for both dialects" (I, 336).

Second, there is no simple way to describe the differences between Negro and Standard English. Sometimes Negro speech extends the rules of Standard English, as when the copula is not just contracted, but deleted. Sometimes, although this is rarer, Negro speech lacks a feature which is present in Standard English. For example, Negro speech seldom employs the third person singular *-s*, as in "He hits." Sometimes there are elements in Negro speech which Standard English lacks. For example, black speech uses a verb *be,* unlike the ordinary verb *be,* which carries subtle meaning and works in complex ways. Negro language is not simply an impoverished or deprived form of Standard English. In general, the two forms of speech are similar; when they diverge, which is not often, the differences are of several sorts.

Third, social factors influence speech in a number of ways. Adults generally show fewer forms of Negro speech than younger people, middle class fewer than lower class, and teen-agers who are not members of gangs fewer than gang members. In other words, the "purest" form of Negro speech is used by young, lower-class, gang members; the least pure is employed by middle-class adults. Thus, even within the black community there is no one form of Negro speech, no "genuine" black dialect. Negroes' speech patterns differ along social lines, just as whites' do (at least in superficial ways).

Fourth, Negro speakers can generally understand Standard English patterns, even when they cannot produce them. In addition to the interviews, Labov and his associates administered a *repetition test*. The subjects' task was to repeat verbatim Standard or nonstandard English sentences, varying in length, which the examiner first produced. The purpose of the test is to estimate how firmly embedded are the subjects' grammatical or phonological rules. If the child can imitate fairly long Standard English sentences, then he apparently has available many of the rules of Standard English, even if he does not ordinarily use them. If the subject cannot imitate, there are two possibilities. One is that he does not understand the model utterance, since his own linguistic system is so different from Standard English. Another is that he understands the model utterance, but cannot produce it.

Labov's results show that in many cases (for example, utterances involving the copula) the subjects were quite capable of repeating sentences in Standard English. Thus they can understand and produce it. In a few cases, however, the subjects could not imitate. For example, the typical response to the sentence "I asked Alvin if he knows how to play basketball" was "I asks Alvin do he know how to play basketball." These distortions seem to occur when the rules underlying the model sentence are strongly at variance with those underlying Negro speech. But even on these occasions, which are rare, the subjects comprehend the model. This is shown by the fact that they make an accurate translation from Standard English into their own mode of speech. So black adolescents and adults almost always have the competence for understanding Standard English, although they might not always be able to produce it.

Fifth, how do the results relate to the hypothesis that lower-class children are characterized by deficient language? They show the following: (1) While the lower-class Negro child has a somewhat distinctive form of speech, it is not impoverished, illogical, syntactically primitive, or semantically empty. Rather, it is quite similar to Standard English, and the differences are in general rather superficial. (2) The lower-class black speaker can comprehend Standard English quite well, even though he cannot always produce it. (3)

The facts of speech are much more complex than theorists like Bernstein imply. For example, blacks can and do produce some forms of Standard English, but not others. Also, their underlying syntax is sometimes identical to that of Standard English; sometimes it lacks Standard English features; sometimes it overgeneralizes Standard English features. (4) The notions of restricted and elaborated codes are not very useful, at least in the case of black speech in America. These ideas do not capture what is important about Negro speech, for example, that it has some unique uses of words and grammatical rules, or that on a deep level of structure it is quite complex, or that it involves unique and highly elaborated functions, some of which I shall describe in the pages to follow. The notion of "restricted" and "elaborated" codes implies social-class differences along a simple unitary dimension of complexity-simplicity, or expressiveness-muteness. This does not correspond to the facts. It is too simple an idea.

Sixth, what implications do Labov's results have for understanding Negro children's school failure, particularly in reading? One type of theory —for example, Englemann and Bereiter's—asserts that poor black children cannot learn to read because their language is massively deficient: they could not possibly understand the words on the page. While Labov has not studied 5- or 6-year-olds, his results strongly suggest that this is not true. Black children have available a mature language, and so a language deficiency hypothesis cannot explain their failure to read.

While views like Englemann and Bereiter's are oversimplified and inaccurate, Labov feels that there are some ways in which Negro speech may interfere with school learning. Such "structural interference," however, is apt to be of rather minor dimensions. For example, the lower-class black child seldom produces the s at the end of third person singular verbs in the present tense. Thus, he says, "He laugh" rather than "He laughs," and this omission may lead to difficulty in learning to read. If he sees "He laughs" in a reading primer, the most natural response is "He laugh." Under these circumstances, the child may be confused about the role of the letter s. From his point of view, one must sometimes sound the letter and sometimes not, and this ambivalence may lead to difficulty in learning to read. The middle-class white child, on the other hand, pronounces the singular s and, therefore, experiences no confusion when he sees it on the page. (On the other hand, suppose middle-class children were required to read black dialect!)

While there may be some cases of structural interference between Negro speech and school English, Labov feels that these are not sufficiently numerous to explain the functional illiteracy of Negro children. Little conflict should arise between the child's way of talking and what he sees on the pages of the reading primer. Negro speech is not deviant enough from Standard English to explain massive reading failure.

What, then, is responsible for the failure of the schools? Labov feels that part of the problem is a conflict between the spontaneous uses of Negro speech and those that are required in the school. Another problem is a clash between black values and the ideology of the educational system. Let us now explore these matters.

THE FUNCTIONS OF SPEECH

To understand the uses of language in the Negro community, we must first try to gain some insight into black children's value system and the social structure which they have developed. Many of Labov's subjects were members of street clubs or gangs. These are organized by the members, without any adult control, and have a well-developed social structure. Each club has (1) leaders, including a president, vice-president, and war lord; (2) members who take pride in the club and feel themselves more worthy than other youths in the neighborhood who are excluded from group membership; (3) a name; (4) a history and mythology explaining the origin of the club; (5) an official song; and (6) a number of associated clubs for younger children. Membership in a club is fairly common and seems to fulfill a number of needs common to most adolescents and pre-adolescents: comradeship, status, and conformity to the peer group. Of course, many youths are not members of such clubs. These boys hold to a somewhat more "proper" set of values, are less often trouble-makers, and are in general more acceptable to middle-class society than are club members.

The attitudes held by boys in clubs are quite deviant from the official ideology of the school system. Club members place high value on fighting, stealing, cursing, drinking, drugs, and sex; their beliefs are diametrically opposed to the conventional morality. As Labov puts it, the ideal club member:

> . . . is a dangerous and effective fighter; he pays no attention to rules of a fair fight; he is a daring and successful thief; he pays no attention to any taboos on language, even in front of older women, and he has a good command of invective; he can handle large amounts of whiskey, and will drink anything in sight, including port; he gets high on reefers, heroin and cocaine; gets all the women he wants by a bold and direct approach, but has no personal regard for women at all (II, 36).

The value system in the black community is, of course, not monolithic. As we have already pointed out, many boys do not belong to gangs and hold to a morality more acceptable to the middle class (or at least to its public beliefs). Also, black nationalist ideology has become increasingly influential in the ghetto. The black Muslims, for example, stress values such as respect for women which are at variance with the beliefs of the clubs. There is thus considerable diversity within a place like Harlem.

Club members, and to a lesser extent others in the community, employ language in ways that are almost completely foreign to the white, middle-class segment of society. One example of the rich verbal culture is *toasts*. These are long epic poems which club members partially recite from memory, and partially invent as they go along. The toasts often achieve a high level of literary value. The clubs usually have verbal leaders—members who are proficient in toasts and others forms of verbal culture which are highly respected in the black community. The verbal leaders exercise their skills for the benefit of the club, and stimulate other members to engage in similar activities. Not everyone can perform toasts with a high degree of skill. The point is not that club members are all literary geniuses; it is rather that they institutionalize and place high value on a function of language which is essentially literary and which is a distinctive product of the Negro community.

The following are excerpts from a toast given by Stevie, a 13-year-old verbal leader of one of the gangs. Stevie's toast is partly original and partly rote. It is not as good, from a literary point of view, as adult toasts, but it serves to illustrate the type of verbal activities that club members engage in, the values they hold, and the level of sophistication in language that they achieve.

The toast begins as a parody of "The Night Before Christmas" (from Labov *et al.*, II, 69–70).

> It was the night before Christmas and all through the pad
> Reefers and cocaine was all we had,
> The nod [dope-addict] in the corner, coppin' a nod
> One more scratch he saw he was God.
> As I went to the phone to dial with care
> Wishing the reefer man would soon be there.
> All of a something I heard the clatter.
> I ran to the door to see what was the matter.
> As I opened the door, in my surprise
> Five shiny badges was shinin' in my eyes.

Note that to this point the poem is simply a parody, substituting drug taking for the tender sentiments of the original verse. Note also that Stevie maintains much of the rhythm of the original, although the parody makes thorough use of Negro speech patterns (e.g., "Reefers and cocaine was all we had"). The poem goes beyond parody, however, when it describes subsequent events.

> Before the cops began to get rough
> I ran to the bathroom, get rid of the stuff.
> As they bang I stuffed into my veins
> All I couldn't stuff I flushed down the drain.
> They caught me. But I didn't give a damn.

The hero eventually escapes from jail, and after some tribulations comes to a bar.

> As I slipped and slide through the mud,
> I came to this place called "The Bucket of Blood."
> I asked this man for a bite to eat.
> He gave me some dirty water and a fucked-up piece of meat.
> I say . . . "*Man,* do you realize who I am?"
> He say, "I don't give a damn."
> I pulled out my forty-four.
> I shot him *all* in his head.
> This bitch ran out there, said, "Is he dead? Is he dead?"
> I say, "If you don't think he's dead count the bullets in his head."

It is hard to find some middle-class values which are not violated by this poem. The hero takes drugs and does not regret it; he escapes from prison; he kills when someone offends him; he insults a bereaved woman; he has no remorse over the murder he has committed; and, of course, he uses profanity throughout. While the school system and middle-class society may deplore these values and the manner of their expression, it is nevertheless true that black youths participate in and contribute to a rich verbal culture. How many middle-class whites enjoy and create epic poetry?

Toasts are not the only form of creative verbal activity which club members engage in. They spend considerable time at *ritual insults.* These are events where one club member uses whatever verbal skill is available to him in order to surpass another member in mutual insult. While many of the insults are somewhat gross, it is important to note that club members place extremely high value on verbal skill. When a successful insult is made, its author is roundly applauded and clearly receives a place of honor in the group.

Not only does the group reward verbal excellence; it also exerts control over the speech patterns of its members. In general, the group reinforces use of the Negro vernacular and discourages Standard English forms. For example, consider the contraction and deletion of the copula. Table 3-3 shows club members' and nonclub members' (or "lames") use of the full form of the copula, the contracted form, and the deletion of the copula. Considering the contraction rule, we see that both club members and lames contract *is* about a third of the time before or after a noun phrase. Also both groups contract *is* in the majority of cases when it follows a pronoun. But there is one major difference between the groups. The club members have a high incidence of use of the deletion rule, whereas lames hardly use it at all. This result is particularly striking in the case of *are.* Furthermore, Labov goes on to show that *within* the club, those members who enjoy high status show "purer" forms of Negro speech than peripheral members. It would seem, then, that the gang encourages use of distinctive forms of Negro speech.

TABLE 3-3   Use of Contraction and Deletion Rules by
Club Members and Lames

	Club Members		
	Full Form	*Contracted*	*Deleted*
is—Before or after noun phrase	43	16	3
is—After pronoun	4	46	29
are	6	7	67
	Lames		
	Full Form	*Contracted*	*Deleted*
is—Before or after noun phrase	9	3	1
is—After pronoun	1	8	1
are	0	6	5

Source: Labov *et al.,* 1968, II, 178.

How does this process work? While Labov's work is somewhat incomplete in this area, it suggests that both modeling and overt sanctions are involved. The toasts and ritual insults that we have already discussed seem to serve as models for the sanctioned mode of speech. The verbal leaders demonstrate through these speech events the "official" ways of speaking. Furthermore, the audience reacts with clear approval or disapproval to a speaker's toast or ritual insult. If the speaker uses socially acceptable forms (and is clever, too) he is apt to be applauded; if he makes too frequent use of Standard English constructions, he will likely be ridiculed. Techniques like these quickly teach new members that the group values a certain type of language and fully accepts only those who speak it.

We have seen, then, that black youth participate in and value verbal activities, such as toasts, of which middle-class society has almost no knowledge; that black speech is "purest" in the gangs which form the heart of the street culture; and that the peer group places high value on Negro speech. We may now ask how use of Negro speech relates to performance in school, particularly in reading.

To investigate this issue, Labov obtained from the school system the Metropolitan Reading Test scores of 75 pre-adolescent and adolescent boys who were subjects for the study. Of these boys, about half participated fully in the street culture (i.e., were members of clubs) and about half did not. These proportions seem to be typical of Harlem as a whole. Consider first the data for boys who were not members of gangs (lames). The results indicate that 11 of the 32 lames read at grade level or above, and conversely that about two-thirds of the boys are below grade level. The data also show that scores at the older grades are higher than at the younger ones, indicating that some learning has occurred. Consider next the results for 43 club members. The data show that not one boy reads above grade level, that only one reads at grade level, and that most boys are three or four years behind. Moreover, no one reads above fifth grade level, regardless of the grade he is in, even ninth or tenth, and there seems to be very little learning taking place. Reviewing the individual cases, Labov discovers that many of the club members are considered to be behavior problems in school, and in fact many were expelled or suspended at one time or another. None of the lames was classified as a behavior problem.

There are at least two ways of interpreting these relationships. One is that club members' academic performance is inferior because they use Negro speech to a greater extent than do lames. This hypothesis would be reasonable if it could be demonstrated that use of Negro speech hampers reading and other aspects of school learning. That is, if black nonstandard English is a cognitive liability, then club members should do more poorly than lames in school. The problem with this hypothesis is that the assumption does not seem to be true. Labov has shown that nonstandard English is basically similar to middle-class speech and that club members value and participate in a rich verbal culture. Negro speech, therefore, does not seem to be a cognitive liability.

A more reasonable interpretation of the data is that black children's school failure is largely the result of motivational and value conflicts, and that alleged cognitive or linguistic deficiency is not the major problem. Labov has shown that club members' values are quite different from those of the school system and, to a lesser extent, from those of the lames. Boys in the street culture place a high premium on toughness, antisocial behavior, and defiance of authority, particularly if it is white. They see education as an institution which is irrelevant to their goals and antagonistic to their culture. Not only that, they believe it is oppressive and brutal. Often teachers do not understand them, treat them with a lack of respect, and expect them to be intellectual failures. According to this hypothesis, then, school failure results primarily from a value or cultural conflict; there is a mismatch between the poor black child's motivation, values, and aspirations, and those of the schools.

What is the role of language in this conflict? According to Labov, language is merely one element of a cultural orientation which clashes with the schools' values; and it is this conflict, not a deficient language, which largely accounts for poor performance in school. By this hypothesis, members of clubs, and particularly the gang leaders, do poorly in school because they participate heavily in a street culture which opposes school values, and not because language handicaps their intellect. Conversely, lames do better in school because they are not dedicated members of street culture. The same is true, although to a lesser extent, of youths who are only peripheral members of the clubs.

Labov's hypothesis is largely based on impressionistic evidence. The portrayal of the street culture and of its values does not rest on systematic techniques of measurement or analysis. It depends, rather, on informal contacts with the boys and on a general familiarity with street culture. Some may find it convenient, therefore, to dismiss Labov's hypothesis as unscientific or unproved. Certainly we need a deeper understanding of the cultural conflicts and the motivational difficulties which poor blacks experience as they contend with the schools. Certainly, too, further research needs to be done. But despite all this, we would be blind not to admit at least the possibility that one major cause of school failure in poor blacks is cultural conflict and that presumed intellectual deficit may play a secondary or even negligible role.

LANGUAGE UNIVERSALS

Thus far, the bulk of the evidence suggests that poor children's language is, in fundamental respects, not deficient or indeed not much different from middle-class children's speech. Consider now some cross-cultural evidence concerning this issue: are there fundamental differences in language among various societies? If there are not, then the lack of differences between social classes within our own society becomes more understandable.

Lenneberg (1967) reports a study of young children, from early infancy to age 3, in three societies: the Dani of Dutch New Guinea, the Zuñi of the American Southwest, and the Bororo of Central Brazil. The investigators made tape recordings of the babies' vocalizations before they learned to speak, as well as of their utterances after language was acquired. In addition, information was obtained from native informants concerning the children's fluency, characteristic errors, syntax, and so on. The general finding was that the children in the three cultures advance through essentially the same sequence of speech development as do Western children. "There seems to be no relation between progress in language acquisition and culturally determined aspects of language" (p. 139). Regardless of culture (and presumably the parents' language training techniques), almost all children utter words at about the time they begin to walk. And again, regardless of culture, by 3 years almost all children have a vocabulary of about a thousand words, and the grammatical complexity of their utterances is comparable to that of adult colloquial language.

McNeill (1970) presents further evidence on this issue. He points out first that there are several language universals which describe the basic syntactic structure of sentences. For example, every language in the world uses the same basic syntactic categories—noun phrases, verb phrases, etc. Every language uses the same basic grammatical relations—subject and predicate, verb and object, and so on. Lenneberg, making a similar point, argues that all languages seem to be of roughly equal syntactic complexity; there do not seem to be any "primitive" languages.

McNeill goes on to review a number of studies concerned with the development of language in children from several cultures. The general conclusion is this: the development of children's language takes remarkably similar forms in various cultures throughout the world. Here are some examples:

Discussing a Russian child, Zhenga, and an American, Adam, McNeill writes:

> Zhenga had a pivot class almost identical to Adam's: both children included demonstrative and personal pronouns, various adjectives, and such determiners as *other*. Presumably the two children passed through a similar series of steps in reaching the grammatical classes of their languages (p. 1093).

Discussing a comparison between American and Japanese children, McNeill writes that there is:

> . . . a similar sequence in a study of the development of negation in Japanese children. An initial incoherent period, where denial seemed to depend on the absence of an object, was followed within a few months by the emergence of a single semantic contrast between the denial of the truth of propositions and the denial of the existence of objects or events—that is, by the form of negation also observed [in American children] (p. 1110).

These are but a few examples. It is hard to present more in great detail because the theory of language is quite complex and technical. But the general point is clear: the development of basic features of language seems quite similar all over the world. On the surface, there are of course many differences: Japanese use different words from English; some blacks have an English dialect different from that of whites. But when one considers the fundamentals, it is the similarities, not the differences, that are striking. If this is so, then Labov's work on Negro speech should not be thought to yield results which are in any way surprising. Quite the contrary: it is the conventional wisdom—that of Englemann and Bereiter, for example—which is hard to explain.

LANGUAGE IN THE OPEN CLASSROOM

Aside from Labov's work, there is little systematic evidence bearing on poor children's verbal culture. In recent years, however, several radical teachers and journalists have produced impressionistic accounts of poor children's literary activities in the "open classroom"—an educational arrangement which attempts to give children the freedom to pursue their own interests.

While lacking in scientific objectivity, these reports nevertheless teach us a great deal, and so we shall review one of them here.

Kohl's Classroom

Herbert Kohl (1967) taught a sixth grade in a Harlem school. The pupils were presumably quite similar to the youths studied by Labov. New to teaching, Kohl at first sought to maintain control of his class by conducting it in the traditional fashion. He gave assignments, attempted to cover the standard subject matter, made the children read textbooks, graded homework, and so on. As one might predict, this was a failure, like countless other traditional classes. The children were bored and sullen, acted stupidly, and were well on the way to another year of academic disaster.

The class would have been the ordinary debacle if Kohl had not paid attention to what the children did in their free time. He saw that in the ten-minute breaks between lessons "everything important" happened. Here are some examples:

One girl learned a few tunes on the piano and taught them to some other girls. One day they asked Kohl to teach them to read music and learned how to do so in one afternoon.

A boy did good art work. The other children told Kohl that the boy had been drawing since an early age and had achieved quite a reputation for his art.

Several children got interested in chess and, failing to learn all of the conventional moves, developed a unique system of their own.

The class had an extended discussion about the Patterson-Liston heavy-weight boxing championship. They read newspaper accounts of the fight and wanted to learn about "ancillary rights," percentages of the gross, the meaning of "promoter," and so on. Many of the children then read Patterson's autobiography.

Kohl saw from all this that the children could have real interests, that they could be intelligent and alert, and that they could accomplish something. Trying to encourage activities like these, Kohl one day discovered the children's interest in language and literature. The incident began when one child insulted another by calling him "psyches," a slang word for crazy. Kohl exploited this by discussing the Greek origins of the word. He told the myth of Psyche, the woman who fell in love with Cupid. The children wanted to know about the history of words stemming from Psyche and Cupid. They saw that words change and one child said, "You mean one day the way we talk—you know, with words like *cool* and *dig* and *sound*—may be all right?" (p. 24)

The children asked to study language. They discussed Greek words—

logos, philos, anthropos, pathos—and myths—Tantalus, the Sirens, the Odyssey, Venus, Adonis. They asked for words to name ideas they had—"What is it called when something is funny and serious at the same time?"

The children began to read. Kohl brought in the *Iliad*, the *Larousse Encyclopedia of Mythology*, J. D. Salinger, the *Bobbsey Twins*, Thurber, O. Henry, James Joyce; and individual children read them.

Most importantly, as the "free periods" between lessons expanded to fill the greater portion of the day, the children began to write. They wrote about their neighborhoods:

> Last night on 17 St. Liebowitz collected the rent. They told him not to come himself but he came for many years. The junkies got him last night. He wouldn't give them the money so they shot him and took it. They was cops and people runny all over roofs and the streets.
> There were people from the news and an ambulance took Liebowitz (p. 35).

They wrote autobiography:

> When I was born I couldn't see at first. But like all families my father was waiting outside after a hour or so I could see shadows. The hospital was very large and their were millions of beds and plenty of people. And their were people in chairs rolling around, people in beds, and people walking around with trays with food or medicine on it. Their was people rolling people in bed and there were people bleeding crying yelling or praying I was put at a window with other babies so my father could see me their was a big glass and lots of people around me so I could see a lot of black shapes. . . . The fifth day we were free to go on the way out all the people said pray for me and I'll pray for you their were tears all over the ground and sniffin so we went out the door my father was waiting for us we took a cab home. For the first time I saw: cars, trees, trains, the sun, and even people without white suits on (pp. 54–55).

They wrote fables:

> Once upon a time there was a pig and a cat. The cat kept saying you dirty old pig who want to eat you. And the pig replies when I die I'll be made use of, but when you die you'll just rot. The cat always thought he was better than the pig. When the pig died, he was used as food for the people to eat. When the cat died he was buried in old dirt.
> Moral: Live dirty die clean (p. 109).

I have cited only a few examples. Kohl's book is largely a collection of the children's work.

What conclusions can we draw from these examples? One is this: Kohl's account demonstrates that in the open classroom, children—even poor blacks, doomed to academic failure—can be *literate* in the finest sense of the word. They can enjoy language and books, and they can write what they want to say. Notice I say that this *can* happen. It does not ordinarily happen, but it can. All we need is one case to demonstrate this. Unless Kohl has fabricated the children's work—which, of course, he did not—the point is conclusively proved: poor children—at least poor blacks in the sixth grade in Harlem— can be literate in school, just as Labov shows them to be literate outside of school. Herndon (1968) and Dennison (1969) find much the same sort of thing.

One may object to this conclusion by saying that Kohl was a very atypical teacher. He certainly was. He did graduate work in philosophy and even wrote a book on it. He knew enough Greek mythology to capitalize on his students' interests. Perhaps ordinary teachers cannot do what Kohl did. Even if this is so, although I doubt it, my conclusion remains true: under special circumstances, poor children can be literate in school; it is not true that intellectual deficit must prevent this.

My second conclusion is that Kohl's success was based mainly on nourishing the children's natural abilities and interests; Kohl did not do compensatory education or remedial training. Perhaps this is a hard distinction, but I think it is crucial. To me, compensatory education involves the assumption that poor children suffer from intellectual and motivational deficits and that these must be overcome by some special educational procedures. One must compensate for poor children's deficit; one must bring them up to the level of the normal child. Did Kohl think this? Not at all. He saw, of course, that the children were listless and dull in school. But he assumed throughout that this was not indicative of the children's real abilities. He assumed that the children were not retarded, that they tried to make sense out of their worlds, and that they were capable of interesting work. He saw, for example, that they were interested in a prize fight, and this led to the discussion of percentages. He saw that they were fascinated with words, and this led to Greek mythology. Of course, Kohl's children had a great deal to learn; I am not saying that they knew it all before he started or that he did not help them at all. But Kohl attempted to let the children follow their interests; he did not try to remedy some alleged deficiency.

He assumed that they were intelligent enough to do the things they wanted to do, such as read Greek mythology; he did not start with the belief that they were retarded and so could not go any further than reading some fourth or fifth grade primer. Kohl knew that they could learn by themselves; he did not think they needed to be taught in the usual way. Kohl tried to let the children be themselves; he did not try to give them the "benefits" of a middle-class education.

In short, Kohl gave the children opportunities to grow, to learn, to develop their own talents and interests, to "find themselves"; he did not try to teach in the usual fashion, to remedy, to remove deficiencies. That is the difference between the radical philosophy of the open classroom and the liberal philosophy of compensatory education.

SUMMARY AND CONCLUSIONS

We began the chapter by reviewing the conventional wisdom concerning poor children's language. Bernstein's early theory proposed that lower-class parents use impulsive and authoritarian child-rearing techniques and employ a "restricted code" which is poorly suited for clear thinking or the expression of meaning. The result is that the lower-class child acquires a deficient language that cannot communicate complex ideas, cannot express logical relationships, and is limited to the concrete. The restricted code is generally a poor vehicle for thought, and it therefore handicaps the child in his attempts to deal with academic work. Bernstein's theory is only an example; many psychologists have proposed outlooks similar to his.

Programs of compensatory education are built on psychological assumptions concerning the child's language and other cognitive abilities. To demonstrate this, we reviewed a portion of Englemann and Bereiter's work. They assume that poor black children are retarded in language. To correct this, they recommend a highly structured series of language lessons for 4-year-olds.

Is poor children's language really deficient in fundamental ways? To answer this question, we first reviewed several normative studies. Templin finds few social-class differences in language. Loban's results are similar. And when his results do indicate social-class differences, these are difficult to interpret for several reasons: the selection of subjects was handled badly, and there is insufficient evidence concerning competence. A second study by Loban describes some aspects of poor black children's dialect.

Robinson's research investigates poor children's competence with respect to the elaborated code. He shows that poor children are capable of the elaborated code, but do not often use it, especially in informal circumstances.

The most interesting research on poor children's language is Labov's. He shows that the syntactic structures of Negro speech and Standard English are basically the same. Labov also describes, in rich detail, the sophisticated verbal culture which blacks in Harlem possess. Cross-cultural studies confirm the trends suggested by these studies: social groups do not differ much in the fundamentals of language.

Finally we reviewed Kohl's open classroom. We saw that in an educational arrangement which attempts to nourish their abilities, rather than provide remedial instruction, poor children can be remarkably literate.

In conclusion, I would like to raise several general points. First, the conventional wisdom is seriously wrong. Poor children's language is not generally deficient in important respects. Poor children have a syntactically complex language, and at least some of them—blacks in Harlem—enjoy a rich verbal culture.

Second, since the language deficit does not exist, one need not expend a great deal of energy in looking for its causes. We do not need to worry about how lower-class parents and how a deprived environment stunt the poor child's linguistic growth since it is basically sound.

Third, in a similar way we do not need to be concerned with how poor children's deficient language results in deficient thought. If the thought is deficient, the cause is not language.[1]

Fourth, Labov's work shows that a proper study of poor children's competence in language must employ flexible methods and must stem from an understanding of poor children. Research on poor children cannot be based exclusively—or perhaps at all—on standard tests given in school. To assess poor children's competence, it is necessary to investigate their behavior outside of school and to use a variety of devious methods. The researcher can do these things only if he has an understanding of and a rapport with poor children. This means, among other things, that he realize how school inhibits their language, that he have insight into the circumstances under which poor children speak freely, and that he accept their language for what it is. Perhaps another way of saying this is that he must abandon the middle-class perspective. By these criteria, few research studies on poor children's language are of great value. Many studies—Loban's, for example—display an insensitivity to poor children and are limited by a middle-class view. As a result they do not tap poor children's competence and hence provide data of limited significance.

Fifth, compensatory education programs such as that of Englemann and Bereiter are based on wrong assumptions. Poor children do not need remedial training in language. Like any other children, they need an environment which nourishes the abilities which they possess and allows their language to develop.

Sixth, Kohl's work conclusively demonstrates that a different kind of education is possible for poor children. In an open classroom they can be literate.

[1] In psychology, there is considerable debate concerning the relations between language and thought. Contrary to Bernstein's hypothesis, many theorists propose that language does not exert strong effects on thought or perception (see, for example, Furth, 1966; Gibson, 1969; Lenneberg, 1967). In this view, even if research showed a deficit in poor children's language, one could draw from this almost no conclusions about their thought.

chapter four

Intellectual Abilities

We have now looked closely at poor children's language, finding that it is far from deficient. The next question refers to their thought: what is the nature of poor children's intellectual abilities?

THE CONVENTIONAL WISDOM

One view asserts that poor children do badly in school because they lack or are deficient in basic conceptual abilities. Many writers no longer describe the deficiency in terms of general intelligence. Instead, they refer to classification, abstraction, and other mental operations. Consider, for example, Klaus and Gray's (1968) views, quite typical of those of workers in compensatory education.

Klaus and Gray's Work

Klaus and Gray were directors of the Early Training Project, a program concerned with the problem of "progressive retardation, which tends to characterize the school progress of children reared in deprived circumstances and attending schools with children like themselves . . . such children enter school at an initial disadvantage and, without special intervention, fall further behind . . ." (p. 1). The Early Training Project's aim was to develop and test an "intervention package"—that is, a set of procedures designed to provide poor children, 3 and 4 years of age, with the skills necessary for later academic success.

The research was conducted in the Nashville, Tennessee, area, where there exist many of the problems which plague cities and towns throughout the United States: poverty, slums, and massive academic failure of the poor, particularly the blacks. The poor families in the Klaus and Gray study were all Negro. They lived in inferior, crowded housing; the parents generally held unskilled or semi-skilled jobs which yielded an extremely low income; the parents' education was only at the eighth grade level, on the average; and past experience showed that the children were likely to do quite poorly in the public schools.

What is the nature of the "initial disadvantage" in intellectual abilities which characterizes these children? Klaus and Gray emphasize deficiencies in perception, concept formation, and language. Since we have already reviewed material on language, let us examine Klaus and Gray's views on perception and concept formation:

> The children, when they came to us [at the age of 4 years] were noticeably deficient in all three areas [perception, concept formation, and language]. This is easily understandable when one remembers that across all modalities, the sensory stimulation provided in the deprived home is basically unstructured and unordered. . . . In the spatially and temporally disorganized homes, full of noise in all modalities, from which our children came, the only coping mechanism readily available to them was "tuning out." . . . Exploration of the qualities of objects and events is difficult for the child in the deprived home. Not only does the disorganization lead to this, but so also do the reinforcement patterns in the home—withdrawing and passive behavior are much more apt to be reinforced positively than is active exploratory behavior . . . such exploration is essential for the development of adequate perception . . . (pp. 15–16).

What is a "spatially and temporally disorganized" home? In Klaus and Gray's view:

> . . . the television set booms all day. There is no one place for any object within the home if that object is moveable. There is no undisturbed occasion for a toddler to explore an object thoroughly. The day is not organized around such standard patterns as mealtime and bedtime (p. 8).

Thus, Klaus and Gray maintain that as a result of "disorganized" stimulation at home during the early years, the poor child "tunes out," is not familiar with objects and events, and in general does not engage in perceptual exploration. In addition, he is incapable of the simplest discriminations: he cannot see the differences among the primary colors, simple geometric shapes, and so forth.

Some of Klaus and Gray's statements are rather extreme. It is hard to imagine a home so disorganized that it contains "no one place for any object." On the other hand, several of the writers' propositions are at least plausible: perhaps for one reason or another poor children have difficulty in visual discrimination or are less prone to engage in perceptual exploration than other children.

Klaus and Gray have this to say about concept formation:

> For our purpose, we defined concept formation as the identifying of common characteristics in different objects and events and the applying of a common label. As might be expected, the children with whom we worked tended to have little categorizing ability except in affective terms; they were highly concrete and immediate in their approaches to objects and situations. Our general purpose over time was to move them to increasingly more abstract levels of classification, since such abstraction is essential in school and life in the Western world today (p. 16).

So in Klaus and Gray's view, poor children are concrete in their thinking. They respond in emotional terms and lack the kind of abstraction which the "Western world" (and presumably not the non-Western) demands. The inability to think abstractly makes poor children incapable of satisfactory work in school; their concrete mentality cannot cope with the subtleties of academic subject matter.

This view of poor children's intellect—a view that is shared by many researchers in this area—leads to programs of compensatory education. Klaus and Gray developed a pre-school program, operated during the summer months, five days a week. The general aim of the school was to provide the children with a "Head Start"—that is, with the intellectual and motivational skills that they ordinarily lack on entrance to school.

The daily schedule was roughly as follows:

9:00 All children arrive by bus.
9:10 Work in small groups, emphasizing, for example, language instruction or perceptual development.
10:00 Snack—wash up.
10:30 Large group activity. All of the smaller groups joined to engage in singing, films, games, etc.
11:00 Small group activities.
12:00 Lunch.
12:30 Small group activities.
12:50 Preparation for leaving.
1:00 Departure.

As you can see, the program stresses small group instruction. Within this framework, there was a heavy emphasis on reinforcement theory. Klaus and Gray felt that because of the general immaturity of the students, it was necessary to begin by using concrete rewards such as candy, and an adult's physically expressed approval, such as hugging. On each occasion when the child made a correct response, such as naming the colors, or even an approximately correct response, the teacher attempted to reward him. As time went on, the teacher became more demanding; she would reward only responses which were precisely correct: "Please give me the milk" instead of simply "milk." Also, the teacher attempted to make the child accept rewards that were less concrete and physical. Instead of candy and hugs she dispensed comments such as "good." The ultimate aim was to eliminate the necessity for any form of external reinforcement—that is, rewards given by the teacher —by getting the child to reward himself.

Reinforcement, then, was the technique used to teach children in the small groups several different kinds of skills, including perception, concepts, and language. In the area of perceptual development, the teacher first attempted to show the children that there are perceptible differences among objects and events; not everything is the same. Then the children learned about certain particular differences, especially visual and auditory. For example, the children were taught the differences between the primary colors, between simple geometric shapes, between easily identifiable sounds, and so forth. As progress was made, the teacher increased the difficulty of the required discriminations until the child was able to perceive rather small differences.

In the case of concept formation, the teacher's general aim was to get the children to advance beyond concrete concepts to abstract ones. This was accomplished by procedures like the following: a child was first shown a green, red, and yellow apple, and learned to call all of them "apples"; then a peach and a pear were added, and he was required to use the word "food"; and finally clothing was placed with the other objects and the child was expected to use the concept of "necessities of life." As you can see, the child began with a simple, concrete concept ("apple"), and gradually proceeded to a rather abstract one ("necessities of life").

Language development was another focus of the small groups. One of the teacher's first aims was simply to get the child to speak—to say anything at all. This was accomplished in most cases by adult reinforcement: the teacher would sit with one child who was ordinarily silent and would encourage and approve of his use of language. Another approach was to devise a situation where a child had to use speech to accomplish some goal. If the child did not have available the necessary language, the adult would tell him what to say and would help him say it. In addition, language was encouraged in several ways typical of most nursery schools: group singing, story reading, toy (and real) telephones, and the like.

In addition to the nursery school project, Klaus and Gray instituted a program of "parent intervention." This involved several years of weekly visits to parents of the children in the Project's pre-school. The visitors, who, like the parents, were Negroes, were women trained in education and child development. The visits were intended to teach the parent to encourage the child's educational endeavors. According to Klaus and Gray, many of the families had no father present, with the result that the mother had to work for long hours and at low pay. This work, and the responsibility of caring for a large family, enervated the mothers. It was, therefore, necessary for the home visitor to plan the mother's schedule with respect to bringing up the children and to provide encouragement and support. The home visitor stressed that the mother should make:

> an interested, encouraging, and reinforcing response to the materials the children brought from school. . . . Every attempt was made to reinforce any indication on the part of the parent of increasing concern for the welfare of the child. The home visitor tried to call attention to a child's characteristics and performance of which his mother could be justly proud. Any indication of the child's showing improvement in the areas of major concern of the project received the special attention of the home visitor" (pp. 20–21).

Another task of the home visitor was to instruct the parent in "educational techniques." The visitor began by asserting that "during a child's pre-school years the parent is the child's most important teacher" (p. 21). Therefore, it is incumbent on the parent to plan "activities of a training nature." The visitor showed the mother how to do this. "To help develop confidence and skill, the home visitor frequently used role playing with the parent, the home visitor acting as parent and the parent as child" (p. 21). Using techniques like this, the home visitor showed the mother how to read books to the child, emphasizing particularly the explanation of the relevant pictures and concepts. The visitor planned trips to the library, the post office, and other points of interest and had the mother provide exhaustive and relevant commentary during the excursion. The visitor arranged activities which would lead to a discussion of cause-effect relations. For example, she had the mother leave a can of water outside in the freezing weather and then engage the child in an "interesting elementary science lesson" (p. 22).

Two Faulty Assumptions

We have seen that Klaus and Gray, like many others in the field of compensatory education, begin with a theory of poor children's intellect. They propose that poor children suffer from deficits in perception, concept formation, and language. To overcome these, Klaus and Gray maintain, it is necessary to provide compensatory education in nursery school and even to change the ways in which lower-class parents rear their children.

Let us begin by emphasizing how severe and drastic is the remedy proposed by Klaus and Gray. Their solution to poor children's academic difficulties is not only to devise programs of pre-school compensatory education; it is to modify the very foundations of family life among the poor. These writers believe that lower-class mothers are so incompetent at child rearing as to damage their children's intellect and destroy their chances of academic success. The only hope is for society to interpose itself between mother and child so as to prevent him from suffering lasting damage.

This solution obviously raises many moral issues. Is it proper for society to prescribe the manner in which mothers relate to their children? Is it acceptable for society to interfere with the privacy of the home? Normally, such steps are taken only when there is real danger to the child—as for example when his physical safety is in doubt. In the case of intellectual development, does a real danger exist? Is the lower-class mother really so drastic an obstacle to the intellectual development of her child?

In the pages that follow, I shall argue that Klaus and Gray's approach to compensatory education is based on two faulty assumptions. The first is that on entrance to school poor children suffer from severe intellectual deficit. I will show that the research evidence gives quite a different picture of poor children. Contrary to Klaus and Gray's opinions, poor children have many intellectual strengths and are not characterized by inadequate perception, concrete concepts, or similar intellectual deficits.

The second faulty assumption is that poor mothers play a major part in retarding their children's intellectual growth. The evidence gives several reasons for rejecting this assumption. The most obvious is that poor children's intellect is not deficient and so we do not have to worry about who stunted it. We shall discuss these matters in Chapter 5.

The major job of this chapter is to examine Klaus and Gray's initial assumption, that poor children suffer from severe intellectual deficit. We shall begin with studies of infant development, since some writers (e.g., Wachs, Uzgiris, and Hunt, 1971) have claimed that the poor child's intellectual deficiencies have their roots in the first few years of life.

INFANT DEVELOPMENT

Before considering poor infants' development, we must first review some general background material concerning infancy.

The untrained observer of an infant usually reports several impressions. The baby, who is much smaller than anticipated, appears weak, fragile, and extraordinarily passive. He does not seem to *do* much of anything. In the first few months of life, the baby spends most of his time in sleep, and usually wakes only to be fed. Even during the feeding, he does not seem very alert; he is half asleep. Since the infant seems to show little reaction to people or things, our observer may even suspect that the newborn does not *see* the world clearly, if at all. Perhaps he can perceive a few blurred shapes and some sharp contrasts in light; but surely the world he sees is not our world.

Our naïve observer of infants is both right and wrong. He is right in assuming that infants lack many of the intellectual and perceptual skills that older children, and certainly adults, possess. The infant does not perceive the world in the same ways we do (although recent research—e.g., Bower, 1964—suggests that he may be more capable than is usually suspected). He must learn to attend, to discriminate, to recognize, to identify. The infant lacks many sensorimotor skills. At the outset he cannot always bring his thumb to mouth when he wants to. And of course the infant lacks language: he cannot understand or produce speech.

So the infant is relatively incompetent. But our observer may be wrong about two things. First, he may be unclear about the ways in which the infant is incompetent. He may suppose, for example, that perception is a major area of weakness for the infant, when in some respects it is not. And he may not be aware of some fundamental deficiencies which do indeed characterize infant behavior. An example is "object permanence" which we shall review below.

Second, the observer is wrong about the infant's passivity. It is incorrect to conclude that the infant does little, is not alert, and pays little attention to what is happening around him. The evidence shows that on the contrary, from the day of birth (and even before), the infant is active. He seeks contact with the environment; he looks for increased levels of stimulation and excitation. The infant quickly learns to distinguish among various features of the immediate environment and to modify his behavior in accordance with its demands. Yet the environment does not simply shape and mould his behavior. As Lenneberg (1967) puts it: "Once the individual mammal attains freedom from the intrauterine influence, he is neither a passive tool that may be put to any arbitrary use nor a tabula rasa [a blank slate] into which behavior can be arbitrarily inscribed" (p. 28). Instead, the infant plays an active role in determining the course of his own development. To a significant degree, he controls the process of learning and interprets the data of experience.

The infant, then, is relatively incompetent—sometimes in unsuspected ways—and yet extremely active. There is much he cannot do and yet much he attempts to do. Consider next a few specific examples of infant development; I will describe in each case what the infant learns and then consider the question of social-class differences. The examples are taken from the work of Jean Piaget, whose careful research and brilliant theories have revolutionized our view of infancy and of intellectual development in general.

His work has focused on some fundamental aspects of infant development. Without skills of the sort that Piaget describes, the infant's intellectual life would be crippled indeed.

Object Permanence

The infant must learn first to perceive objects and then to realize that they enjoy a relatively permanent existence quite apart from his immediate perception of them. Suppose the infant has a toy duck. Perceiving it involves many activities. The child must distinguish it from other toys; he must recognize it when he sees it; he must identify it as a duck and not something else. All this he rapidly learns in the first year of life. He has difficulty, however, with the notion that the duck has a reality of its own quite separate from his perception of it. For adults, this is no problem. For example, a man who has hung his coat in a closet knows several hours later that in all likelihood the coat is still there. Although he cannot see or touch the coat, he knows that it remains behind the closet door. The "concept" of an object, therefore, involves more than the direct perception of external reality; the adult knows that the object exists independently of his own perception of it. Strange as it may sound, the infant is at first incapable of this apparently simple notion; and it is only after a long process of development that he elaborates the cognitive skills necessary for a mature object concept.[1]

During approximately the first month of life (Stage 1 of sensorimotor development in Piaget's theory), the infant reacts only to immediate sensations, both internal and external. Feeling the pangs of hunger, the infant cries; experiencing a touch on the lips, he sucks. The same holds true in the case of visual perception. If the mother's face suddenly appears in his visual field, the infant stares at it. But when the face is just as suddenly withdrawn, the infant immediately stops looking and resumes other activities. It is clear that he has no conception that the face continues to exist when he loses visual contact with it. Instead, the infant merely perceives a series of images or *pictures,* as Piaget calls them, which appear and then disappear.

From approximately 2 to 4 months (Stage 2) there appear certain behavioral patterns which are a first step toward the acquisition of the object concept. For example, the infant begins to exhibit *passive expectation.* At this stage, but not before, he can follow a moving object with his eyes. And once the object leaves the visual field, the infant continues to stare at the spot where the thing disappeared. One might almost be tempted to state that he already has the object concept and is hoping for the thing to return. But this interpretation, Piaget feels, is fallacious, since the infant does not actively

[1] The astute reader will notice that this paragraph is taken from Ginsburg and Opper, 1969, p. 42. See pages 1–41 and 43–237 for further details.

search for the vanished object as he will do in later stages. Instead, the Stage 2 infant merely pursues an action (looking) which has been interrupted. If after a short while the thing does not reappear, the infant discontinues his passive watching and turns his attention to other elements of his surroundings. Although ineffectual, passive expectation is the first step toward the later active search for the missing object.

In Stage 3 (about 4 to 10 months) we see the beginnings of object permanence. The infant shows visual anticipation of the future positions of objects. If, for example, an object drops very quickly and the infant cannot see all of the movement, he can nevertheless anticipate the final resting place of the object: his eyes move to where the object should be. The infant no longer continues passive viewing of the place where he saw the object vanish, as he did in the previous stage, but now visually searches for it in a new location. This behavior shows that the infant anticipates that the object's movement will continue even though he himself is unable to see it. In this sense the infant confers on the object a preliminary sort of intrinsic permanence. But the infant's object concept is quite "subjective." It is closely tied to his own actions: the infant visually searches for the object chiefly if he himself has caused its disappearance.

From about 10 to 12 months (Stage 4), there is marked progress in the acquisition of the object concept. The infant is now better able to coordinate his hand and eye movements. As a result, he can explore objects more adequately than before. Grasping an object, he brings it closer to or farther from his eyes; he turns it around in his hand. All this leads him to become aware that the object remains the same even though many visual changes have taken place. This discovery causes the infant to attribute to the object qualities of permanence and substance. As a result, when the object vanishes, the infant tries to find it again by active search. He no longer attempts to rediscover the object by merely prolonging or repeating the actions underway when the object disappeared. Instead, the infant now initiates *new* movements and actions to find the object. Thus, the object concept is less "subjective" than before: it is not related solely to the infant's ongoing activities.

Under certain conditions, however, the object concept continues to retain some of its subjective qualities. This is particularly true when *displacements* are involved. For example, suppose an adult takes a toy and, as the infant watches, hides it under a blanket at point A. The infant in Stage 4 goes to point A and searches for the toy. Suppose the adult does this again. Once more the infant searches at point A. But now imagine that the adult takes the same toy and with the infant again watching hides it under a towel at point B, some distance from point A. When this happens, the infant searches for the toy at the place where it had previously been hidden, namely point A.

We see, then, that in certain situations, the infant is unable to take into account the number or complexity of an object's movements; and he attempts to look for it in the place where he had previously succeeded in discovering it. In other words, if the situation is too complex, he tends to attribute to the object a sort of absolute or privileged position—a position associated with previously successful discoveries. If on the other hand, the object simply disappears in one spot, the infant searches for it in the right place.

In Stage 5 (approximately 12 to 18 months), the infant has no difficulty in following correctly a series of visible displacements. He now understands positional relationships between the object and other elements of the environment. Therefore, even if the object disappears successively in a number of places the infant will search for it in the place where it was last seen. He does not, as in Stage 4, look for the object in the place where he had previously been successful in discovering it. In Stage 5, the object is no longer connected with a practical situation (the infant's past successes), but has acquired a permanence of its own.

At this stage, though, the infant can understand only visible displacements of the object. If unable to see all the displacements, he reverts to the earlier reaction—looking for the object where he had been successful in finding it in the past. For example, suppose an adult hides a toy, as the infant watches, under a blanket at point A. The infant immediately goes to that point and searches for the object. Next the adult makes the toy invisible by placing it under a small towel. He then moves the toy, covered by the towel, to a new hiding place, point B. The infant, of course, cannot see the toy itself being moved; he sees only the towel. Asked to find the toy, the infant searches at point A.

We see that the object seems to be endowed with a dual nature. On the one hand, if the infant is able to see the object's movements, he believes in its permanence and continued existence. If, however, he cannot follow the movements visually but must imagine them, the infant no longer endows the object with the property of permanance. The object reverts to its earlier status of having a privileged or absolute position.

In Stage 6 (18 months to 2 years), the infant has no difficulty with invisible displacements of the object. The concept of the permanent object is fully elaborated. The infant can form a mental image of the object and can follow it through a series of invisible and complex displacements.

Such then is the development of the object concept. I wish to make several general comments about it. First, it is a good illustration of the complexity and beauty of infant development. The object concept has its origins in the elementary coordination of sight and hearing in the young infant: he learns to look at what he hears. From this simple beginning, there evolves a series of stages, each more complex than the one before: the infant looks at the place where an object disappears; then he searches for it; then he follows its displacements. And the object concept is only one feature among the many which comprise the infant's development. The infant also learns, again through a series of stages, to understand causal relations, to categorize objects, to use mental imagery, and to develop effective behavior patterns for dealing with the environment. It is Piaget's genius to have penetrated beyond the infant's apparent passivity and to have discovered these extraordinary accomplishments in the development of mind and behavior.

Second, the notion of object permanence is undoubtedly quite essential to intellectual functioning. It is the first step in the child's abandonment of egocentrism. At the outset, his view of the world is entirely subjective: objects exist only when he sees them. But he soon attempts to go beyond this primitive egocentrism. He begins to appreciate that things have an existence apart from his own consciousness of them. When the object concept is mature, then a fuller appreciation of the world is possible.

Third, most parents know nothing about the development of the object concept. They are surprised when they hear about it and so they could not possibly teach it to their children. I shall elaborate on this argument in chapter 5.

Recently there have been a few attempts to examine poor children's sensorimotor functioning in terms of Piaget's theory. Golden and Birns (1968), part of a research team at the Albert Einstein College of Medicine, have conducted a very careful study of the development of the object concept. The basic question was this: do there exist social-class differences in infants' sensorimotor development? According to writers such as Klaus and Gray, poor children are handicapped early in life. A deprived environment and inadequate mothering combine to retard the child's perception, thinking, and language. Is this really so?

To answer such questions, Golden and Birns examined the development of the object concept in 192 Negro children at 12, 18, and 24 months of age. Approximately a third of the infants at each age level were from the following groups: (1) welfare families, where neither father nor mother was employed; (2) lower-class families, where at least one of the parents held an unskilled or semi-skilled job; (3) higher-status families, where at least one of the parents had schooling beyond high school or had a skilled or professional job. All of the babies were normal and healthy, having no history of serious illness, birth complications, or prematurity.

The infants were tested either at home or in the laboratory. (The results showed that the place of testing made no difference.) Each child, with the mother present, was given 11 items from an object concept scale developed by the research team. The items are simply standardized forms of Piaget's original tests. For example, item 4a is as follows: "Using both hands,

E [the experimenter] hides an object in one hand without allowing S [the subject] to perceive which hand the object is in. On subsequent trials the object is randomly left in one hand or the other" (p. 143). Golden and Birns took great pains to provide proper testing conditions. They used as much time as necessary, repeated items if the child seemed not to attend, had the mother help if the infant did not respond to the examiner, and used cookies or candy as the hidden object if the child did not find a toy attractive. While the administration of the tests was flexible, the scoring of responses was standardized and reliable.

The results showed no significant social-class differences in object concept development. The 12-month-old infants, regardless of social class, were capable of dealing with visible displacements of the object and were beginning to understand invisible displacements; the 18-month-old children were competent in simple aspects of invisible displacements; and the 24-month-old children had generally mastered complex invisible displacements.

Wachs, Uzgiris, and Hunt (1971) have investigated further aspects of sensorimotor development in the poor. They studied not only the object concept but also the development of means-ends behavior and the development of behavior patterns for dealing with objects. Consider briefly each of these facets of sensorimotor behavior.

At Stage 4 (about 10 to 12 months) the infant acquires the ability to coordinate two independent patterns of behavior in order to achieve some goal. Piaget describes several interesting observations on the development of means-ends behavior in his own son Laurent. The infant showed an interest in a small matchbox, which he enjoyed manipulating. He had developed patterns of behavior for playing with the matchbox; he grasped it, opened and closed it, and so on. We shall call these the "goal behaviors." Piaget often performed the following experiment. He shows Laurent the matchbox, and the infant naturally wants to play with it. But Piaget interposes a physical obstacle between Laurent and the matchbox. Laurent wishes to play with the matchbox—wishes to exercise the goal behaviors—but the obstacle stands in the way. What does he do? In Stage 3 (before approximately 10 months) Laurent can do nothing effective. He fails to utilize any means for removing the obstacle: he simply reaches in a futile manner for the matchbox. In Stage 4 (after 10 months), however, the infant uses one behavior pattern to remove the obstacle and a second to play with the matchbox. Now the infant does not simply head directly and blindly for the goal. Although he has the goal in mind from the outset, he delays implementing the goal behaviors until he has first used other behavioral patterns—the means behaviors —to deal with the obstacle. Piaget also observed that Laurent's means-ends behaviors were not limited to the specific actions involved in obtaining the matchbox. After reaching Stage 4, Laurent could employ the means-ends technique as a general strategy in a variety of situations. Obviously, such behavior is adaptive and indeed essential for ordinary interaction with the environment.

Wachs and his colleagues use the term "behavioral patterns for dealing with objects" to refer to a variety of sensorimotor acquisitions, like the exploration of objects or curiosity. Piaget has observed that curiosity undergoes an interesting evolution. In the early stages of infant development, curiosity is relatively passive. When the environment presents something relatively novel, the infant visually explores it, sometimes with great intensity. For example, at 3 months, Laurent continually stared at new toys hanging from the hood of his cradle but at the same time ignored the cradle itself which was already quite familiar to him. At Stage 5 (about 12 to 18 months) the infant does not simply respond to novelties which the environment presents; instead, he engages in behavior which is designed to produce novelties. He takes a toy and drops it from varying heights and onto various surfaces in order to produce novel results: will the toy bounce, will it break, will it make new sounds? The child makes the object do new things; he no longer waits for some interesting event to occur.

Wachs and his colleagues examined the development of the object concept, means-ends behavior, and behavior in relation to objects in 102 infants at 5 different age levels—7, 11, 15, 18 and 22 months. Half of the subjects—about 10 at each age level—were from lower-class families, mainly Negro, and half were middle class and apparently white. The infants were tested at home only when they seemed in a cooperative mood. Aside from this precaution, Wachs and his associates did not seem to use as much care as did Golden and Birns in arranging adequate testing conditions.

The results show that in the case of the object concept, the middle- and lower-class children perform equally as well, except at the age of 11 months, when the middle-class infants show superior performance. The lower-class infants catch up, however, by the age of 15 months. These findings—essentially no difference between the groups—corroborate Golden and Birns' results. In the mean-ends test, however, the middle-class children receive higher scores than the lower-class infants at all age levels except 15 months, when the groups are equal. While the differences are significant, the report does not indicate their magnitude. In the case of behavior in relation to objects, no significant differences between the social-class groups were found.

The results then are mixed. Two tests (object concept and behavior in relation to objects) show essentially no differences between the two social classes. The means-end problem shows significantly superior performance on the part of middle-class children. Why the inconsistency? Why should poor children lag behind in the development of means-ends behavior and not the others? At present there seem to be no good answers to these questions.

All I can do is make the obvious statement that further research is needed to replicate the results and, if this can be done, to explain them.

What conclusions can we draw from the Golden and Birns study and from the Wachs, Uzgiris, and Hunt research? The obvious conclusion is that in some respects poor children advance through the stages of sensorimotor development in roughly the same manner as middle-class children.[2] The research of Bayley on infant intelligence (cited in chapter 2) corroborates this view. A possible exception may be the development of means-ends behavior, where poor children may lag behind. But suppose that this result were replicated. What would it mean? At the most it would mean, I think, that poor children are a little slow in one aspect of sensorimotor development; but eventually they must surely master it. Is it conceivable that poor children after the age of, say, 2 years cannot use means to obtain ends? Not at all. Poor children may simply attain this strategy some months later than others. Another way of saying this is that the stages of sensorimotor development which we have described are cognitive universals. Just as all infants acquire the basic features of language, so do all develop the fundamentals of sensorimotor functioning.

EARLY CHILDHOOD

At the end of infancy (2 years), poor children seem to have available the basic sensorimotor skills. But what happens during the years 2 to 5? Do poor children fall behind, so that on entrance to school they are already deficient?

Frank Palmer (1970) has performed an extensive study of social-class differences in intellectual development during the years 2 to 3. Palmer was interested in assessing what he considered to be certain fundamental abilities in the perceptual, motor, and intellectual areas. It was assumed that these skills were important for the child's interaction with the world and for his ultimate success in school.

The subjects were 310 Negro boys, both middle and lower class, born

---

[2] I should point out that Wachs *et al.* reach a different conclusion. They assert that their data indicate that a deficient environment retards poor children's intellect, and so on. For example, "The findings of this investigation indicate that deficiencies in the psychological development of children from the disadvantaged background of poverty are manifest earlier than has heretofore been supposed." This, I think, is an interesting example of Kuhn's (1962) thesis that in science facts derive their meaning from theoretical presuppositions or "paradigms." Wachs *et al.* start with the assumption that a deprived environment must lead to intellectual retardation. The writers then emphasize the *few* facts in their study which support this view and ignore the rest. Starting with a different paradigm, I focus on the facts—I think a majority—which are consonant with my view and downplay or attempt to discredit the dissonant evidence. The idea of science as an objective machine leading inexorably to the truth is fallacious.

in Harlem. Each child was tested several times, at the ages 2-0, 2-8, 3-0, and 3-8. Palmer and his associates administered to each child a large battery of tests and went to great lengths to assure that he was comfortable in the testing sessions. Before beginning the actual testing, they took as much time as was necessary to put the child at ease so that he would not be frightened by his mother's absence from the room. Also, they tested each child only as long as he was alert and responsive. The result of these precautions was that nine or ten separate sessions were required to test each individual child (remember that there was a total of over 300 children). The amount of labor involved in the assessment was immense, but such is the price of doing things properly.

Table 4-1 lists *some* of the tests given to children at ages 2-8 and 3-0. The tests cover a wide variety of skills, from "intelligence" as measured by

TABLE 4-1   Some Tests Given to Children at 2-8 and 3-0
in the Palmer Study

Concept Familiarity Index
Stanford-Binet IQ
Peabody Picture Vocabulary
Persistence
Embedded Figures
Sequence
Simple Perceptual Discrimination
Motor Battery
Labeling
Location Discrimination
Simple Form Discrimination
Varied Form Discrimination
Color Discrimination
Body Parts
Body Position
Delayed Reaction

the Stanford-Binet IQ test, to motor abilities. In general, the testers used verbal techniques, in a fairly flexible manner, to assess the child's ability. Consider Palmer's (1969) description of some of the tests:

> *Concept Familiarity Index (CFI)*—tests a child's knowledge of various concepts. Two procedures were used. For some items, the child is presented with two objects and is required to select (point to, touch, etc.) the object that is an instance of the concept being tested. For example, to test the concept "big," the instructor puts a big and a little horse on the table and asks the child to give him the big horse. With other items, the child must demonstrate his knowledge of the concept by using the materials provided appropriately. For example, to test the concept "on top of," the instructor places a piece of wood on the table

and says, "Look at the wood." Then he shows the child a dog and says, "Watch the dog; the dog is jumping." He gives the dog to the child and asks him to "Make the dog jump on top of the wood."

Delayed Reaction Test—a box with six drawers is presented to the child, and a cup is placed in one of the drawers. The task is to find the cup after an immediate, one-minute, and four-minute delay period. Questions from other tests are administered during the delay periods.

Persistence Measure—tests a child's persistence at a boring task. The child is shown pictures of two clowns, one sad and one happy, and the facial differences between the two are pointed out. Following this discrimination training, the child is presented with pictures of a sad and happy clown and is asked to take one. The pictures are presented and the same request repeated until a total of 48 trials has been reached or until the child refuses to continue.

Grouping—tests a child's ability to select objects on a given dimension. The child is presented with two objects and asked to select that object from another group which belongs with the first two.

Motor Battery—is a battery composed of various tasks such as paper folding, paper cutting, drawing, buttoning, and bead stringing, which measure the child's fine motor coordination.

In addition, there were several discrimination problems in which the following is done: the child is shown several objects, such as a blue ball on the left, a red car in the middle, and a yellow box on the right. He is asked to pick out the yellow one. After the first trial, the objects are shifted around so that now the blue ball is on the right, the red car on the left, and the yellow box in the middle. The child is again asked to select the yellow one. On other trials, it is possible for the examiner to insert new objects entirely: a yellow submarine, blue watch, etc. If the child is to be consistently correct, he must base his choice only on the color and not on the objects' positions or other factors.

The study showed that from ages 2-0 to 3-8, there are essentially no social-class differences in performance on the perceptual, verbal, motor, and intellectual tests used. The only exception was the Peabody Picture Vocabulary Test, where middle-class children did better at ages 3-0 and 3-8. We have some confidence in these results since the testing was done with care, every effort being made to motivate the children properly. There is, of course, a general moral to be drawn from this, and Palmer (1970) states it as follows:

A methodological explanation for the fact that differences do not emerge by age 3-8 may reflect the considerable efforts of the present study to ascertain that each child was comfortable in and responding to the testing situation. Many studies showing differences by class do not exert such efforts. Instead, they begin testing the child the first, and frequently the only, time he is exposed to the testing environment. It is possible that middle-class children are more adapted to conditions where such testing ordinarily occurs and consequently perform better in those situations, but that the lower-class child when given the opportunity to adapt performs as well. Indeed, these results raise a question about differences related to SES [social class] at any age (p. 9).

While I think Palmer's study is well done, and while it supports my position, I have one criticism to make: the study relies too heavily on verbal methods of assessment. For example, to test the concept "on top of" the examiner shows the child a piece of wood, gives him a toy dog, and says: "Watch the dog; the dog is jumping. Make the dog jump on top of the wood." If the child does this, then he is said to have the concept of "on top of." If he fails to perform the task, then he is considered to lack the concept. My argument is that this is not necessarily true. Failure to perform the task may indicate only that the child does not understand the *words* "on top of," not that he lacks the concept.

In fact, I wish to carry the argument one step further. If we use nonverbal techniques, we find that even young infants are capable of many of the concepts and discriminations which Palmer investigates in 2- and 3-year-olds. It should not be surprising, then, that 2- or 3-year-olds can do "on top of" since, in fact, they are capable of this and similar concepts in the first year of life.

My argument is based partly on the work of Piaget. Consider an example involving the coordination of behavior patterns, which we have already discussed. Recall that in Stage 4 (10 to 12 months) the infant acquires the ability to use one behavior pattern as a means and the other as ends. For example, Laurent removes an obstacle in order to grasp a matchbox. Piaget points out that behavior like this implies a primitive appreciation of certain relationships. Laurent has learned something of the relation between obstacle and goal. For example, the pillow is *in front of* the matchbox, which conversely is *behind* the pillow. Or the cushion is *on top of* the cigar box which in turn is *under* the cushion. Of course, the child's "understanding" of relations is not abstract as is the adult's; instead, it is entirely implicit in his means-end behavior patterns.

Piaget's theory of infancy is based on his careful observation of his three children. Some psychologists object to this on the grounds that the observations are uncontrolled, that statistics are not used, and so on. I do not take these objections very seriously for many reasons (which are given in Ginsburg and Opper, 1969, chapter 2 especially). Nevertheless, there has recently been performed a number of controlled experiments which support the general proposition that infants possess far more sophisticated perceptual abilities than we ordinarily suspect. Gibson (1969), in a review of the literature, discusses experiments which show, for example, that newborn infants can discriminate among several degrees of brightness (Hershenson, 1964); that infants between 70 and 85 days old can pick up stimulus variables specifying size and distance (Bower, 1964); that at the age of crawling, about 9 months, infants can perceive depth (Walk and Gibson, 1964); that 3-month-old infants discriminate some shapes from others (Saayman, Ames, and Moffett, 1964); and so on. Infant perception is far more sophisticated than we usually suppose.

Let me return now to the main argument. We saw that, using mainly verbal procedures, Palmer finds no social-class differences in several perceptual and conceptual skills in 2- and 3-year-olds. But using nonverbal techniques, experimenters have found that infants possess many of the skills which Palmer describes. It should, therefore, come as no surprise that 2- or 3-year-olds can do these things. And if verbal data failed to show this, we could only conclude that verbal data are misleading in this area.

So now we can place the Palmer study in proper perspective. It is not concerned only with discrimination and concepts; it deals mainly with children's ability to use and comprehend words. We should take it for granted that by the end of infancy, children can do most of the things that Palmer describes. The only remaining question is whether they can understand and use words connected with these abilities. One may or may not think this is an important question. (I think it is not.) But one should be clear on what the question really is and on what children's abilities are really like.

Consider an example of how the emphasis on verbal skills affects compensatory education. *Sesame Street,* a popular television program for children, contains "commercials" which are designed to teach children the "concepts" of up-down, big-small, etc. Children are shown a big object and a small one and the accompanying song stresses the size difference between them. I think it is incorrect to claim that this teaches children the concept of up-down or big-small. On a nonverbal level, children can make these discriminations early in infancy. In fact, I doubt that without these abilities any child would live long enough to watch *Sesame Street.* The program simply teaches him to attach certain words to what he already knows.

Conclusion

Palmer's study suggests that at least until the age of 3-8, lower-class urban blacks are not very different in a variety of intellectual skills from middle-class children. Yet the research focuses too strongly on verbalizations. We need further study to examine nonverbal skills and concepts in 2- to 5-year-old children from a variety of backgrounds and to provide a broader view of poor children's intellect on their entrance to school.

THE CHILD AFTER 5 YEARS

Deutsch's Work

Martin Deutsch, a psychologist at New York University, has conducted many studies which have had an important impact on compensatory education. Consider one of Deutsch's research studies concerned with this question: What is the nature of linguistic and intellectual functioning in elementary school children (aged 5 to 12 years)?

To answer this question, Deutsch (1967) performed an extensive study of 127 first grade (about 6 years old) and 165 fifth grade (about 11 years old) children. He and his colleagues assessed over 100 variables intended to measure home background, language skills, concepts, IQ test performance, reading, and so forth.

While Deutsch's presentation is not entirely clear on this point, it seems to be the case that the children were tested in school and that the tests were administered in a standardized way. Here is a description, in Deutsch's own words, of *some* of the measures:

> *Verbal Identification Test*—The child is shown 20 simple drawings one at a time and given a set [i.e., indirectly told] to enumerate the objects in the pictures. The child is then shown the 20 pictures a second time and asked to give the one word that best describes each picture. . . .
>
> *Concept Sorting Test*—The child is presented 16 cards in random order (four each, representing: modes of transportation, housing, occupations, and animals) and asked to sort the cards into piles. He also is asked to explain his grouping.
>
> *Concept Formation Test*—The child is presented with a booklet consisting of pictures representing concepts of identity, similarity, class specificity (persons or animals), and class generalization (living things). He is instructed to choose stimuli which belong together and to give a verbal explanation for the grouping.
>
> *Orientation Scale Test*—A measure of the child's general knowledge, e.g., what state does he live in? (pp. 362–64).

Within each of these tests, it is possible to derive several different kinds of scores. For example, in the concept formation test, one is the *"Class Generality Score*—The number of items correctly matched when the items to be matched belong to different classes which are subclasses of a more general category, e.g., a dog and a rose are both living things" (p. 363). In other words, the examiner determines whether the child can see that objects such as a dog and a rose are similar in a certain way.

Once the tests have been administered to all subjects, it is possible to perform a large number of comparisons among the 100 variables. Table 4-2 shows *all* of the data which Deutch presents in his paper. The figures in the Table are correlations. Recall that a correlation can range from −1.00 to +1.00. If the correlation is close to zero, then there is little or no relationship between the two variables. For example, there is probably little relation between a child's height and his grades in school. If you know a child's height,

TABLE 4-2   Comparisons between First and Fifth Grade Children

Variables	Correlations * with race		Correlations * with social class	
	First Grade (N=127)	Fifth Grade (N=165)	First Grade (N=127)	Fifth Grade (N=165)
1—Age in months				
2—L-T IQ Score				−.21
3—L-T subtest #1		−.36	.42	.38
4—L-T subtest #2		−.34	.35	.25
5—L-T subtest #3		−.30	.26	.32
6—L-T raw score		−.30	.26	.38
7—WISC Vocab. score		−.35	.34	.37
8—Gates score		−.31	.22 (test not given)	.49 .44
9—Verbal Ident., noun enumer. score	−.25	−.28		
10—Verbal Ident., action enumer. score	−.28	−.20		
11—Verbal Ident., combined enumer. score	−.27	−.27		
12—Verbal Ident., noun gestalt score			.33	.24
13—Verbal Ident., action gestalt score			.24	
14—Verbal Ident., combined gestalt score			.32	.27
15—PPVT raw score			.32	(test not given)
16—PPVT IQ			.33	(test not given)
17—Concept Sort., # piles score	.21			
18—Concept Sort., verbal score			.23	
19—Concept Sort., verbal score/# piles (ratio)	−.21			.23
20—Concept Form., percept. similarities scores				.22
21—Concept Form., verbaliz. score, class specificity	−.25	−.36	.26	.20

TABLE 4-2   Comparisons between First and Fifth Grade Children (*cont.*)

Variables	Correlations * with race		Correlations * with social class	
	First Grade (N=127)	Fifth Grade (N=165)	First Grade (N=127)	Fifth Grade (N=165)
22—Concept Form., verbaliz. score, class generaliz.		−.24		.21
23—Concept Form., total verbaliz. score	−.24	−.32		.21
24—Word Knowledge score		−.24		
(Verbal Fluency)		−.24		
25—Verbal Fluency, all rhymes score		−.20	.24	.28
26—Verbal Fluency, meaningful rhymes		−.24	.28	.33
27—Verbal Fluency, sentence fluency		−.20	.25	
28—Orientation Scale		−.30	.36	.51
29—Wepman test of auditory discrimination	.24		−.24	
30—Word Assoc., form class score				.27
31—Word Assoc., latency score		.35		
32—Cloze test, grammatical score			.26	.33
33—Cloze test, correct score			.25	.33
34—Cloze test, popular score			.30	.37

* Only correlations significant at p< .01 are shown.
Source: Deutsch, 1967, pp. 360-61.

you cannot predict—at a level better than that expected on the basis of chance —his grades. If a correlation approaches +1.00 or −1.00, then there is a strong relationship between the two variables. For example, the grades on children's first report card are probably highly correlated in the positive direction with those on the second. If the first English score is high, you can predict fairly safely that the second will be, too. Conversely, there is probably a high negative correlation between the child's grades and his deportment scores. If the grade is high, he will be low on a score like classroom disruption, and vice versa.

Consider now Deutsch's data. All of the correlations shown are "significant" in the statistical sense; that is, the observed correlation is probably not a fluke; if you replicated the study, you would get similar results. Where no figures are shown, the correlation is not significantly different from zero.

The results show several things. We could easily have predicted the results for variables 1–8. Negroes have lower Lorge-Thordike IQ scores than whites; and as social class gets higher, so does the IQ.

Variables 9–14 describe the results for the verbal identification scales described above. On about half of these scales, there are no racial or social-class differences. On the other half, there are some differences. Whites have a greater tendency than blacks to use nouns and action words to describe the pictures (variables 9–11). And the higher the child's social class, the greater is his tendency to use an appropriate single word to describe the picture (variables 12–14). I should point out that these "significant" relationships are quite small: the correlations are in the .20s and low .30s. This means that knowledge of the child's race or social class does not allow one to predict his intellectual status with great accuracy.

Variables 15 and 16 involve the Peabody Picture Vocabulary Test. The results show that at both age levels the races do not differ in this measure. At the first grade level, middle-class children do slightly better than lower-class children on the test. At the fifth grade level, the test was not given. So again, the data show a few small differences.

Consider next the concept sorting task (variables 17–23). Again, we see the same pattern: on about half the variables there are significant differences among the races or social classes. For example, considering class generality (variable 22), we find that at the first grade level there are no differences between the races in ability to identify abstract similarities among objects; at the fifth grade level whites do this slightly better than blacks. Similarly at the first grade level, there are no social-class differences in abstract similarities; at the fifth grade level there are, with middle-class children doing better. Again all of the correlations are quite small.

I could go on to discuss the remaining statistics in the Table. But they do not add anything to what we have already seen: in Deutsch's study, there are social-class and racial differences in about half the cases; and these differences are quite small—correlations generally in the .20s and .30s.

I think that studies like these are of small value. First, the tests themselves are of little interest. Deutsch's measures rely quite heavily on verbalizations. The child must understand the examiner's language and use it well himself to get a high score on the test. The verbal identification test simply requires the child to name pictures of objects. The Peabody Picture Vocabulary test does the same. Both the Concept Sorting task and the Concept Formation task require two things. One is that the child must be able to use concepts; he must identify the similarities among disparate objects, as when he sees that apples, pears, and oranges are all fruits. The second requirement is that he use certain labels to name the concepts.

These tests can be criticized by the same arguments that I applied to some of Palmer's tests. A verbal measure of concept formation is misleading. First, concepts may operate on a nonverbal level, so that if a child does poorly at naming a concept, we cannot infer that he necessarily lacks it. Second, there is considerable evidence—verbal and nonverbal—demonstrating that concept formation and similar activities begin in infancy. Piaget (1952b) shows this and so do others using more controlled techniques (for example, Ricciuti, 1965). The child's first words are used to label concepts which he already possesses (Piaget, 1951; Lenneberg, 1967). For example, the 2-year-old often has the concept of *man*. He is able to see the similarity among all men, even though each looks different in some respects from all others. Often he uses the word "daddy" to communicate this concept to us. While the word is used incorrectly by conventional standards, it does signal the availability of a concept.

In brief, the first argument is that Deutsch's tests are superficial because they over-emphasize verbalizations and because we already know that even very young childern can do the things which the tests try to measure. If a child does poorly on Deutsch's tests, it may mean only that he lacks certain vocabulary items, not that he fails to form concepts or to think.

A second criticism is that the tests seem to have been administered in a standardized way in school. You will no doubt recall Labov's experience in this regard. Black children in ghetto schools may not be sufficiently motivated to work hard under these circumstances and, as a result, may appear stupid when they really are not. This factor alone—the standardized testing and resultant poor motivation—may be enough in itself to account for the small social-class and racial differences uncovered by Deutsch.

In my view, we should interpret Deutsch's study and similar work in the following way: On the measures employed, there are few social-class and racial differences, and those that exist are small. Moreover, the measures are superficial, relying too heavily on verbalizations, and the testing procedures are inadequate, failing to motivate poor children as well as could be done. Given all this the results show only that, when unmotivated, poor children use a less adequate vocabulary (by middle-class standards) than do middle-class children. The results do not indicate severe intellectual deficiencies.

Lesser's Study

Lesser, Fifer, and Clark (1965) begin with the assumption that intelligence is not a single dimension but is composed of several different cognitive skills. If so, some interesting questions arise concerning the *patterning* of mental abilities. What is the configuration of mental abilities in children from different social-class and ethnic groups? While poor children generally receive low IQ scores, they may reveal unsuspected strengths in particular cognitive abilities. Moreover, one group of poor children may show a different arrangement of strengths and weaknesses than another group.

To examine issues like these, Lesser *et al.* gave tests of several different mental abilities to children from different social-class and ethnic groups. The subjects were 320 first grade children, ranging from 6 years 2 months through 7 years 5 months. Eighty children were from each of four ethnic groups: Chinese, Jewish, Negro, and Puerto Rican. Half of each cultural group (40 children) were middle class and half lower class. Thus, we have 40 lower-class Chinese, 40 middle-class Chinese, 40 lower-class Jewish, and so forth. All of the subjects attended public schools in New York City.

Lesser *et al.* went to extraordinary lengths to assure that the testing of each subject be done fairly. The following is a *partial* list of the precautions they took.

1. All tests were administered individually, and no reading or writing was required of the children.
2. Directions were as simple as possible.
3. Each child was tested by an experienced examiner who spoke both English and the appropriate foreign language (Spanish, Yiddish, several Chinese dialects).
4. Before the formal testing, each child was given practice materials to familiarize him with the directions and requirements of the task.
5. The child was given time to get familiar with the examiner.
6. The examiner was from the child's own cultural group.
7. Children were eliminated as subjects if they had health or emotional problems.
8. The test items were designed so as to include content which is familiar to all the cultural and social groups in New York City.
9. There was an attempt made to measure the degree to which the child was influenced or persuaded by the tester.
10. The child's interest in the test problem was measured.
11. The child's effort and persistence were measured.
12. Testing was terminated, and completed at a later date, if the child appeared fatigued or otherwise unable to continue.
13. All examiners were carefully trained to administer the tests in essentially the same way.
14. Time limits were not set on responses to the test. Children did not need to hurry through the task.

I have elaborated on the methodology because it is so good. These aspects of the Lesser research should be a model for other investigations.

Each child was given four scales—Verbal, Reasoning, Number, and Space Conceptualization—derived from the Hunter College Aptitude Scales for Gifted Children. Each Scale consisted of several sub-tests containing a large number of items.

The *Verbal Scale* measures "memory for verbal labels" (p. 36) and includes thirty Picture Vocabulary items and thirty Word Vocabulary items. (In a picture vocabulary test, the child is asked to name a picture, and in a word vocabulary test, the child is given a word and must describe its meaning.) The words were familiar to all ethnic groups and had Spanish, Chinese, and Yiddish equivalents.

The *Reasoning Scale* measures "the ability to formulate concepts, to weave together ideas and concepts, and to draw conclusions and inferences from them" (p. 36). The scale includes several sub-tests. Among them is *Picture Arrangement.* The examiner presented the child with several series of three to five drawings each. In each series, the drawings were out of sequence, and the child had to arrange them so that they made a good story or were in the proper order.

The *Numerical Scale* measures "skill in enumeration and in memory and use of the fundamental combinations in addition, subtraction, multiplication, and division" (p. 36). The addition sub-test involved showing the child a picture of a street scene with houses, trees, cars, children, and so forth. The child was asked such questions as: "There are four boys. If three more boys come, how many boys will there be altogether?" (p. 101)

The *Space Conceptualization Scale* "refers to a cluster of skills related to judging spatial relations and sizes of objects and to visualizing their movements in space" (p. 36). The jigsaw sub-test, for example, involved two identical triangles. One was cut into several pieces and the child had to put it together so as to match the other.

We may make several comments on the tests. First, they are rather superficial. The Numerical Scale measures simple calculations that can be performed by rote, and fails to assess "deeper" skills such as the understanding of equivalence and others we shall describe in some detail below. Similarly, the Verbal Scale measures vocabulary, and there is much more to language than that. Second, the tests are not pure measures of the abilities they purport to assess. For example, the Reasoning Scale correlates .46 with the Verbal Scale, .61 with the Number Scale, and .47 with the Space Scale. In other words, the Reasoning Scale measures not reasoning alone, but abilities which the other Scales measure, too.

With these comments in mind, we can turn to the results. Consider first each group's performance on the four scales. Table 4-3 presents the major results. They show first that middle-class children were significantly superior to lower-class children on all scales. Second, there are significant differences among the ethnic groups in performance on various scales. In the case of the *Verbal Scale,* Jewish children received the highest scores, followed by Negroes, Chinese, and Puerto Ricans, in that order. On *Reasoning,* there was a different ranking of the groups: Chinese first, then Jews, Negroes, and Puerto Ricans. Considering the Numerical Scale, we see that the ordering from highest to lowest is Jewish, Chinese, Puerto Rican, and Negro. On the Space Scale, Chinese ranked first followed by Jews, Puerto Ricans, and Negroes. So there is a different patterning of groups for each scale.

TABLE 4-3   Mental Ability Scores by Ethnic Group and Social Class

	Chinese	*Jewish*	*Negro*	*Puerto Rican*
			Verbal	
Middle Class	76.8	96.7	85.7	69.6
Lower Class	65.3	84.0	62.9	54.3
			Reasoning	
Middle Class	27.7	28.8	26.0	21.8
Lower Class	24.2	21.6	14.8	16.0
			Number	
Middle Class	30.0	33.4	24.7	22.6
Lower Class	26.2	23.5	12.1	15.7
			Space	
Middle Class	44.9	44.6	41.8	37.4
Lower Class	40.4	35.1	27.1	32.8

Source: Lesser, Fifer, and Clark, 1965, p. 60.

Consider next the pattern of abilities within each ethnic group. Figure 4-1 portrays this. In the case of Chinese children, the best ability is spatial, with reasoning and number skills following close behind. The worst performance is on the verbal scale. Contrast this with the performance of Jewish children, whose best ability was verbal, and worst spatial. Negro children show most ability in language, then spatial ability, then reasoning and number. Puerto Rican children are highest in language, then spatial skills, and then, like the blacks, are about the same on number and reasoning.

Notice that the *pattern* of scores of lower-class children is quite similar, in all four ethnic groups, to the pattern of middle-class children. While this is so, the middle-class children receive higher scores in all cases. In other words, lower-class children are a weaker carbon copy of middle-class children in their own ethnic group. For example, both lower- and middle-class Negro children receive their highest scores in the area of language and their lowest scores in number ability. The only difference between the social-class groups is that middle-class children in general receive higher scores on all scales.

The patterns we have just discussed describe *groups* of children. In other words, taking the average of Jewish children's scores in number, language, and so on, yields a certain pattern of abilities. But now we should ask this question: Do individual children within each group show the same

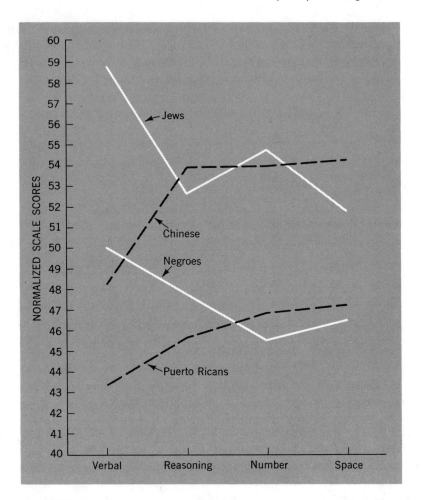

FIGURE 4–1 Pattern of Mental-Ability Scores for Each Ethnic Group. *Source:* Lesser, Fifer, and Clark, 1965, p. 64.

pattern of abilities as is shown by the group as a whole?[3] Table 4-4 gives the relevant data. It shows that 23 of 40 middle-class Chinese showed the same pattern of scores as the middle- or lower-class Chinese group. Twenty of

[3] It is easy to show that group data can be different from individual data. Here is a proof. Suppose you give two tests to three children. Child 1 scores 10 on test A and 10 on test B; child 2 does the same; and child 3 scores 10 on test A and 20 on test B. The averages show that as a group, children score higher on test B than A. But, as you can see, this is true of only one child of three; the majority does not show the pattern.

TABLE 4-4   Number of Individuals Showing Group Patterns *

Group	Group Patterns							
	MCC	LCC	MCJ	LCJ	MCN	LCN	MCP	LCP
Middle-Class Chinese (MCC)	13	10	6	1	5	1	2	2
Lower-Class Chinese (LCC)	6	14	2	4	3	1	1	9
Middle-Class Jewish (MCJ)	4	0	32	4	0	0	0	0
Lower-Class Jewish (LCJ)	0	1	9	18	7	4	0	1
Middle-Class Negro (MCN)	5	1	11	10	11	0	0	2
Lower-Class Negro (LCN)	1	3	0	3	0	28	0	5
Middle-Class Puerto Rican (MCP)	6	6	3	6	4	0	3	12
Lower-Class Puerto Rican (LCP)	0	7	1	1	0	8	3	20

* Figures to read across as follows: The scores of 13 middle-class Chinese subjects fit the middle-class Chinese group pattern and level on the four mental ability scales; 10 middle-class Chinese perform like lower-class Chinese; six perform like middle-class Jews, etc.

Source: Stodolsky and Lesser, 1967, p. 572.

40 lower-class Chinese children show patterns of scores like the middle- or lower-class Chinese group. For middle-class Jewish children, the figure is 36 out of 40; for lower-class Jewish children, 25 out of 40. The figures for middle- and lower-class Negroes are respectively 11 out of 40 and 28 out of 40; for middle- and lower-class Puerto Ricans, 15 out of 40 and 23 out of 40. In brief, these figures show that in general only about one half of the children in each ethnic group show the same pattern of mental abilities as does the group as a whole. The only major exception to this is the fact that 90 percent of middle-class Jewish children show the same pattern as their group.

What can we make of all this? First, consider the social-class differences, regardless of ethnic group, in intellectual performance. Lesser *et al.* propose that one interpretation of the data is that lower-class children are genuinely less able or competent than are middle-class children in the areas of verbal, number, reasoning, and spatial abilities. The alternative explanation is that the results show merely a performance difference between the two groups. By this view, lower-class children may do poorly because they are not properly motivated to take the tests.

It seems to me, and to Lesser too, that at present it is difficult to decide between the alternative interpretations. On the one hand, the investigators took great pains to motivate each child. They found empirically that certain motivational factors—effort and responsiveness to the tester—could not explain the observed social-class differences. On the other hand, Lesser suggests that a variety of performance factors—impulse control, attention span, etc.—which were not measured, may have contributed to the poor children's inferior performance and may have, therefore, obscured their real competence.

The research also showed that, regardless of social class, the ethnic groups displayed different *patterns* of mental abilities. Each group, however, was not monolithic: about half the children in each group showed the group pattern of mental abilities. With this qualification in mind, it is possible to say that ethnicity affects the organization of mental abilities; social class may determine their level (although it is not clear whether this reflects performance or competence). This is an intriguing hypothesis, and a convincing rationale can be given for it. Perhaps each ethnic group must adapt to an environment which is in some respects distinctive and which, therefore, requires a unique pattern of mental abilities. While this is a useful perspective with which to view cultural differences, the Lesser results are hard to interpret in detail. For example, why should Chinese children excel in spatial ability and not in verbal skills? All that Lesser *et al.* can say is that the Chinese environment must reinforce spatial skills at the expense of verbal ones. This explanation does not get us very far: it is completely speculative and after the fact. Would anyone with knowledge of the Chinese environment have *predicted* the pattern? Also, we do not know whether the patterns of mental abilities continue to exist at older age levels. More data are needed.

In sum, the Lesser study, extremely well designed and executed,[4] shows that the facts may be complex: the social classes may differ in level of mental abilities, whereas ethnic groups may differ in *pattern* of skills. However, the social-class difference in level is difficult to interpret in terms of competence and performance; the ethnic difference in pattern is hard to understand. Perhaps the chief difficulty with the Lesser study, which in many respects is a model for research, is that the tests are rather superficial and atheoretical. In these measures, language is conceived of as labeling, number as counting, and the line is not firmly drawn between knowledge and behavior. This is no longer satisfactory.

PIAGETIAN STUDIES

The foremost theory of thinking is Piaget's. What does it tell us about the fundamentals of lower-class children's knowledge? To answer this we must first review some general features of Piaget's theory, although what fol-

---

[4] The study has been replicated in remarkable detail by Jane Fort. See Stolsky and Lesser (1967). After this was written, I came across a study by Sitkei and Meyers (1969) who studied social-class and racial differences in patterns of thinking. The results differed from those of Lesser *et al.*: there were no ethnic differences in the pattern of abilities, and only a few social-class differences (on the use of Standard English). The most obvious explanation of the discrepancy between the two studies is that they used different tests. Ethnic differences in *patterns* of abilities are probably limited to a few areas of cognition.

lows is bound to be incomplete. It is not possible to present in one chapter a comprehensive account of Piaget's voluminous and complex work. I will be content to review here a few of his major ideas.

Pre-Operational and Concrete Operational Thought

After the period of sensorimotor development in infancy, the child passes through three major periods of intellectual development. The first is the period of *preoperational thought,* lasting from about 2 to 6 years. (The ages are only approximate and not very crucial.) During this period, the child develops the rudiments of thought. He learns to create mental symbols, to reason, to employ memory. But his thought is as yet primitive and takes a form qualitatively different from adult cognition.

Consider the example of *conservation of liquids* or continuous quantities. The examiner presents the child with two identical beakers (A and B in Figure 4-2), each filled with equal amounts of liquid, and asks him whether

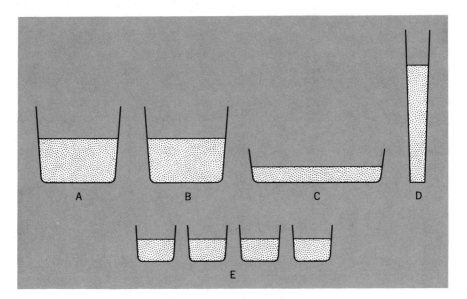

FIGURE 4–2 Conservation of Continuous Quantities.

the two glasses contain the same amount to drink or not the same amount to drink. After the age of 3 or 4 years, the child is almost always able to assert that the amounts are the same. Next, the examiner asks the child to watch closely what is about to happen and pours the liquid from one of the two identical beakers (say B) into a third, dissimilarly shaped beaker (C). Notice that the child observes the pouring; nothing is hidden from him. The result, of course, is that the column of liquid in glass C (and the glass itself) is both shorter and wider than that in the remaining original glass (A). The examiner now asks again whether the amounts are the same. Do beakers A and C contain "the same amount to drink"? The pre-operational child now asserts that the amounts are *not* the same. He usually thinks that beaker A has more to drink because, he says, "it is taller."

The Piagetian examiner conducts the interview in a flexible manner. He uses alternative phrasings of the questions; he follows up on a child's idiosyncratic answers; he sometimes repeats the same problems. He makes every effort to clarify the problem to the child, to get him interested in it, to explore the full meaning of his answer, and to determine whether the child really believes his own explanation. Moreover, the examiner usually gives several conservation problems. For example, after the initial problem, the examiner again presents the child with beakers A and B and the child agrees that the amounts are the same. Then, as the child watches, the examiner pours the liquid in beaker D, which is taller and thinner than the original glasses A and B. Now the child typically asserts that D has more liquid than A because the former is taller.

But the examination is not yet complete. The examiner gives a new problem. Once the child agrees again that beakers A and B have the same amount to drink, the examiner pours the contents of B into four small beakers, set E in Figure 4-2. What does the child say now? Sometimes he asserts that beaker A has more since it is taller. But sometimes he maintains that set E has more since it includes four beakers as opposed to one in the case of A.

Late in the pre-operational period, the child begins to acquire *conservation,* the tendency to recognize that the initial equivalence (established when the liquid is in A and B), is maintained or conserved despite the visible transformation (the pouring from B to C, D, or E). He is inconsistent, sometimes maintaining that the liquid is conserved and sometimes not. For example, when the examiner pours the liquid from B into a third beaker only slightly different from A, the child may conserve. On the other hand, if the new beaker is much different in appearance from the first, then the child may well deny the equivalence. Also, his answers are not very firm. When the examiner, using the technique of counter-suggestion, challenges the child's correct response, it is easily abandoned.

The failure to conserve is not limited to liquids. During this period, the child fails to appreciate equivalence in a variety of areas: weight, substance, number, volume, and others. Consider the conservation of substance. Here the child is presented with two identical balls of plasticene (or clay, etc.). He is first asked whether there is the same amount of plasticene in both balls. If he thinks there is, the examiner changes one of the balls to a sausage shape. The child must now decide whether or not the ball and the sausage have equal amounts of substance. Again, the question is this: Can the child pene-trate beyond an apparent difference to detect a deeper similarity?

Like everyone else, psychologists tend to ride hobby horses; and con-servation, poor beast, is by now almost exhausted. The over-emphasis on con-servation results in several difficulties. One is a neglect of other fascinating Piagetian experiments which also illustrate pre-operational thought. Consider this study of imagery.

The examiner shows the child a container of liquid, A in Figure 4-3.

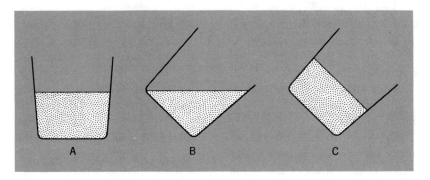

FIGURE 4–3   Imagery Experiment.

Then he uses a cloth to cover the container so that the child cannot see it. He tilts the container on its side, as in B, and asks the child to draw what it would look like if uncovererd. The child draws something like C. Then the examiner removes the cloth, showing the child that C is incorrect. He removes the container from sight and again asks the child to draw it tilted. Again, the pre-operational child produces C. Such is the impact of "objective fact" on the child's mind.

A second difficulty stemming from the over-emphasis on conservation is that psychologists tend to forget that it is a test for underlying thought processes. Piaget's main interest is not so much in the child's success or failure at the task but in the patterns of reasoning which produce his response. The main questions are these: In the conservation experiments, what leads the child to deny the real equivalence? In the imagery experiment, why does he anticipate incorrectly and then ignore the evidence of his senses?

In Piaget's view, the pre-operational child's thought shows several unique qualities. One general characteristic of his cognitive activity is *cen-tration*. He tends to focus on a limited amount of the information available. In the conservation of liquids, he attends mainly to the heights of the columns of liquid. When they are the same (as in A vs. B in Figure 4-2), he judges the amounts to be the same. When they are different (as in A vs. C), he considers that the taller has the greater quantity.

The pre-operational child's thought is *static* in the sense that it centers on states. In the conservation of substance, he focuses on the shape of the plasticene (sometimes a ball and sometimes a sausage) and ignores the transformation, that is, the change from one state to the other. In the conservation of continuous quantity he focuses on the heights of the columns of liquid and not on the act of pouring. In the area of imagery, he lacks adequate representation of an object's shift from one position to another. Thus, when the container is tilted, he sees the situation as unchanged: the water level is still parallel to the bottom of the container.

The pre-operational child's thought lacks *reversibility*. In the conservation of liquids, he fails to appreciate that if the water were returned from C to B, the original equivalence would be restored, proving that it was not destroyed in the first place. In general, he cannot perform a certain mental operation and then reverse it.

These three aspects of thought are interrelated. If the child centers on the static aspects of a situation, he is unlikely to appreciate transformations. If he does not represent transformation, he is unlikely to reverse his thought.

Gradually there is change. Over a period of time, the child achieves *concrete operational thought*. He must do this by himself; training by adults has little effect. At about the age of 7 or 8 years, there is a major change in his thought processes. Their symptoms are easy to describe. In the conservation of liquids, the child recognizes that the amounts stay the same despite the pouring. No amount of counter-suggestion can get him to abandon this belief. In fact, he now thinks that the result is quite obvious and that it is absurd for the examiner to ask him the question in the first place. Similarly, in the imagery problem he can generally anticipate that the water level in B (Figure 4-3) must remain parallel to the floor. If he does not predict this, then a quick glance at the real situation is enough to correct his error and get him to produce an accurate drawing.

In Piaget's view, these successes are made possible by a significant alteration of the child's patterns of thought. The concrete operational child is characterized by *decentration*. He tends to focus on several dimensions of a problem simultaneously and to explore their relations. In the conservation of liquids, he coordinates both the height and the width of the columns of liquid. He recognizes that the amounts are equal when one column of liquid is at the same time taller but narrower than the second.

His thought is *dynamic,* being attuned to changes. In the conservations, he concentrates on the transformation: the act of pouring the liquid or deforming the ball into a sausage. No longer does he attend only to the static states which precede and follow the transformation. He forms more or less accurate representations of the changes which have taken place. He can therefore reason that as the plasticene increases in length, it simultaneously descreases in width. Similarly, in the imagery problem the child can recognize where the change occurs and see what effect it must have on the final outcome.

The concrete operational child's thought is *reversible*. He recognizes that pouring liquid back from C to B reverses or negates the action of pouring B to C. He is aware that it is the same action performed in another direction and concludes from this that equivalence between B and C must be true. In general, he can perform a mental operation which leads to a certain conclusion and then do the reverse of this operation, enabling him to return to the original starting point.

So the concrete operational child focuses on several aspects of a situation simultaneously, is sensitive to transformations, and can reverse the direction of his thinking. Again, all these traits of thought are interrelated, forming a system. If the child focuses on several aspects of the situation, he is likely to appreciate the transformation, and he must do this to reverse his thought.

The Importance of Piaget

As I mentioned earlier, we have reviewed only a minute portion of Piaget's voluminous work. He has produced some forty books on different aspects of cognitive development, so that you have seen only a smattering of his theory in the last several pages.

Here I want to discuss why it is so important for us to study Piaget's ideas as they relate to poor children. You will recall that earlier I described aspects of Palmer's and Lesser's work as superficial. I said that it was not particularly important to know that a child can attach the label "ball" to the proper object or that he can remember that two and two are four. I maintained that other aspects of thought are more fundamental. Now I must answer this question: Why is Piaget's work more basic than the others?

I will give two arguments. The first can be approached through a simple example concerning arithmetic. According to Lesser *et al.*, the child shows a high degree of arithmetic ability when he can consistently solve problems such as finding the sum of three and four objects. What is the minimal set of skills needed to do something like this? First, the child must be able to count the objects properly so that he knows that there are three here and four there. Second, he must have some way of finding the sum. He can use a rote method, simply holding in memory the addition facts for small numbers. If the objects are all visible, he can use a counting procedure, simply combining the two sets and enumerating the elements.

Is all this fundamental? From one perspective, it is: The child cannot do arithmetic and succeed in school without being able to count and without remembering some basic number facts. So Lesser's work is important from this point of view. But from another perspective, counting and adding may be based on little understanding; arithmetic skills may function without the child's appreciating the underlying mathematical concepts which Piaget's work focuses on. For example, in one interview Piaget presented a child of 5 years with two sets of objects, arrayed as in A in Figure 4-4, and asked the

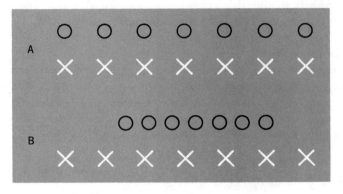

FIGURE   4–4   Conservation of Number.

child to count them. He did so and correctly maintained that each set had seven. Then, as the child watched, the examiner performed the classic conservation experiment, bunching up one of the sets. Again the child was asked to count the elements in the sets, and again he correctly reported the numbers: seven in each. Then the examiner asked whether the sets had the same number or whether one had more. The child maintained that the lower set had more because it was longer (Piaget 1952a, p. 45)!

The example shows what nearly everyone who has been through school knows quite well: you can correctly execute various calculations without understanding the ideas involved. In this case, the child could count, but the results were meaningless to him.

Piaget's work attempts to focus on the basic concepts of various areas of knowledge. In dealing with number, for example, Piaget examines the concepts of equivalence and of a series; he largely ignores counting and mastery of the addition or subtraction facts. This, then, is the first reason that Piaget's work is fundamental: it concentrates on the basic ideas of a discipline, not on the superficial aspects which schools often stress.

A second reason is that the mental operations which Piaget's theory describes underlie the child's thinking in a variety of areas. For example, Piaget has studied the "formal operations" which characterize adolescent and adult thought. Briefly, this kind of thinking involves the ability to imagine hypothetical possibilities, to consider in an exhaustive way the various combinations of events that may occur, to reason in a logical fashion, and so on. Piaget shows that the formal operations manifest themselves in several areas of endeavor. For example, when the adolescent acquires the formal operations, he can handle certain types of scientific problem solving (Inhelder and Piaget, 1958); he elaborates theories of society and of religion (1958); and he engages in advanced forms of moral judgment (Piaget, 1932). In brief, formal operations subsume many areas of content: they make possible scientific, social, religious, and moral thought. This, then, is the second reason for the importance of Piaget's theory: the mental activities it describes are central to many areas of intellectual endeavor.

Indeed, some of the mental activities which Piaget describes are almost essential for human survival. For example, some of Piaget's work deals with the development of basic categories of mind: concepts of space, time, causality. Without these, the child would have a difficult time surviving his first several years.

Cross-Cultural Studies

Piaget's theory proposes, with a few minor qualifications, that the stages and order of cognitive development are universal. All children, regardless of culture, progress through the stages of the sensorimotor period, as in the case of object permanence, and proceed from there to pre-operational thought, then concrete operational thought, and finally, in all but the most primitive societies, to the stage of formal operations.

The cultures may differ in the ages at which the various stages are attained, but not in the basic course of development. For example, in one culture children may acquire the conservation of number at age 6 whereas in another they cannot conserve until age 8. But in both cultures, all children eventually acquire the mental operations which make conservation possible. Also, in both cultures children first must progress through pre-operational thinking before the concrete operations will appear. What evidence is there to support these claims, and what bearing does it have on problems of poor children's intellect?

Goodnow (1962) attempted to determine whether children in a non-Western culture show cognitive abilities similar to those of Western children. The subjects were a large number of boys, from 10 to 13 years of age, all of whom lived in Hong Kong. One group consisted of 148 Europeans, mainly English and mainly middle class. A second group involved 151 Chinese boys of middle-class origin. They attended exclusive schools where instruction was in English. A third group involved 80 lower-class Chinese boys, whose parents had unskilled or semi-skilled jobs and who attended schools in which Chinese was the language of instruction. A fourth group consisted of 80 Chinese boys of lower-class background who had a mininum of schooling, education not being compulsory in Hong Kong. Each group had approximately equal numbers of subjects at ages 10, 11, 12, and 13. To summarize, Goodnow's four major groups of subjects were Europeans, Westernized middle-class Chinese, lower-class Chinese attending school, and lower-class Chinese with a minimum of education. Presumably the last two groups represent a non-Western culture, whereas the first two groups are Western or at least Western influenced.

Each boy was given four Piagetian tasks: conservation of weight, volume, and area, and a test of combinatorial reasoning. As we have seen, the conservation of weight involves showing the child two identical clay balls which are of the same weight. When the child accepts this fact, one of the balls is transformed into a different shape, for example, a sausage, and he is asked whether the weight remains the same. The conservation of volume involves the same materials. The child is first shown that the two identical balls, placed in two identical beakers of liquid, displace the same volumes. Then both balls are removed from the water, one is transformed in shape, and the child must predict whether it will still displace the same amount of liquid. The conservation of area involves placing on two identical rectangular surfaces two identical arrays of objects (for example: houses arranged in the same way on two fields). After the child agrees that the objects cover up the same amount of surface, one set of objects is transformed so that it is arranged differently on the surface. The three conservation tasks are intended to assess the child's concrete operational thinking. The tasks are not of equal difficulty, however. Piaget has found that the conservation of area is mastered at about age 7 or 8, weight at about 10 years, and volume at about 12 years.

The fourth problem involved presenting each child with a collection of poker chips of six different colors. The task was to construct from the six colors all possible combinations of two colors at a time. There are 15 such combinations of elements. If we symbolize the six colors as A, B, C, D, E, and F, then the combinations are: AB, AC, AD, AE, AF, BC, BD, BE, BF, CD, CE, CF, DE, DF, EF. (Order does not count. Thus BA is not a legitimate combination since we already have AB). Note that the sequence in which the combinations are listed is systematic. First, A was paired with each of the others, then B with each (except A), and so on. Without some system, it is easy to lose track of what has been paired with what. The test is intended to tap one aspect of formal operational thought, namely the ability to combine things in an exhaustive and systematic way. From the point of view of formal operations, the task is relatively simple, since it involves concrete objects. All four tasks were administered in a standard way, the questions being taken from published protocols of Piaget's clinical interviews.

The findings showed that on the conservation tasks there were only minor differences among the four groups. For example, in the conservation of weight, Europeans and Chinese children with a minimum of schooling received almost identical scores at all ages. Interestingly, the children who did most poorly, on the average, were not the Chinese children with a minimum of education, but the middle- and lower-class Chinese children who attended school: they tended to parrot "scientific" explanations referring to mysteries such as "center of gravity" which they did not understand and which were inappropriate. Further, the Chinese subjects' incorrect and correct answers generally took the form predicted by Piaget. A minor discrepancy with Piaget's results involved the sequence of mastery of the tasks. Piaget maintains that conservation of area is mastered first, then weight, then volume. Goodnow found, however, that area and weight were of about equal difficulty, and (in agreement with Piaget) that volume was hardest of all. Goodnow speculates, though, that the area task may have been presented in an especially difficult manner. In sum, the cultural and social-class differences on the three types of conservation are generally quite minor.

The results for the combinatorial task were much different. Europeans and Chinese boys of middle-class origin who attended Western type schools performed much better than did lower-class Chinese with or without schooling. Goodnow found, however, that lower-class Chinese, while doing poorly on the combinatorial task relative to the middle-class subjects, nevertheless improved with age. This suggests that in due course the lower-class Chinese acquire formal operations, too, albeit more slowly than the others. The lower-class boys lag behind but are not completely deficient in combinatorial thought.

To summarize, Goodnow finds that on the three conservation tasks, all cultural and social-class groups perform at about the same level. On the combinations task, middle-class Chinese and European boys are superior to lower-class Chinese, although the latter show signs of improvement with age.

I wish to make several comments on these findings. First, while cultural and social-class factors have little effect on conservation, the meaning of the combinatorial reasoning results is not clear; several interpretations might account for them. One possibility is that success at the task depends on Westernization. The Europeans and the middle-class Chinese in Western type schools, both of which groups one might consider to be Westernized, performed at a higher level than the two non-Westernized groups, the lower-class Chinese. The difficulty with this interpretation is the postulate that the middle-class Chinese were Westernized. We do not know for a fact that they really were.

Another possibility is that social class is crucial. Those showing superior performance were middle class, and inferior performance, lower class. But is the middle class in Chinese culture really similar to the middle class in European culture? Does not cultural difference override class similarity?

A third possibility is that schooling is involved. Those doing well at the task attended English schools; those doing poorly either did not go to school or attended inadequate lower-class schools. But can schooling be a more important influence than either social class or culture?

Another interpretation still, which Goodnow originally offered, is that IQ is the important factor. She found that groups superior in the combinations task had higher IQs than the groups who did poorly on it. If the effect of IQ is eliminated by statistical means, then there are no major differences among the groups. But the IQ interpretation is ambiguous, too. What do IQ scores in foreign cultures mean? And are not the IQ findings confounded with social-class differences, the high IQ subjects being middle class and the low, lower class? As you can see, each interpretation is complex. Furthermore, there is the possibility that some combination of factors—not just a single one—is involved. Perhaps lack of schooling and social class and culture are all related to the observed differences.

My second comment is that it is hard to see why there were no group differences on the conservation tasks, while there were differences on the combinations test. Whatever the factor—culture, social class, schooling, or IQ—responsible for the group differences in the combination tasks, why should it not affect conservation tasks as well?

Further research clarifies some of these issues. Price-Williams (1961) found that West African children from 5 to 8 years of age showed roughly the same progression as European children in the development of conservation of continuous and discontinuous quantities.

These children were not in school, nor were they of European culture. The study indicates, then, that neither schooling nor Westernization is necessary for successful conservation in these cases.

Vernon (1965a) gave a battery of Piagetian tests, in a standardized fashion, to 100 British and 50 West Indian boys. All children attended school and were from 10½ to 11 years. The middle and lower classes were represented in each cultural group. First, consider overall cultural differences on the Piaget tasks. On several tests there were negligible or small differences between British and West Indian children: conservation of substance, conservation of volume, inclusion relations (classification), and imagery. The largest differences occurred in the case of conservation of continuous quantities, where 6 percent of the English children and 18 percent of the West Indian children were wrong on the standard problem; conservation of length, where 5 percent of the English and 40 percent of the West Indians were incorrect; conservation of area, where the error rates were 7 percent for the English and 18 for the West Indians. Of the three "large" differences, only conservation of length seems important. The Vernon results must be viewed with caution since the method of administration was extremely inflexible. Nevertheless, the findings suggest that on most of the tasks, with the possible exception of conservation of length, West Indian and British children perform at roughly equivalent levels. In a second paper (1965b), Vernon reports that West Indian boys of different social classes did not differ on the Piagetian tasks. (He does not give social-class data for the English.)

Greenfield (1966) studied the conservation of liquid in West African children (Senegal). There were three groups: village children who did not attend school, village children who did, and urban children who attended school. In all groups there were three age levels: 6 to 7 years; 8 to 9; and 11 to 13. The results showed that the schooled children, both rural and urban, followed the typical course of development with regard to conservation: relative success at age 6 or 7 and almost perfect performance by the age of 11 to 13. By contrast, the unschooled rural Senegalese failed to improve after the age of 8 or 9: only about 50 percent succeeded at this age level and at ages 11 to 13. Thus culture does not affect the development of conservation; the urban-rural distinction is not important, either. What seems to matter is schooling.

Opper (1971) has performed what I think is the most thorough study in this area. Her aim was to examine Thai children's acquisition of the intellectual stages and types of reasoning described by Piaget. She studied two groups, one involving 142 children from the city of Bangkok, and the other involving 140 children from a small rural community engaged mainly in rice farming. The children in both samples ranged from 6 to 16 years of age. Opper administered to all children from 6 to 11 years of age a battery of 10 Piagetian tasks measuring concrete operational thought: class inclusion, conservation of length, conservation of liquid, one-to-one correspondence, and seriation. They also received tasks of mental imagery. In addition, she administered to children from 6 to 16 years of age two tests of formal operational thinking: conservation of volume and permutations. In testing the children, the examiners, who were native speakers of Thai, used Piaget's clinical method. This procedure produces data both on the children's stage of cognitive development (for example, whether or not they can conserve volume) and on the mental processes used to solve the problems. Too few studies of cross-cultural differences in cognition have employed the clinical method to examine the mental processes themselves.

Consider first the results concerning concrete operational tasks. On each task, both the urban and rural samples showed the same three-stage progression described by Piaget and displayed by Western children. Furthermore, at each stage of development, the Thai children used the same types of reasoning shown by Swiss children and often verbalized the reasoning in identical words.

In the tasks of mental imagery, there was a slight difference between the Thai and Swiss children. The Thai children do approximately as well on both static and dynamic problems, whereas Swiss children find the static tasks easier. Nevertheless, Thai children develop each type of imagery in the manner Piaget describes and in general make the same types of errors as do Swiss children.

In the case of formal operational tasks, Thai children again show the pattern of development described by Piaget.

In general, the similarities between Thai and Swiss children are remarkable when one considers the stages of development, and the similarities are especially striking when one considers the types of reasoning. Children from Geneva and children raised in rice paddies in central Thailand often justify their solution of a conservation problem in precisely the same manner!

At the same time, there were some differences between Thai and Swiss children. The rural Thai children develop at a slower rate than do either Genevan or urban Thai children. In general, the urban Thai and Swiss children acquired the various concepts at about the same age (although there were a few exceptions) whereas the rural Thai children acquired these concepts about 2 or 3 years later. Opper presents some evidence suggesting that the older the child, the less the lag between rural Thai children and the others. Thus, as the rural Thai child grows older, he becomes more similar to the urban Thai and Swiss child.

In brief, Opper's research shows overwhelming similarities in stages of development and types of reasoning between Thai and Swiss children (who are of course quite similar to American and other Western children). The major difference is in the age of acquisition of the various concepts: rural Thai children acquire them at a later age than do the others. Unfortunately there is no simple explanation for the Thai urban-rural difference in rate of cognitive development. Both groups go to school; both speak the same language. Presumably, some as yet unidentified differences in environment or experience can explain the results.

Table 4-5 summarizes the results from various studies. What do they show? First, consider the hypothesis that culture produces important differences in certain cognitive skills. The evidence does not support this hypothesis. Goodnow found minimal effects of culture; Price-Williams showed that conservation develops "normally" in West African children; Vernon found that culture had little effect on many tasks; and Greenfield's data indicate that schooled African children are similar to Europeans in performance on the conservation task. There were a few exceptions to the general rule: Goodnow found some differences, possibly attributable to culture, in a combinatorial reasoning task; and Vernon found West Indians to be inferior in conservation of length. These results need to be replicated; all we can say now is that the bulk of evidence indicates little effect of cultural factors on the Piagetian tasks investigated.

Is social class a crucial factor? In general, the evidence seems to show that it is not. Goodnow found no such effects in the case of conservation,

TABLE 4-5   Cross-Cultural Studies of Cognitive Development

I. Goodnow (1962), Hong Kong.
   Groups: Middle-class Europeans; middle-class Chinese attending English Language School; lower-class Chinese attending Chinese School; lower-class Chinese with a minimum of education.
   Tasks: Conservation of weight, area, volume, and combinatorial reasoning.
   Results: All groups were about the same on conservation tasks. On the combinatorial task, the middle-class Europeans and Chinese were superior to the lower-class Chinese, schooled or unschooled.

II. Price Williams (1961), West Africa.
   Groups: Unschooled African children of various ages.
   Tasks: Conservation of continuous and discontinuous quantities.
   Results: Performance is similar to what is found in Europeans.

III. Vernon (1965a, b), England and West Indies.
   Groups: Middle- and lower-class British and West Indian children.
   Tasks: A battery of conservation, classification, and imagery tasks.
   Results: There were negligible differences in the case of conservation of substance and volume, inclusion relations, and imagery. There were small differences in the case of conservation of continuous quantities and area. The West Indian children did poorly on the conservation of length. There were no social-class differences within the West Indian group.

IV. Greenfield (1966), Senegal.
   Groups: Urban schooled, rural schooled, rural unschooled.
   Task: Conservation of continuous quantity.
   Results: The schooled groups showed the normal pattern of development, and the unschooled group did poorly.

V. Opper (1971), Thailand.
   Groups: Urban schooled, rural schooled.
   Tasks: Concrete operational, imagery, formal operational.
   Results: Both groups were similar to the Swiss in developmental stages and types of reasoning. The rural group acquired the concepts at a later age than did the urban Thai or Swiss, both of which were similar.

although social class might underly some of the obtained differences in the combinatorial task. Vernon found no social-class differences on Piagetian tasks and neither did Greenfield (if one interprets the urban-rural factor as social class). The only discrepant finding is Opper's. She found social class differences in Thai children (if one interprets the urban-rural factor in this way). Of course, social-class differences in cognition may exist for tasks not yet studied or for groups within Western countries; not enough research has been done to rule out this possibility. Nevertheless, much of the evidence does not support the hypothesis.

Consider next the effects of schooling. Here the situation is ambiguous. Goodnow finds that schooling may make a difference for the combinatorial problem but not the conservation tasks. Price-Williams finds no effect of schooling in the case of conservation. Greenfield, however, shows that lack of schooling has marked effects on conservation. On the other hand, in Opper's study, both groups were schooled and yet there was a difference between urban and rural children. The picture seems confusing; schooling may or may not have an effect.

Finally, there is the hypothesis that IQ can account for observed cultural differences in cognitive development. Since the observed differences seem minor, this hypothesis has little work to do.

It should be pointed out that the cross-cultural studies, while in some respects illuminating, suffer from a major weakness. Much of the research does not obtain a clear measure of the reasoning process used in the solution of various problems. The conservation problem, for example, can be solved in a variety of ways, and Piaget is not interested so much in the fact that a child solved it, but in his method of doing so. He repeatedly points out that even complex problems, like Goodnow's combination task, can be solved by ontogenetically primitive modes of thought. To rule out this possibility, one must probe the child's thought by administering several problems in a flexible way. Only Opper's study does this. Such research is the only hope for clarifying some of the ambiguities posed by cross-cultural studies—for example, that West Indian children do well on conservation of substance but not length. If we had some idea of the reasoning process employed in both cases, we might be able to interpret the confusing results.

Western Studies

What does Piagetian research tell us about social-class differences within Western culture? Several studies have compared the social classes on various Piagetian tasks. The results may be summarized as follows. Some studies find no social-class differences; some find minor ones; none of the research shows that lower-class children entirely lack the skills Piaget describes.

Here are a few examples of research showing a social-class difference. Beilin, Kagan, and Rabinowitz (1966) studied visual imagery in 7-year-olds (the water level problem described earlier). They found significant social-class and racial differences in the imagery problems. Unfortunately, the writers do not tell us how large the differences were or whether lower-class or black subjects are completely deficient in the skills under consideration.

Rothenberg and Courtney (1969) investigated social-class differences in the conservation of number. Table 4-6 shows the percentage of children passing four different conservation of number problems. The table shows that few young children (2-5 to 3-4) of either social class are consistent conservers and that at ages 3-5 to 4-4 a significantly greater percentage of middle-class children conserve consistently than do lower-class children. Of course, the study has nothing to say about what occurs after the age of 4-4. Do poor children eventually catch up?

Consider next a few studies showing no social-class differences. Beilin (1964) studied lower- and middle-class children's performance on a task analo-

TABLE 4-6   Percentages of Responses to Four Conservation Problems

Problems	Lower Class		Middle Class	
	2-5 to 3-4	*3-5 to 4-4*	*2-5 to 3-4*	*3-5 to 4-4*
1. CONS *	0.0	13.3	0.0	17.1
CNC	10.0	30.0	37.5	58.5
INC	90.0	56.7	62.5	24.4
2. CONS	3.3	10.0	6.3	31.7
CNC	10.0	23.3	12.5	24.4
INC	86.7	66.7	81.2	43.9
3. CONS	0.0	6.7	0.0	17.1
CNC	10.0	16.7	31.3	56.1
INC	90.0	73.3	68.7	24.4
4. CONS	0.0	3.3	0.0	12.2
CNC	6.7	26.7	37.5	56.1
INC	90.0	66.7	56.2	29.3

* CONS means consistent conserving, CNC means consistent nonconserving, and INC means inconsistent.

Source: Rothenberg and Courtney, 1969, p. 497.

gous to Piaget's problem of the conservation of area. According to Beilin, "performance in the MC Kindergarten [about age 5] is not appreciably different from that of the LC Kindergarten groups on all measures" (p. 221).

What happens in the case of older children? Mermelstein and Schulman (1967) investigated the effect of lack of schooling on lower-class children's conservation performance. These writers studied 6- and 9-year-old Negro children. About half of the subjects at each age level were from a lower-class background in the American South and did not attend school. Another group (again both 6 and 9 years of age) was from a similar background in the North and did attend school. The question was whether the first group's lack of schooling affected its performance on the conservation of continuous quantity. The results showed that both groups performed at about the same level: by 9 years of age, children from both the North and South did well at the conservation problem. The data are given in Table 4-7. They plainly show that on the various forms of the conservation tasks, poor 6-year-olds, schooled or unschooled, do badly, whereas a high proportion of older children show evidence of an ability to conserve. The results are of interest in two ways. They show first that extremely deprived black children in the South eventually acquire conservation and, second, that attendence in school apparently makes no difference for this aspect of development.

CONCLUSIONS

In general, the available research supports Piaget's views. The cross-cultural studies show that the basics of cognitive functioning, at least as

TABLE 4-7   Number of Schooled and Unschooled Children
Showing Conservation or Its Lack on Five Conservation Tasks

	Task	6-year-olds	
		Unschooled	Schooled
1	Nonconservers (NC)	17	23
	Conservers (C)	9	6
2	NC	25	28
	C	4	1
3	NC	27	29
	C	3	1
4	NC	24	26
	C	6	4
5	NC	24	29
	C	3	0
		9-year-olds	
1	NC	6	5
	C	24	25
2	NC	17	14
	C	9	13
3	NC	13	14
	C	14	14
4	NC	6	5
	C	21	20
5	NC	8	9
	C	21	18

Source: Mermelstein and Schulman, 1967, p. 47.

Piaget describes it, are quite similar in a variety of cultures throughout the
world. The ages at which children master the Piagetian tasks may not be
precisely the same in Geneva as in Hong Kong, but in both cases cognitive
development seems to follow the same general course. In view of this, it seems
unlikely that the minds of lower-class children within Western societies differ
in remarkable ways from those of middle-class children. The available research supports this conjecture. Some studies show no social-class differences
in intellect; other studies show minor differences.

The bulk of the evidence suggests that certain aspects of cognition are
universal: all children acquire certain basic categories of thought. This is
not to deny that there may be individual and social-class differences in other
aspects of thought. Surely the *content* of poor children's thought must include
unique features. Poor children in the ghetto often know about the numbers
racket, whereas middle-class children may think of numbers in the context of
adding lollipops.

Perhaps, too, poor children's *patterns* of thinking (not the content) are
in some ways unique. The Lesser research suggests that this may be true of
different ethnic groups. But as yet we know little about this possibility, how-

ever plausible it may be. As I pointed out earlier, the tests used in the Lesser research were rather superficial. To detect subtle differences in thought, we need subtle research—research which attempts to measure fine aspects of the reasoning process. It will benefit us little simply to tabulate the number of problems on which middle- and lower-class children are correct or incorrect. We should save wasted effort by attempting to measure instead the types of reasoning that both kinds of children employ.

So there must be social-class differences in the content of thought, and there may be some social-class differences in the pattern of thought. But we must not permit these differences to obscure the basic similarities—the cognitive universals. Taking this perspective we see that much current theory concerning poor children's intellect is often misleading and incorrect: poor children do not suffer from massive deficiencies of mind. If this is so, then a basic question remains. How do poor children develop powerful intellectual skills despite an apparently deprived environment?

chapter five

Development
In the preceding three chapters I have attempted to portray the intellectual abilities of poor children at various points in their lives: their intelligence, language, and thought. The next question, I think, is this: How does poor children's intellectual life develop? How do they acquire the cognitive skills which research shows they possess?

The way in which I pose the developmental question is, of course, influenced by my conclusion that poor children's intellect is far from deficient. If this is so, then our chief job is to come to an understanding of how poor children develop as adequately as they do. Contrary to the opinions of many writers on the issue, it is health we must explain, not pathology.

This chapter deals with four topics. We begin by discussing the ways in which child-rearing practices affect intellect. The second section reviews evidence on poor children's learning, and the third describes a study on the natural process of development. The fourth section attempts to provide a general perspective on problems of development.

COGNITIVE SOCIALIZATION

How does the mind of the child develop? What determines its growth and its nature? One point of view emphasizes the power of culture: mind is very much a product of society. The child's intellect is moulded by social forces, and one of the most important of these is his parents' child-rearing practices. Consider some recent research on the application of this principle to poor children.

Hess and Shipman's Work

Like Bernstein, Hess and Shipman (1965, 1967) begin with the general assumption that child-rearing techniques—particularly the mother's—have a major impact on the child's cognitive development. In the case of poor children, this view asserts that inadequate socialization produces deficient intellect which in turn produces school failure. In Chapter 3, we have already reviewed many of the early Bernstein hypotheses, and so we shall not repeat them here in detail. Suffice it to say that in Bernstein's view, the lower-class mother employs a restricted code, fails to plan for the future, discourages or does not promote in the child impulse control and rational thinking, and in general engages in a variety of child-rearing practices which retard the child's intellectual development.

Accepting Bernstein's general orientation, Hess and Shipman attempted an empirical test of his hypotheses and related ideas. The subjects, all Negroes, were 163 nonworking mothers and their 4-year-old children. The families were selected according to social-class criteria: Group A (40 mother-child pairs) came from professional, managerial, and executive levels; Group B (42 pairs) had no more than a high school education and came from skilled blue-collar occupational levels; Group C (40 pairs) generally had only an elementary school education and came from unskilled or semi-skilled occupational levels; Group D (41 pairs) was the same as Group C, that is, relatively unskilled and uneducated, but the fathers were absent from the home and the families were consequently supported by welfare (Aid to Dependent Children or ADC). Within each group, about half the children were boys and half girls. The children ranged in age from 3 years 9 months to 4 years 4 months.

The first phase of the research project involved two interviews, about one and one half hours each, of all mothers in their homes. The interviewers were trained Negro social workers. The questions concerned the mother's activities with the child, her daily schedule, the kinds of intellectual stimulation—e.g., books—that were available in the home, and attitudes toward school and the child's chances of academic success. Responses to this last topic were tape-recorded.

In the second phase of the project, the mothers and children were brought to the University of Chicago for two testing sessions. The tests included adult and child intelligence scales, concept formation tests, a curiosity task, and the like.

The third and last part of the study involved the direct observation of mother-child interaction. This took place in a specially designed room which contained a microphone for recording speech and a one-way mirror through which observers might secretly view and score the mother-child interaction. In this session, the mother was required to teach the child three simple tasks that one of the researchers had previously explained to her in the absence of the child. One of the tasks was to classify a number of toys (cars, spoons, chairs) by function. For example, eating implements might go in one category and transportation devices in another. This is a simple concept formation task, as described in Chapter 4. The second problem, also involving concept formation, but perhaps more complex than the first, was to classify eight blocks, differing in color, size, shape, and design, by two attributes simultaneously (e.g., large red blocks vs. small, green ones). The third task required mother and child to work together in copying five designs.

Hess and Shipman have analyzed their extensive data in a large number of ways, and we cannot describe all of the findings here. We will consider two major topics: the nature of maternal child-rearing strategies, as assessed by interviews, and their relations to cognition; and the connections between observed maternal behavior and children's intellectual ability.

MATERNAL CONTROL AND COGNITIVE DEVELOPMENT

Hess and Shipman distinguish among three types or strategies of maternal control. One is essentially an *appeal to authority*, to unchallengeable norms, decrees, and rules. The mother uses authority to impose her will on the child's behavior. Typical statements are: "You'll do that because I said so" or "Don't do that—girls don't act that way." This kind of control, appealing blindly to the norms of the status quo, does not require the child to think about his actions, the reasons for them, or the rationale which presumably underlies the moral code. Bernstein has hypothesized that this approach characterizes the lower class.

A second kind of control involves an *appeal to feeling*. The mother justifies commands or prohibitions on the basis of the effects of the child's behavior on the feelings of others. Typical statements are: "How do you think your sister will feel if you do that?" or "When you do that, it makes me sad." This kind of control orients the child not so much to a rational understanding of rules but to a sensitivity to the feelings of others. The child must learn to take the point of view of others and anticipate their reactions to his behavior. This seems more complex than the simple behavior demanded by appeals to authority.

A third approach is the *appeal to reason*. The mother attempts to direct the child's attention not to arbitrary rules or feelings, but to the possible outcomes of his behavior. The mother urges him to imagine the consequences of his actions and to consider alternative plans. For example, if the child wants to play with a friend rather than do school work, the mother might say: "Will you have enough time to do your homework?" This remark forces the child to think about the future and may lead him to understand the rationale underlying certain rules. This is the type of discipline which Bernstein feels is a characteristic of middle-class parents.

To measure the mother's use of the various kinds of controls, Hess and Shipman included in the interview several specially designed questions. One asked the mother to describe what she would tell her child before he left for his first day in school. Another question dealt with the mother's response to hypothetical misbehavior on the part of the child in school. Responses to these questions and others were tape-recorded and later coded into several categories, including the dimensions of control (authority, feeling, and reason) described above.

Table 5-1 shows some of the results. Part A describes the mother's re-

TABLE 5-1 Class Difference in Control Strategies of Authority, Feelings, and Reason (Mean Percent) *

| Method of Control | A. School behavior question | | | |
	A Professional	B Skilled	C Unskilled	D ADC
authority	27.8	36.9	40.7	51.1
feelings	36.9	31.6	26.4	20.9
	B. First day at school			
authority	14.9	48.2	44.4	46.6
reason	8.7	4.6	1.7	3.2

* Figures for other strategies are not given.
Source: Hess and Shipman, 1965, pp. 877, 878.

sponses to hypothetical questions involving the child's misbehavior at school. It shows that in the interview, middle-class parents used significantly fewer appeals to authority than did any of the other groups and that the ADC mothers used significantly more such appeals than did any of the others. In the case of appeals to feelings, the middle-class parents received significantly higher scores than any of the other groups, which did not differ among themselves. The data for appeals to reason are not given since they were relatively infrequent.

Part B shows similar findings with respect to the question concerning the mother's advice to the child on his first day in school. The middle-class group uses fewer appeals to authority than the other groups. In the case of appeals to reason, the middle-class mothers scored significantly higher than the lower-class groups, which again did not differ significantly among themselves. It is clear, however, that few appeals to reason were made by any of the groups; most mothers depended on authority or tried to point out to their children the effects of their action on the feelings of others. If we consider appeals to feelings a kind of rational approach, then the findings seem to support Bernstein's hypothesis concerning social-class differences in parental discipline.

The next issue is the effects of maternal control strategies on children's intellectual ability. Table 5-2 shows correlations between mothers' scores on various measures of control strategies and their children's performance on

TABLE 5-2   Correlations between Maternal Control Strategies
and Children's Intellectual Performance

| | Control Strategies | | |
Intellectual Performance	Authority	Feelings	Reason
8-block verbal score	−.32 **	.18 *	.30 **
8-block physical score	−.26 **	.12	.25 **
Binet IQ	−.32 **	.22 **	.18 *
Sigel nonverbal	.36 **	−.17 *	−.09

* Significant at $p < .05$.
** Significant at $p < .01$.
Source: Hess and Shipman, 1967, p. 66.

several tests. The 8-block verbal score reflects the child's ability to verbalize the basis for his sorting. The 8-block nonverbal score measures the child's ability to sort correctly, without giving a verbal response. The Sigel nonverbal score is a measure of the child's *inability* to verbalize about sorting. The table shows that if the mother uses appeals to reason or feelings, there is a slight tendency for the child to do well on the intellectual tests. If the mother employs appeals to authority, then the child tends to score poorly. Hess and Shipman conclude that the data support Bernstein's theory: in disciplining children, lower-class mothers tend to use appeals to authority, and these fail to stimulate intellectual development.

I wish to make several comments concerning this aspect of Hess and Shipman's study. First, it relies on interviews for data concerning mothers' disciplinary techniques. This is not a sound procedure. A number of writers have shown that interviews are inconsistent and often inaccurate. For example, Crandall and Preston (1955) compared psychologists' ratings of mothers' behavior with mothers' self-rating and found that there is little relation between the two. Zunich (1962) obtained similar results. For an account of other relevant studies reaching similar conclusions, see Freeberg and Payne (1967, pp. 75–76). The moral is simple: we must be skeptical of studies which employ interview techniques to obtain data on child-rearing practices. As a result of this skepticism, I have not reviewed in this chapter the many studies correlating IQ and interview measures of child rearing.

Second, the correlations between control strategies and children's performance are quite small: at best, they are in the range of .30. While some correlations are statistically significant, they show little relation between child rearing and intellect.[1] Statistical significance is not the same as psychological significance. Another way of stating Hess and Shipman's results

[1] In statistical terminology, a correlation of .30 accounts for only 9 percent of the variance.

is this: factors other than maternal control strategies account for most of the variation in children's intellectual performance on the tests used. (Of course, it is conceivable that if other tests were used, the results might be different.)

Third, the interpretation of correlational studies is always ambiguous with respect to cause and effect. Did the mothers' discipline affect the child's intellect or vice versa? Or could there be other factors which influence both intellectual functioning and discipline? In conclusion, the soundest interpretation one can make about this aspect of the Hess and Shipman study is that it tells us little about the effects of discipline on intellect. If anything, there is little relation between the two.

MOTHER-CHILD INTERACTION

Fortunately, Hess and Shipman's study offers not only interview data on maternal discipline, but also direct observations of mother-child interaction. To study this, Hess and Shipman brought mother-child pairs to university facilities. The experimenters first taught the mother (without the child present) the simple tasks which we have already described: toy sorting, block sorting, and copying designs. The mother was then required to teach the child to sort the objects in certain ways and to verbalize the principle for the grouping (e.g., "Blue ones go here"). In the third task, the mother had to instruct the child in making certain designs. After the interaction session, the experimenter took the child aside and tested him on the sorting tasks.

The interaction sessions and subsequent tests yield large amounts of data. The experimenters recorded the speech of mother and child, coded their nonverbal behavior, and scored the child's performance on the tests. We will focus on mother-child behavior on the block-sorting task. (This is typical of the rest.)

In scoring mother-child interaction in the block task, Hess and Shipman concentrated on the "teaching aspects" of the mother's behavior. Every statement that the mother made to the child was coded according to the following categories: (1) *Informing.* This concerns the mother's imparting specific information concerning the blocks, e.g., "These blocks are the same height." (2) *Motivating.* These are statements which try to interest the child by promising rewards, by describing the intrinsic value of the task, etc. (3) *Orienting.* These are statements which prepare the child for the task, e.g., "Let's try it again," or "I'm going to show you how to do it." (4) *Seeking physical feedback.* This refers to the mother's attempt to get the child to sort the blocks, e.g., "Where does this block go?" or "Put this one here." (5) *Seeking verbal feedback.* These are statements which ask the child to verbalize aspects of the task. "Why did you put the block there?" (6) *Positive reinforcement.* "Yes, that's right," and the like. (7) *Negative reinforcement.*

"No, that's wrong," and similar remarks. (8) *Requiring discriminations.* These are messages which require the child to attend to and discriminate relevant aspects of the problem. "Find a tall block with an *x* on it" is an example.

Following Bernstein, Hess and Shipman's hypothesis is that middle-class mothers are better teachers than lower-class mothers: the former give valuable information, force the child to deal with problems, and encourage intellectual activity. Data on social-class differences in mothers' teaching are presented in Table 5-3. Statistical analysis shows no significant differences

TABLE 5-3   Social-Class Differences in Mean Number of Teaching Behaviors

Types of Behavior	Groups			
	A	B	C	D
	Middle Class	Upper Lower Class	Lower Class	Lower Class, Father Absent
Informing	23.46	22.87	20.82	22.26
Motivating	5.30	3.46	2.73	3.08
Orienting	8.12	6.45	5.78	5.44
Seeking Physical Feedback	8.17	13.91	13.16	14.06
Seeking Verbal Feedback	21.05	20.45	20.89	19.65
Positive Reinforcement	53.10	35.37	40.75	46.27
Negative Reinforcement	44.73	44.80	53.82	58.24
Requiring Discriminations	48.20	42.56	44.72	39.17

Source: Hess and Shipman, 1967, p. 72.

among the groups on *informing* and *seeking verbal feedback.* Middle- and lower-class mothers give information and request verbal explanations to about the same degree as lower-class mothers. In the case of the other variables, there are statistically significant differences. Usually, the middle-class group significantly differs from the other groups, all of which receive roughly equivalent scores.

Let us examine the "significant" differences more closely. In the case of *motivating* and *orienting,* the absolute size of the differences is quite small. For example, the middle-class mothers make an average of about 8 orienting statements and the ADC mothers about 5½. *Requiring discriminations* shows a moderate difference: 48 for the middle-class and 39 for the ADC mothers. There are fairly substantial differences on only three variables of the eight: *seeking physical feedback, positive reinforcement,* and *negative reinforcement.* In comparison with other groups, middle-class mothers less frequently asked their children to sort the blocks, more often told the children that they were right, and less often told them they were wrong. On the whole, then, it would seem as if the social-class differences are far from massive. Certainly there is not a complete absence of what Hess and Shipman define as teaching behaviors in lower-class parents; in fact, on four of the eight measures the groups are quite similar. On the other hand, one might argue that the four variables—*requiring discriminations, seeking physical feedback, positive reinforcement,* and *negative reinforcement*—on which the groups differ are quite important.

Let us see if this is indeed the case: How do the various measures of teaching behavior relate to the child's performance on the block-sorting task? Table 5-4 presents correlations between maternal teaching variables and two

TABLE 5-4   Correlations between Maternal Behaviors and
Child's Performance on the Block Task

Mother's Behavior	Placement Score	Verbal Score
Motivating	.06	.07
Orienting	.20 *	.16 *
Seeking Physical Feedback	—.39 *	—.30 *
Seeking Verbal Feedback	.18 *	.24 *
Negative Reinforcement	—.09	—.03
Positive Reinforcement	.12	.01
Requiring Discriminations	.16 *	.30 *

* $p < .05$.
Source: Hess and Shipman, 1967, p. 74.

measures of children's performance on the block-sorting task. Note that this analysis combines mothers from all social classes. The question here is not how social classes differ in maternal behavior, but how maternal behavior, regardless of social class, relates to children's intellectual performance.

The data show very little correspondence between the mother's behavior and the child's. Consider first the variables on which, according to the previous analysis, the social classes differ. The correlations for positive and negative reinforcement are essentially zero. This means that social-class differences in this area are of no interest since maternal reinforcement has no effect on the child's behavior.

One variable that might have a convincing and consistent relation with block sorting is *seeking physical feedback*. The correlation shows that if the mother insisted that the child sort, he tended to sort poorly. It seems to me that this result is hardly in line with Bernstein's perspective. One simple hypothesis is that children react poorly to pressure and need to pace themselves.

Requiring discriminations shows a small correlation with block sorting. This supports Bernstein's position.

The other correlations are extremely low. Further, the social classes do not differ much—if at all—on these variables so that the results are of little significance in any event. My overall summary of the results is this. The social classes differ on some aspects of maternal behavior (e.g., negative reinforcement), but not others (e.g., informing). When a difference does exist, it sometimes has no effect on intellectual activity (e.g., negative reinforcement), and it sometimes has a small effect (e.g., requiring discriminations). In general, Bernstein's hypothesis does not get much support.

FURTHER EXAMINATION OF THE HESS AND SHIPMAN DATA

Brophy (1970) presents a further analysis of the Hess and Shipman data. His study examines several aspects of maternal behavior on the block-sorting task. The general question is this: Are there social-class differences in the mother's tendency to provide the child with help during different phases of the task?

Consider first the mother's behavior. Brophy coded two aspects of the maternal communications: *verbalizations of labels* and *focusing*. The first referred to the extent to which the mother supplied a specific label referring to the attributes of the blocks. If she said "same height" or "tall," etc., she was considered to have verbalized a label. If she said nothing or referred to the blocks in vague terms—e.g., "this one," "the block over there," etc.— she was considered not to have verbalized.

Focusing referred to the mother's attempt to draw the child's attention to the relevant attributes. The mother was considered to have focused if she pointed to an attribute, asked the child to look at a block, placed a tall and a short block side by side so as to make salient the difference in height, etc.

Brophy proposes that maternal behavior varies according to the phase of the task. He suggests that there is first an *orientation period* in which mothers explain or demonstrate the task as the child watches. Then the child makes his responses and the mother might give instructions before each one. These are called *pre-response instructions*. Then there is *post-response feedback;* the mother may confirm or correct the child's response, give him additional information, etc. The different phases of the task—orientation, pre-response instructions, and post-response feedback—may require different kinds of maternal behavior. And the question is whether there exist social-class differences in maternal behavior on different phases of the task.

Some of the data are presented in Table 5-5. Consider first the *orientation period.* The differences between the middle-class mothers (Group A) and the rest were all highly statistically significant, if not particularly large. The middle-class mothers tended to label and focus more extensively than did lower-class mothers. In the *pre-response instructions,* the social-class differences are again statistically significant, and here they are also large. Middle-class mothers tended to focus and verbalize far more frequently than lower-

TABLE 5-5   Mean Scores on Maternal Teaching Measures for
Four Social-Class Groups

	Group			
	A	*B*	*C*	*D*
	Middle Class	*Upper Lower Class*	*Lower Class*	*Lower Class, Father Absent*
Orientation period:				
Verbalizes and focuses on one attribute	2.1	1.8	1.8	1.8
Verbalizes and focuses on another	1.9	1.3	1.1	1.2
Pre-response instructions:				
Verbalizes both labels (%)	27.2	14.1	10.7	8.2
Verbalizes any label (%)	39.5	22.1	22.3	20.1
Focuses (%)	15.3	4.7	5.5	6.4
Post-response feedback:				
Verbalizes labels after error (%)	86.1	75.3	72.3	65.2
Focuses after error (%)	36.9	33.0	29.9	40.8
Verbalizes labels after success (%)	41.5	40.2	30.7	24.8
Focuses after success (%)	20.7	14.7	8.7	9.7

Source: Brophy, 1970, p. 89.

class mothers. In the *post-response feedback* phase, the differences were smaller and sometimes not statistically significant. For example, middle-class mothers generally did not differ from the others on focusing after error.

We may summarize the results in the following way: middle-class mothers *prepare* their children for the task more adequately than do lower-class mothers. After the child responds, however, the different groups of mothers act in similar ways, although here too there are a few social-class differences (favoring the middle class) in the extent to which mothers verbalize or focus the child's attention. Lower-class mothers let the child shift for himself more frequently before the task than do middle-class mothers; after the task, this difference is less pronounced.

Note two features of the Brophy study. First, his data are far more convincing than those of Hess and Shipman. Apparently, in a structured learning situation there are some fairly substantial social-class differences. What these imply for other situations, however, is not yet clear, and we shall return to this issue below. Second, Brophy does not report on the link between child rearing and cognitive development; he does not demonstrate a relation between differences in maternal behavior and children's intellect.

Bee's Study

A study by Helen L. Bee and her associates (1969) provides further data concerning maternal teaching behavior. These investigators studied 38 upper-middle-class families (University of Washington staff and students, all white) and 76 lower-class families (two-thirds black). The mothers and their children, whose average age was about 4 to 6, were observed in two situations: in the waiting room of the University laboratory and in a task in which the children were required to build a house with blocks. The first situation was unstructured in that mothers and children were free to do what they liked. Toys were available, so that the children could play and the mothers would help.

The second task, like Hess and Shipman's, was structured: the children were required to build the house and the mothers were told to give "as much or as little help as you like" (p. 729).

Table 5-6 gives the results for the unstructured situation. There are no

TABLE 5-6   Comparison of Middle- and Lower-Class Mothers and Children on Behavior in the Waiting Room

Variable	Lower Class	Middle Class
Mother's rate of control statements	.565	.258
Mother's rate of suggestions	.667	.614
Mother's rate of approval	.753	.987
Mother's rate of ignoring	.449	.440
Mother's rate of disapproval	.234	.139
Mother's rate of questions	1.287	1.424
Mother's rate of information statements	1.582	2.107
Mother's rate of attention		
Level 0	1.567	1.195
Level 1	.961	.700
Level 2	1.346	1.839
Level 3	.541	.639
Child's rate of acceptance	.806	.565
Child's rate of rejection	.134	.144
Child's rate of general seeking	.572	.613
Child's rate of ignoring	.339	.304
Child's rate of questions	1.261	1.252
Child's rate of demands	.252	.226
Child's rate of information statements	2.683	3.445
Child's rate of toy shifts	1.040	.823
Child's rate of space shifts	.807	.627

Source: Bee *et al.,* 1969, p. 730.

social-class differences in: mothers' rate of suggestions, approval, ignoring, and questions; child's rate of rejecting his mother's suggestion, his rate of general seeking (i.e., requesting mother's help), ignoring the mother, asking questions, and demanding mother's help. By contrast, the significant social-class differences were these: in comparison with the middle class, lower-class mothers were more controlling ("in pre-emptory fashion"), more disapproving, gave fewer information statements, and attended less carefully to their children; lower-class children more frequently accepted the mother's suggestion, less frequently gave information, played with more toys, and moved around more than did middle-class children.

In sum, on about half the measures, differences appear and on the other half, they do not. Some of the differences seem to "favor" the middle class: mothers are less controlling, less disapproving, give more information and attention. Other differences are harder to evaluate: lower-class children move and play with toys more frequently than middle-class children. Does this indicate greater curiosity or greater distractibility?

Table 5-7 presents data on the structured task. Again, on about half

TABLE 5-7   Comparison of Middle- and Lower-Class Mothers and Children on Problem-Solving Behavior

Variable	Lower Class	Middle Class
Total time spent on problem (sec.)	435.513	523.421
Mean specificity of mother's suggestions	2.684	2.521
Mother's rate of nonquestion suggestions	6.568	5.778
Mother's rate of question suggestions	2.254	3.120
Mother's rate of positive feedback	2.067	3.073
Mother's rate of negative feedback	1.855	1.018
Mother's rate of specificity		
Level 1	2.591	3.816
Level 2	4.027	3.332
Level 3	2.385	1.886
Mother's rate of nonverbal intrusions	2.373	.695
Child's rate of acceptance	1.027	1.129
Child's rate of rejection	.481	.470
Child's rate of dependency bids	1.217	1.252

Source: Bee *et al.,* 1969, p. 730.

the variables, there are no social-class differences: specificity of mother's suggestions; rate of suggestions; levels 2 and 3 of suggestions (i.e., very specific ones); child's rate of acceptance and rejection of suggestions; and child's attempts to get help. There are social-class differences on other variables: lower-class families spent less time on the problem, mothers made fewer question suggestions (e.g., "Where does this one go?"), were less approving (positive feedback) and more disapproving (negative feedback), gave fewer level 1 specificity statements (these were orienting and focusing statements, like "Look at the lady's house"), and made more nonverbal intrusions (placing a block for the child). These differences seem generally to "favor" middle-class families.

It is difficult to compare these results with Brophy's, since he divided the session into several phases and scored mainly verbalization and focusing. The Bee *et al.* results might agree with Brophy's in that both find middle-class mothers give more orienting suggestions than do lower-class mothers. Also, the Bee *et al.* results agree with Hess and Shipman's in finding that lower-class mothers criticize more and reward less than do middle-class mothers.

The Bee *et al.* study does not consider the relations between maternal behavior and children's intellect.

Conclusions

Enough data. It is now time for us to consider their meaning and place them in perspective. I wish to make several points.

First, the various studies show that there are social-class differences in some aspects of maternal behavior. Yet one should not exaggerate them. The differences are often small and nonsignificant and sometimes trivial.

Second, we do not know whether the observed differences are at all typical of maternal behavior in a variety of settings. The data in all the studies were obtained in the laboratory or in the waiting room adjacent to it. There is no way of telling whether the results apply to the home as well. It is quite conceivable that the mothers—particularly middle-class mothers—perceived the situation as evaluative and tried to behave in ways that would secure the psychologists' approval. The only way to settle the issue is to study mother-child interaction in the home.

Third, the laboratory task and the behavior it elicits may not have been typical of either children's learning or the way in which parents help it. The 8-block problem, for example, is artificial and probably unrelated to the usual concerns of the mothers and children. In the Hess and Shipman and the Brophy studies, the experimenter imposed on the mothers a strategy for teaching and a set of goals to be achieved. The mothers were required to have the child sort the blocks in several specific ways and to verbalize the solution. It is possible that the observed social-class differences apply mainly to cases where there is an artificial and imposed task which does not elicit a great deal of interest on the part of mothers or children. If this is so, the findings would, of course, be of little interest. On the other hand, the Bee *et al.* study goes part way toward meeting this objection. Their research included observations on spontaneous behavior in the waiting room. We need further research of this type: How do parents help their children learn in more natural situations?

Fourth, the research studies do not devote sufficient attention to the interaction *process*. Most of the results concern the frequencies of a given behavior—e.g., questions or negative reinforcements—in either mother or child but do not explore in more than a gross way the effects of one person's be-havior on another's. For example, what does a child do when his mother tries to guide his exploration of an object? What does a mother do when the child asks for help? Both of these questions refer to the interactions be-tween mother and child—to the contingencies between A's behavior and B's. Neither question can be answered merely by counting the overall frequencies of A's acts or B's. Table 5-8 gives a simple example which proves the point. A and C show the same total frequencies of responses: both ask two questions

TABLE 5-8   Hypothetical Interaction between A and B, and C and D

A	B		C	D
1. Question → Statement			1. Question → Statement	
2. Question → Failure to respond			2. Question → Statement	
3. Statement → Statement			3. Statement → Failure to respond	
4. Statement → Failure to respond			4. Statement → Failure to respond	

	A	C	B	D
Number of questions	2	2	0	0
Number of statements	2	2	2	2
Number of failures to respond	0	0	2	2

and make two statements. Similarly, B and D show the same total: two statements and two failures to respond. Looking just at the totals, one would conclude that the interactions between A and B, and between C and D were the same. But they obviously are not. When C asks a question, he always gets an answer; when he makes a statement, he never gets a response. On the other hand, when A asks a question or makes a statement, he sometimes gets a response and sometimes does not. In short, research on cognitive sociali-zation in the poor needs to give more detailed attention to problems of inter-action.

Fifth, the Hess and Shipman study fails to demonstrate that maternal behavior, particularly teaching, bears any clear relation to cognition. The results show trivially significant or insignificant correlations between maternal behavior and several measures of block sorting and other alleged cognitive variables. (I am not convinced that the cognitive measures are very informa-tive or interesting, but that is another story and not crucial to my argument here.) Yet the existence of a strong link between maternal behavior and the child's intellect is the basic assumption underlying all of the studies and also many programs of compensatory education.

So, we are left with several unanswered questions. We do not know the extent to which the social-class differences observed in the laboratory are typical of other settings or of more "natural" learning situations. We do not know much about mother-child *interaction* in the learning situation. And, finally, we do not know how the mother's behavior relates to the child's intellectual growth—to his strengths, which I emphasize, as well as to his weaknesses, which Hess and his associates and Bee and hers tend to stress.

Absence of Parental Effect

Apart from the studies already described, there seems to be little research [2] or theory which can clarify the issues I have raised. Consequently, I wish to offer a few speculations based on indirect evidence or my own observations.

First, it is already obvious that child-rearing practices have no important effect on *some* aspects of cognition. For example, we have seen in Chapter 4 that children in all societies studied develop the various patterns of thought described by Piaget. Presumably, these societies differ in child-rearing techniques, and yet the children still develop conservation and other aspects of thinking. Perhaps child-rearing affects the rate at which the cognitive universals develop, but they will eventually develop regardless of whether the parents reinforce, suggest, train, ignore, and all the rest.

Second, parental *teaching,* in the sense described by Hess and Shipman, could not possibly be important for many basic features of cognition. The reason is simple: almost no parent knows what cognitive development is really like. Unless familiar with psychology, parents do not know that infants acquire object permanence, that 2-year-olds develop syntactic structures, that 6-year-olds acquire conservation of number, and 12-year-olds combinatorial reasoning. Parents are not alone in this respect. Psychologists, too, are surprised by these phenomena. When I first read psycholinguistics, I could not believe that by the age of about 4 or 5, children have almost all of adult grammar; and when I read about perceptual development, I could not believe that infants possess some perceptual constancies (e.g., an object is seen to have the same size even when it is viewed from varying distances). But these phenomena now seem well established. My disbelief was not well founded; I should have known (as future psychologists will know) that it is "obvious" that infants have certain constancies, etc.

In brief, my expectations concerning cognitive development were quite incorrect. I have no reason to suppose that I am at all unique in this respect. Almost all parents must have similarly inaccurate expectations of intellectual development. And if this is the case, then they could not systematically *teach* and control intellectual growth. In fact, if cognitive socialization were as important as Hess and Shipman suppose, then parents would be positively

[2] Alfred and Clara Baldwin are conducting a study which promises a real break-through in the area of cognitive socialization. Unfortunately, as this book goes to press, their data are not yet available.

dangerous on two counts. On the one hand, they would fail to teach some essentials. They would not know, for example, that infants need to learn some constancies. On the other hand, they would teach some essentials in the wrong way. For example, some parents might walk around reinforcing their child's language. This would serve mainly to confuse (or amuse) the child since reinforcement has little to do with the acquisition of language.[3]

In sum, teaching could not possibly be important for some aspects of cognitive development, since parents often do not know what to teach or how to teach.

Third, it is unlikely that parental personality factors have much to do with the child's acquisition of the cognitive universals. A study by Gold-schmid (1968) is relevant to this issue. He attempted to examine the relations between the child's ability to conserve and parental child-rearing attitudes. The subjects were 102 7-year-old children. Goldschmid tested each of them in the following areas: conservation of weight, substance, quantity, etc. (There were 14 conservation scores in all.) He also gave to their parents (both father and mother) the *Parental Attitude Survey*. This is intended to measure the extent to which the parents hold dominant, ignoring, and possessive attitudes. (Thus, there are six scores, three for each parent.)

The chief question of the study is how parental attitudes relate to the child's ability to conserve. The answer is that there is almost no relation. Of the 84 correlations computed (14 conservation scores with each of six parental measures), 74 are essentially 0, and 10 are statistically significant. But the "significant" correlations are quite small. For example, there is a correlation of $-.21$ between the child's ability to conserve discontinuous quantity and the extent to which the mother is dominant. This is a trivial relationship.[4]

The Goldschmid study seems to point to the conclusion that there is little if any relation between parental attitudes and the child's acquisition of conservation. I readily grant, however, that the Goldschmid study is far from conclusive. For one thing, it examines parental attitudes, and we do not know how these relate to behavior. For another, Goldschmid may have focused on the wrong attitudes. Had he measured others, then stronger relations with conservation might have been demonstrated. Perhaps, but I doubt it. Why *should* parental personality relate to the child's acquisition of the cognitive universals? As I shall demonstrate below, much of children's learning is self-directed and self-motivated. They themselves control a major part of the learning, not the parents.

---

[3] Imagine what would happen if we depended on the schools to teach children how to speak!

[4] The statistically inclined reader will note that the number of significant correlations (10 of 84) does not differ too much from what is expected on a chance basis anyway. At the .05 level, one would expect 4.2 of 84 correlations (i.e., 84 $\times$ .05) to be significant by chance.

The Role of the Parent

Thus far, the evidence suggests that parents could not strongly affect the development of the cognitive universals. On the one hand, parents do not know what they are; on the other, teaching is not an effective method for inducing them. On the basis of this line of reasoning alone, I think it is wrong to believe that parents foster intellectual development by acting as teachers in the traditional sense—that is, society's agents who *impose* knowledge on the child. But if teaching is ineffective and largely irrelevant to a major portion of the child's cognitive development, what is the parent's role?

Few if any writers have considered cognitive socialization from this perspective. Consequently, all I have to offer in response to these questions are some speculations based on my own observations. Consider a few examples concerning my twin girls. The first describes an episode which occurred a few days before their fifth birthday. (The entire sequence was recorded on television tape, so that my report is quite accurate.)

Deborah and Rebecca were seated at the kitchen table in the late morning. (I had asked them to sit there because it was a good place for television taping, but otherwise I gave them no instructions or suggestions about what to do.) For the preceding several months, they had been interested in learning to count. Deborah counted on her fingers, "One, two, three, four."

Rebecca (R) shows Deborah (D) three fingers and says: "Know how many this is?"

D: "Three." And she counts on her own hand, "One, two, three."

R: "Know how many sixes is six?"

D: Counts five fingers on one hand and one finger on the other: "One, two, three, four, five, six."

R: Counts the fingers on both hands: "One, two, three, four, five, six, seven, eight, nine, ten."

D: "One, two, three, four, five, six, seven, eight, nine, ten." She holds up both hands and says: "Ten, this many is ten."

R: "You got ten fingers." And counting her own, she says, "One, two, three, four, five, six, seven, eight, nine, ten."

D: At the same time, counts her fingers: "One, two, three, four, five, six, seven, eight, nine, ten, eleven, twelve, thirteen, fourteen, fifteen, sixteen. Sixteen!"

R: "Uh uhh [no]. We don't got sixteen. Want me to count your fingers?" She does so: "One, two, three, four, five, six, seven, eight, nine, ten. Got ten fingers, right? Want me to count them again?"

D: Counts the fingers of one hand, touching each to her mouth as she says the number. She did the counting incorrectly: "One, two, three, four, five, six. Six. That's six. Was six."

R: Counts five fingers on one hand and one on the other: "This is six."

D: Holds up both hands and says: "This is six, too. This is six, too." [Apparently she meant that each hand had six fingers.]

R: Again counts five on one hand and one on the other to make six.

Up to this point, the girls were alone at the table, (I was partially hidden behind the TV camera at some distance and they paid no attention to me, not even looking in my direction.) Their counting was self-motivated and self-directed. No one told them to count or rewarded them for it. Their play (work) is a good and typical example of spontaneous intellectual activity. Piaget theorizes that there is a universal tendency toward "functional assimilation": people tend to repeat or to practice patterns of behavior and thought which are not well learned. This is a kind of self-imposed "urge toward mastery," and it does not depend on parental encouragement, reinforcement, or direction.

Of course, one may argue that the girls really were aware of me and that the entire performance was for my benefit. Or one may argue that I had partially reinforced them for counting in the past and that the current episode is merely the result of this. These arguments lack force, however, since they ignore a few crucial facts. First, the parents do not necessarily reward these activities. For example, at this time the girls would often lie in bed counting and thereby delay going to sleep. My wife and I would have to tell them to stop. "No more counting!" If reinforcement is so effective, then they should have gotten the idea that counting is not a good thing to do. Second, and as I pointed out earlier, parental reinforcement cannot be very important since children often learn to do things which the parents do not know about. So I stick to my conclusion that the counting in this episode is mainly self-motivated; it is not simply imposed by the parents.

This is not to say that the parents are irrelevant to the acquisition of counting. We must have given them the numbers in the first place. The numbers one through ten are completely arbitrary. They are a legacy of culture, and the child does not and cannot invent them for himself. The child has to get the numbers from a parent or from TV or some agent of culture. Obviously this is true. But my point is this: granted that the numbers are a cultural product, the motivation for learning them must come from the child.

Next, the girls became interested in other matters. They compared their heights and speculated on how tall they would be on their thirteenth birthday; they copied letters from cards. Soon it was time for lunch, and mouths filled with peanut butter uttered the following remarks:

D: "One, two, one, two, one, two."

R: "One, two, three."

D: "No, not like that. I said, 'One, two, one, two, one, two.'"

R: "One, two, three, four, five, six, seven, eight."

D: "One, two, one, two, one, two, one, two, one, two, one, two."

R: "One, two, three, four, five, six, seven, eight."

D: "One, two, three, four, five, six, seven, eight, nine, ten, eleven, twelve, thirteen, fourteen, fifteen, sixteen, seventeen, eighteen, nineteen. Nineteen."

Rebecca asked her mother, "What's after nineteen?"

You can see that the girls had learned the numbers one through nineteen very well, seldom making mistakes. They knew that there were more numbers (no doubt because they had heard some) and wanted to go on. This was not the first time they had asked for numbers above nineteen.

M (Mother): "Twenty."

R: "Twenty, twenty-one, twenty-two, twenty-three, twenty-four, twenty-five, twenty-six, twenty-seven, twenty-eight, twenty-nine."

D: "Twenty, twenty-one, twenty-two, twenty-three." [Here D said something very inaudibly because her mouth was stuffed. Probably she said the numbers twenty-four through twenty-nine.]

R: "What's after?"

M: "Thirty."

R: "Thirty-one, thirty-two, thirty-three, thirty-four, thirty-five, thirty-six, thirty-seven, thirty-eight, thirty-nine. Now forty."

M: "Good."

R: "Forty-one, forty-two, forty-three, forty-four, forty-five, forty-six, forty-seven, forty-eight, forty-nine."

D: "Ten."

R: "Fifty."

M: "Good."

R: "Fifty-one, fifty-two, fifty-three, fifty-four, fifty-five, fifty-six, fifty-seven, fifty-eight, fifty-nine." [Here R paused and looked toward her mother apparently in search of the next number.]

M: "Sixty."

R: "Sixty-one, sixty-two, sixty-three, sixty-four."

At this point, Rebecca's counting was interrupted by my son, who, obviously uninterested in questions of cognitive development, put his feet on the table. There followed a somewhat lengthy discussion of the propriety of putting feet on the table and other places.

Before going on, we must consider two issues. What was the mother's role? And how did Rebecca know the numbers forty and fifty? In regard to the mother, it seems clear that her main function in this was to offer assistance when it was requested. The girls asked for information only at difficult points—when they did not know the next number in the sequence. She also "reinforced"—that is, offered praise when the children accomplished something interesting or surprising, as when Rebecca knew forty. Is the reinforcement important here? Yes and no. On the one hand, it may not be important for learning since it comes after the child has produced the accomplishment. On the other hand, it may be important as a signal to the child that she was right.

How did Rebecca know that forty comes after thirty-nine, and fifty after forty-nine? There seem to be two possibilities. One is that she merely remembered the numbers as steps in a sequence of rote material. Another possibility is more interesting. Perhaps Rebecca was in the process of formulating a rule about the construction of numbers, and her responses "Forty" and "Fifty" were products of that rule and not the results of rote memory. The rule is relatively easy to describe. In essence, to get the numbers twenty, thirty, forty, etc., you simply take the digits from two to nine, modify them slightly, and add "-ty." Thus, "two-ty" becomes twenty, "three-ty" becomes thirty, "five-ty" becomes fifty, etc. Then, when you have these numbers, you simply take the first nine digits and add them to each: thus, twenty-one, twenty-two, etc. When you get to twenty-nine, you switch to thirty and repeat the whole process. We see then that counting need not be simply a rote procedure. While the numbers zero to at least ten must be memorized, numbers after that point (and particularly from twenty on) follow relatively simple rules.

The remainder of the episode casts light on the question of whether Rebecca merely memorized or whether she *constructed* the numbers as she went along.

D: "Becky, you know what, Becky? I can count to fifteen. One, two, three, four, five, six, seven, eight, nine, ten, eleven, twelve, thirteen."
R: "Fourteen."
D: "Fourteen, fifteen."
R: "Sixteen."
D: "Seventeen, eighteen, nineteen."
R: "Eleven."
D: "Eleven, twelve."
R: "Eleven, twelve, thirteen, fourteen, fifteen. What's after fifteen?"

Rebecca's performance was inconsistent. She had many times previously counted to sixteen. But such inconsistency seems typical of children's learning.

D: "Sixteen."
R: "What's after sixteen?" [This was directed at her mother.]

M: "Seventeen."
D: "Eighteen, nineteen."
R: "Eleven, eleven, twelve."

Note that the girls had gotten themselves into a trap. After nineteen, they returned to eleven and started all over again. This could go on indefinitely.

Perhaps disturbed by this possibility, my wife said, "Twenty, twenty." This remark, unlike those preceding, was an unsolicited attempt at offering information. Nevertheless, it was quite relevant to the children's work and was assimilated at once.

D: "Twenty."
R: "Twenty, twenty-one, twenty-two, twenty-three, twenty-four, twenty-five, twenty-six, twenty-seven, twenty-eight."
M: "You do an awful lot of counting."

Now Rebecca did a strange thing. She returned to fifteen.

R: "Fifteen, sixteen, seventeen. What's after twenty-one?"
M: "Twenty-two."
R: "Twenty-two, twenty-three, twenty-four, twenty-five, twenty-six, twenty-seven, twenty-eight, twenty-nine." [At this point, she indicated by a glance that she wanted her mother to supply the next number.]
M: "Thirty."
R: "Forty, fifty, sixty, seventy, eighty, ninety, tenny, eleven."

My interpretation of this is that Rebecca was making an attempt to discover the rule for constructing the tens (ten, twenty, etc.). One piece of evidence is that she counted by tens. Another is the word "tenny": this implies that her numbers were constructed by rule, not memorized. She had never heard "tenny" before; it must have been the result of a rule such as "add -y to the digits." I am not claiming, of course, that she could verbalize this rule or was even aware of it, but it does seem to have been the force behind her behavior.

I think that this episode can teach us something about cognitive socialization. The example emphasizes the child's contribution to the learning process. It shows that the child is active in several senses: she initiates the activity, sustains it over a long period of time, practices, asks questions, and above all tries to make sense out of the world, tries to discover the regularities underlying the surface. Given all this, the parent can serve useful functions—supplying information and correcting errors. But I believe that for genuine learning to occur, the parent must build on the child's activity and interests:

this is a useful form of cognitive socialization. It is incorrect, I think, to postulate, as for example Hess and Shipman seem to do, that the parent's role is or should be that of a teacher in the traditional sense—the conveyer of information and the reinforcer of correct responses.

Here is another episode, again recorded on TV tape, which illustrates the child's active search for order in the world and her resistance of adult absurdities.

One evening, Rebecca was playing at "reading" a story to her younger brother. At that time (5 years 7 months) she could not really read and was instead telling him what she remembered of the story and what the pictures suggested.

R: "Now want me read this, Jonathan? I'm going to read this to you. Watch. OK? Molly's birthday, today. She makes things for her birthday. And she helps her mother make the presents. She writes, she cuts out things, balloons, animals, dogs, gooses, duck-duck gooses. I mean quacks. What are these called?" she asked me.

A (Author): "Ducks."

R: "These."

A: "I can't see."

R: "These."

A: "That's a goose."

R: "Goose. What's a goose? There's no gooses."

A: "Geese."

R: "Geese. What's a geese?"

A: "Well, there's one goose and lots of geese."

R: "What's a geese? This is a goose?"

A: "Yes, one goose, two geese."

R: "Two geeses and this a geese?"

A: "No, a goose."

R: "This a geese."

A: "No, you say one goose, and two geese, and three geese. (Jonathan, don't eat the book, please. No, we don't eat books.)"

R: "Three geeses. This is a goose."

A: "Yes."

R: "And that's a geese."

A: "No. That's a goose, too. They're both geese."

It is hard to describe the emotional tone of these proceedings. Rebecca was becoming steadily more frustrated, and I could not keep from laughing.

R: "This is a geese, and that's a geese."

A: "No, that's a goose, and that's a goose, and that's a goose, and that's a goose, and that's a goose . . . and you know what they all are? They're all geese."

R: "These are all geese?"
A: "Isn't that funny?"

In retrospect that does not seem to have been a very smart thing to say.

R: "These are geeses?"
A: "No."
R: "These are all geeses? Are these all geeses?"
A: "No. You know what you do? You say 'one goose.' Let's hear you say 'one goose.' "

Teaching! (Repeat after me, class . . .)

R: "One goose."
A: "And two geese, and three geese. Each one is a goose."
R: "This is a goose."
A: "Yes."
R: "This is geese."
A: "Yes, these are geese."
R: "What's a geese?"
A: "It's not *a* geese. You say 'many geese.' "

At this point, Rebecca was quite at a loss to understand the absurdity of the English language. But she then developed an elegant solution and showed an enviable defiance. She said: "I have two gooses and one duck." Then she shouted: "You're wrong!" and the lesson was over.

I did not cite this example only for amusement. In its own way it is quite serious. It shows a child making a prolonged and serious attempt to understand. She wants to capture the essence of things; she is not satisfied with empty slogans. She does not take the easy way out—the unquestioning acceptance of adult authority and institutionalized nonsense. So much for teaching.

The next episode illustrates the child's control over the *content* of learning, and how the parents can stimulate development. But first, I must give some relevant background. About a year before the episode in question, I conducted a study of children's printing in a local kindergarten. The general finding was that in an unstructured environment, children do a great deal of printing—and indeed teach themselves to print—if you give them a notebook and pen. At about the same time, I also read Sylvia Ashton-Warner's (1963) description of her method for teaching Maori children to read. In brief, she set aside a portion of time each day when the children could ask her to write words that they wanted to read. They often asked for words that writers of reading primers would consider somewhat unusual if not indecent. In any event, the children seemed to learn to read this way. Fortified with these techniques, I decided to give my own children (the twins, who were then about 4 or 4 years and 6 months) the opportunity to read and write. I brought home notebooks, pens, small cards on which to write words, and even extracted my typewriter from storage. Unlike O.K. Moore's, it did not talk; but I thought that playing with it might also help the girls to read and write.

The general result of all this was about nothing. The girls scribbled a little in the notebooks but soon ignored them completely. They showed no interest in writing words on cards. And they broke the typewriter. It became very clear to me then that a stimulating environment—even one which promotes free choice—is a necessary but not sufficient condition for children's learning. Certainly, the child cannot learn without an environment. And certainly the environment can stimulate learning. But unless the child wants to learn, there will be no genuine learning.[5]

About a year after the disaster involving the typewriter's innards and my ego, the girls became interested in reading and writing. They spontaneously showed an interest in making letters and in reading words. A few days before their fifth birthday, the following occurred. My wife offered to make words or drawings on small cards.

D showed a card to her mother and asked, "What does that say?"

M: "Which one? It's upside down."

D: "What does that say?"

M: "Ian."

D: "What does that say?"

M: "You got it upside down."

D: "What does that say?"

M: "Debby."

D: "What does that one say?"

M: "It says Deborah Beth Ginsburg."

D: "You said we could make some more. I want some more to make. I want some more pictures to make."

M: "We'll make some more later." [This is an example of a parent's *discouraging* (negatively reinforcing) the child's work.]

D: "Right now. I want some more to make."

M: "What would you like to make?"

---

[5] It is, of course, possible to *train* the child, to *force* him to do certain things. Piaget calls this "learning in the narrow sense," and points out that it is most often superficial and temporary. This may be true of much school learning.

D: "Mmm, this." She pointed at the card and made a circular motion. The meaning of this was not clear.

M: "What do you want me to write? Tell me what to write."

D: "Jonathan."

M: "Jonathan. J-O-N-A-T-H-A-N. Jonathan." She showed the card to Jonathan. "See, that's your name."

D: "Give it to me. That's for me. I want it."

M: "Let him look at his name." There followed a small dispute over whether Jonathan or Deborah should keep the card with his name on it.

M: "O.K. What should I write on this one?"

D: "Becky."

M: "Becky."

R: "I want one for me."

M: "B-E-C-K-Y. Becky." She gave the card to Deborah.

D: "That's for me, right?"

R: "I want to make mine."

M: "Now we'll make one for Becky. What do you want to write?"

R: "Jay." There followed another dispute over ownership of cards.

M: "I wrote Jay here [on another card]. That's Jay."

R: "I want to write it again."

M: "You want me to write Jay again."

R: "Yes." My wife wrote it.

D: "My turn."

M: "All right, what do you want me to write?"

D: "Daddy. Daddy and Mommy, too."

M: "D-A-D-D-Y. Daddy."

And so it went. The girls asked for Mommy, Grandma, Grandpa, and Jay's last name.

Like the other episodes cited, this one illustrates the child's initiative, self-motivation, activity, attempt to understand, and the mother's role of supplier of information when it is requested by the child. But two additional points should be made. First, the children exert strong control over the learning process. As I indicated above, the twins had earlier shown no interest in reading or writing. But in this episode they not only wanted to read, but they had very clear notions about *what* was to be read. They wanted names of people and little else. Similarly, I have observed that in printing, there are times when they want to make say A or B and will not try the other letters even when I ask them to. So the child sometimes has far more power in determining the content of learning than does the parent.

The second point is that the parent can perform a useful service in stimulating the child's spontaneous interests. In the present instance, the children indicated a desire to read. This may, of course, come about in many ways. Deborah and Rebecca have at various times asked what traffic signs mean, what is written on a box of cereal, what written words on television say, and so on. However and whenever the desire to read emerges, the parent can foster the child's interest by providing an environment suitable for learning. This does not mean that the parent necessarily teaches. Rather he provides the necessary "aliment" (to use Piaget's phrase) for the child's intellectual activity; he gives "food for thought." Given the aliment—the necessary environment—the child can learn what he wants to learn in a self-directed way. Note that the aliment is not imposed on the child; it is provided when he indicates that he needs and wants it. If the aliment is given prematurely, the child may well reject it.

The entire process is further complicated by the fact that the provision of an environment stimulating in certain respects may lead to the child's developing a need for a new environment stimulating in other respects. To return to the example of reading, my children began by experiencing a world containing traffic signs and cereal boxes and written words on television. This experience—that is to say the interaction between the children and their environment (aliment)—then *created* further needs, like reading names, for which new aliment was required. The new experience—the interaction between the children and the aliment (their mother and the cards)—then partially satisfied the current needs but also created new ones for which additional new aliment is required.

In brief, development is complex and only partially understood. But several factors stand out. In many cases parents do not teach in the traditional sense. They provide information when the child asks for it, stimulate new interests in the child, satisfy current needs which the child initiates, and in general attempt to provide for him an environment with which he can interact and in which he can grow. In all of this, the child's contribution is paramount. In interaction with the environment, he initiates, directs, controls, and motivates his own learning. He shapes as much as he is shaped.

These, then, are some speculations on the nature of cognitive socialization. I have tried to indicate the complexity of the process and to stress the contribution of the child. According to this perspective, much of the research in the area is both short-sighted and misdirected since it employs the model of parent as traditional teacher.

Back to Poor Children

We know little about cognitive socialization in the poor (or not so poor, for that matter). For one thing, the dominant theory in the area is misguided in ways I have tried to describe. For another, cognitive socialization is very difficult to study. Laboratory research may not be appropriate since we should be interested in the child's spontaneous interests in his natural environment. Teaching tasks in the laboratory are apt to be of little value. But it is hard to study cognitive socialization in the home. What does the presence of a stranger-observer do to the natural interaction between mother and child? Perhaps the only possibility is to use anthropological techniques. The observer should spend a great deal of time with individual poor families, living with them if possible, until he blends into the background and is fully accepted. Then he can begin his videotaping. Until such studies are done, we can only hope that child psychologists will resume the practice, largely abandoned in the early part of this century, of performing careful observational studies of their own children.

In sum, there is little to say about cognitive socialization in the poor. Current research is based on an inadequate conceptual framework and shows little in any event. Also, we know that differences in cognitive socialization cannot be important for some aspects of intellectual development (the universals) and that in some instances parents do not know what or how to teach. Finally, I should observe that in all likelihood poor parents must be doing something right: in many respects their children enjoy a healthy and vigorous intellectual life.

LEARNING

How do poor children learn? There are essentially two views on this matter. One holds that poor children learn differently or more slowly than others. Jensen, for example, maintains that poor children learn in a rote fashion ("associative learning"), whereas middle-class children are capable of "conceptual learning." The other view is basically that all children learn in the same ways, although what is learned may vary according to social class. Consider first Jensen's distinction between associative and conceptual learning.

Jensen's Theory

Jensen (1969) proposes that until the age of about 5 years, middle- and lower-class children use similar techniques of learning. Both groups are characterized by "associative learning." This occurs when the child forms a connection or an association between some stimulus and a response. An example is when the child learns the names of the letters. He sees the letter B (the stimulus) and must associate with it the sound "bee"; similarly, F and "eff," etc. In this case, the child must learn the arbitrary connections between stimuli and responses. Associative learning may occur in other situations too, as when the child learns the first nine or ten digits. In this task, the first number ("one") may be considered a stimulus which is associated with a response ("two'); after the response is made, it becomes a stimulus for the next response ("three"), and so on.

In Jensen's view associative learning is a mechanical, unthinking process. The child experiences a stimulus which, after a period of training, automatically elicits his response. A history of reward and punishment, and the co-occurence of stimulus and response produce a bond between the two, and no thinking or conceptual activity need be involved. According to Jensen, children below the age of 5 years develop many aspects of behavior through associative learning and both social classes are equally adept at it.

After 5 years, however, middle-class children begin to surpass poor children on "conceptual learning." This involves some kind of cognitive activity which mediates between the stimulus and the response. Jensen gives an example involving memory. Suppose children are asked to remember a list of 20 words, presented in random order. Of these, five refer to items of furniture, five to animals, etc. Because of the random presentation, the words for animals do not all occur adjacent to one another on the list, and the same is true of the words for furniture and the other categories. The list then might be *duck, chair, pen, table, dog. . . .* According to Jensen, such a list might be memorized in essentially two ways. If the child uses an associative process, then he must learn the connections among pairs of items on the list. *Duck* serves as a stimulus for the response *chair*, *chair* as a stimulus for *pen*, and so on. Another procedure involves conceptual learning. On hearing the random list, the child conceives of the similarity among *duck, dog, lion*, etc., seeing that all fall into the category *animal*. He groups these words together in memory (even though they did not occur together in the random list). When asked to recall the original words, he produces an organized (nonrandom) arrangement: the animal words are clustered together, and so on. In this case, we may conceive of the words in the list as the stimuli, the child's mental categorization as the conceptual activity, and his recall of an organized list as the response. Here each stimulus is not simply tied to a response; rather conceptual activity (the categorization) mediates between the two.

In Jensen's view, middle-class children's superiority over poor children in conceptual learning is the result of genetic inheritance. Since this is so, Jensen proposes, poor children require a radically different form of education from what is appropriate for middle-class children. The former need a heavier emphasis on drill and other procedures appropriate for rote learning than do the latter. As you shall see, there is little point to pursuing Jensen's ideas concerning heredity and education, since his basic notion of social-class differences in conceptual and associative learning is so thoroughly misguided. To see why I say this, let us begin by examining some of the evidence which Jensen cites in support of his view.

Glasman (1968, cited in Jensen, 1969) working under Jensen's direction, performed an experiment in which middle- and lower-class "schoolchildren" (the exact age is not given) are given two different word lists to memorize. One list contained twenty "unrelated familiar objects," such as *doll, toy car, comb, cup,* etc. The other list involved five words from each of four categories—*animals, clothing, furniture,* and *food.* In this case, the words were, of course, presented in a random order so that words in one category did not necessarily appear adjacent to one another on the list.

The results are that middle- and lower-class children do equally as well at memorizing the unrelated words. Jensen's explanation is that this task requires associative learning, and both social classes can do that. The results are different for the second list. Here the poor children perform at about the same level as they did when memorizing unrelated words, whereas middle-class children do much better. Not only do they remember many words; they also tend to cluster them into the relevant categories. Jensen claims that by age 10 or 11 years social-class differences on the recall of categorized lists are quite large. Jensen's interpretation is that middle-class children have a greater ability than do poor children to learn in a conceptual fashion.

Do Jensen's data support this conclusion? I think the answer is no. Consider first what it takes to memorize a list of "unrelated" words such as *doll, toy car, comb, cup* (Jensen's example). One possibility is the associative method Jensen describes. But researchers in verbal memory (see, for example, Tulving, 1968) find that such a procedure is simply not a very adequate explanation of how humans perform a task like this. Instead, people tend to use various idiosyncratic methods for categorizing the words. For example, a subject may remember the words by saying to himself: "the *doll* and the *toy car* put their *comb* in the *cup.*" While this mnemonic device is highly idiosyncratic, it is nevertheless quite conceptual and does not involve simple association in the sense Jensen describes. Another way of putting the argument is this: although Jensen may not see similarity in the list, the child may.[6] In brief, the Glasman data concerning unrelated (to whom?) word lists do not conclusively demonstrate associative learning in either social-class group.

What happens in the case of the categorized word lists? Here subjects may proceed in several ways. One is to use a category system like the one Jensen describes. In other words, the child groups the words according to the categories that Glasman had in mind when he constructed the list. Middle-class children did this more often than poor children. But in this task, too, it is also possible to cluster the words according to some idiosyncratic strategy —for example, the *dog* jumped on the *couch* holding the *pen.* Such a procedure may not be as effective as Jensen's, but it is nevertheless conceptual. It takes as much intellectual activity (if not more) to imagine a dog jumping on a couch with a pen as it does to discover that a dog and a cat are both

[6] The example makes one wonder. *Doll* and *toy car* are both toys, and *comb* and *cup* are accoutrements of the bath. Who is incapable of conceptual learning?

animals. Perhaps then Glasman's data show only that lower-class children have a greater tendency than do middle-class children to use idiosyncratic methods of categorization in free recall. (In fact, Jensen seems to admit this [1969, p. 113].)

Of course, I do not know for a fact that lower-class children did indeed use such procedures. My main point is not that they did, but that Jensen does not know that they did not. The Glasman experiment is far from conclusive insofar as the issue of associative vs. conceptual learning is concerned. It fails to demonstrate with any degree of precision that associative learning occurred in *any* of the subjects. Jensen's rather grandiose theory turns out to be based on extremely inadequate empirical data.

His position is even further weakened when we place his notions of associative and conceptual learning in a wider theoretical perspective. I think that much of what we know about children's cognitive development tells us that Jensen could not possibly be correct about the importance of associative learning early in life. We have learned from many researchers that children below the age of 5 years do indeed think and learn in conceptual ways. We know that children begin to categorize even in infancy (Piaget, 1952b), that by the age of 5 years they employ a complex grammar which does not consist of mere associations (Brown, 1965), that young children employ sophisticated strategies for detecting and processing information, and that such perceptual learning has little to do with associations between stimuli and responses (Gibson, 1969). These few examples should suffice to convince us that Jensen's position is without merit. It is simply incorrect to suppose that associative learning is the chief component of mental life during the first five years.

It is equally incorrect to propose that poor children above the age of 5 years are weak at conceptual learning (assuming even that there is such a thing as one type of conceptual learning). We know, for example, that poor children in this age range are capable of the kinds of logical reasoning that Piaget describes and that black youths possess a sophisticated verbal culture. Surely these do not involve the mechanical association of stimuli and responses.

In conclusion, Jensen's notions appear to be without empirical or theoretical foundation.

Different Kinds of Learning

An experiment by Stevenson, Williams, and Coleman (in press) shows how complex are the facts of children's learning and, therefore, how naïve is a simple distinction between associative and conceptual processes. The investigators were interested in determining the relations among various measures of learning in children. If a child does well on a paired associates task (e.g., learning the name of each letter), will he also do well at a concept formation test and on a task of serial memory (e.g., learning the first 10 digits in order)? On the one hand, suppose that his performance on all tasks is similar; then one might suppose that a common learning process underlies all of them. On the other hand, if performance varies across the tasks, then different learning processes may be involved.

The subjects in the experiment were 50 lower-class children (40 blacks) whose average age was about 5 years. Each child was given the following tasks:

1. *Paired associates.* The child was asked to form associations between five pairs of animals depicted by drawings. Thus *lion* is arbitrarily paired with *mouse,* etc.
2. *Serial memory.* The child had to learn a series of five common objects (e.g., first *spoon,* next *table,* etc.).
3. *Oddity learning.* The child was required to determine which one of three objects was different from the other two (which were the same).
4. *Concept formation.* The child had to identify toy flowers that had the same color and shape.
5. *Observational learning.* The child first watched the experimenter put together a puzzle and then had to do it himself.
6. *Incidental learning.* The experimenter began by telling the child a simple story which was illustrated by some pictures. The story called attention to some aspects of the pictures but not others. After this, the experimenter questioned the child to determine whether he had learned those aspects of the pictures which were *not* emphasized in the story.
7. *Problem solving.* In one task, the child had to learn to move some toy cheese at one end of a maze to a toy mouse at the other. The task was further complicated by the requirement that the child use different combinations of rods to move the cheese.[7]
8. *Category sorting.* The child had to categorize objects by two attributes simultaneously (e.g., *large* and *red* vs. *small* and *blue*).

Each child, tested by a black examiner, was given each of the tasks. It took four testing sessions to do this.

Table 5-9 presents the relevant data. The major result is that in general there is little commonality among the various measures of learning. Only six of the 36 correlations were significant. Scores on paired associates and

---

[7] The University of Minnesota, where this experiment was conducted, was at one point the Mecca of the rat psychology movement. As you can see, Minnesota psychologists so fervently revere the rat that they make the cheese come to him.

TABLE 5-9 Intercorrelations among Learning Tasks

Task	1	2	3	4	5	6	7	8
1. Paired associates								
2. Serial memory	.43 **							
3. Oddity learning	.13	.16						
4. Concept formation	.17	.06	.07					
5. Observational learning	.31 *	.47 **	.03	.03				
6. Incidental learning	.02	.08	.08	.26	.21			
7. Problem solving I	.09	.06	.04	.11	.13	.04		
8. Problem solving II	.09	.06	.25	.18	.05	.19	.23	
9. Category sorting	.43 **	.30 *	.11	.09	.35 *	.19	.03	.19

* $p < .05$.
** $p < .01$.
Source: Stevenson, Williams, and Coleman, in press, p. 7.

serial memory were correlated, and at first glance this seems to support Jensen's notion of associative learning. But the paired associates score is also correlated with observational learning and with category sorting, both of which seem to involve some kind of conceptual activity. Taken as a whole, the results of this study imply that there are many different kinds of learning processes (although it does not clarify what they are).

The writers point out that the results are quite similar to those obtained in another investigation concerning middle-class children. The latter study (Friedrichs *et al.*, 1970) involved the same learning tasks and same procedures. In both cases, the pattern of significant and nonsignificant correlations was almost the same. There seem to be many different kinds of learning processes in both social class groups. As Stevenson, Williams, and Coleman conclude: "From these data, it appears that there is little utility in positing differences between the two groups in the operation of associative and cognitive learning abilities" (p. 9).

So the relations among measures of learning seem to be similar for the two social classes. This implies that the groups do not differ in the tendency to use many different learning processes on these tasks. But this is not to say that the groups behaved in an identical fashion. In general, the poor children did not achieve as much success on the tasks as did middle-class children. Is this finding typical? Unfortunately, the evidence is inconsistent. For example, Scholnick, Osler, and Katzenellenbogen (1968) found that middle-class children did better than poor children on a simple discrimination learning task but that both groups did equally as well on a more complex concept learning task.

In any event, how can we interpret social-class differences, if indeed they occur, on laboratory learning tasks? Stevenson and his colleagues attribute such differences to factors having little to do with the learning process itself:

Generally, the disadvantaged children had more difficulty than the ad-
vantaged children in understanding what they were being asked to do,
they required more preliminary instruction to familiarize them with
the materials and procedures, and appeared to find some of the tasks,
such as paired-associates and category sorting, much more boring [than
did middle-class children]. In the paired-associates and serial memory
tasks, many of the [lower-class] children did not know the name of the
animals and objects (p. 9).

Thus, poor children enter such situations at a disadvantage. They may
be easily bored with the tasks; they lack experience with formal learning situations; and they may not possess certain vocabulary relevant to the tasks. All
these factors combine to lower poor children's chances of success. But this
does not necessarily indicate a deficiency in poor children's learning ability.
Were poor children motivated, experienced in such tasks, and so forth, their
learning scores might well improve.

Incentives

Suppose that poor children are better motivated to do well on laboratory
learning tasks. Do the social-class differences then disappear? The evidence
on this issue is inconclusive.

Zigler and DeLabry (1962) compared middle- and lower-class children
on a learning task which provided two different incentives. Half of the
children, both middle and lower class, were simply told they were correct
("intangible" incentive) when they did well. The other half were given a
"tangible" reward such as a piece of candy or a prize. The results were that
middle-class children reached their highest level of performance when intangible incentives were used, and lower-class children reached their highest level
(equal to that of the middle-class children) when tangible rewards were
given. Terrell, Durkin, and Wiesley (1959) found much the same thing.
These two studies, then, indicate that social-class differences in amount of
learning (that is, degree of success) disappear when both groups receive
appropriate incentives.

There is, however, some discrepant evidence. Unikel, Strain, and
Adams (1969) found that type of incentive (tangible or intangible) had no
effect on poor children's learning. Unfortunately, these investigators did not
study middle-class children's performance on the same task, so that no social-
class comparisons can be made. Spence and Dunton (1967) found that both
middle- and lower-class children did more poorly under conditions of tangible
reward (candy) than when simply told when they were right and wrong.

The evidence is inconsistent, so that the available laboratory research
permits us to come to few conclusions concerning the effects of incentives on

social-class differences in learning. I hope that future research efforts of this type will use more powerful procedures for motivating poor children. A piece of candy may not be enough. Perhaps the children should be brought to the laboratory for several visits before beginning the experiment; perhaps they should have a chance to familiarize themselves with the experimental materials; and perhaps the experimenter should offer as incentive large amounts of money!

NATURAL DEVELOPMENT

The experimental studies we have just reviewed fail to provide information on a number of crucial aspects of poor children's development, particularly their self-directed learning. We saw earlier in this chapter (when we discussed Deborah and Rebecca's work with numbers and reading) that in their natural environment children seem to direct their own learning, to choose some tasks to work on (play with) but not others, to seek information when they require it, and to attempt to come to an understanding of the world's regularities. The question I wish to raise now is whether self-directed learning characterizes poor children's development as well as that of middle-class children. And if self-directed learning does occur, what is it like?

The Development of Printing

With Mary Wheeler and Edward Tulis, I have done a study of the natural development of printing in middle- and lower-class children (Ginsburg, Wheeler, and Tulis, 1971). So far as I know, this is the only study which examines social-class differences in natural development. Before considering the social-class comparisons, however, we must review some general aspects of printing and its development.

GENERAL FEATURES OF PRINTING

When a child sets out to print the alphabet or words for the first time, he usually experiences considerable difficulty. The letters do not come out right: they are too big or too little; they do not fit together properly; they wobble. Yet after a period of time, almost every child can print reasonably well, and it is easy for an adult to read what the child puts on the page. How does printing develop?

At first, the answer to this question seems both obvious and uninteresting. Children learn printing through instruction in school. And because of this, the particular ways in which printing develops are strongly influenced by the mode of teaching which the school favors. If the teacher makes O before *E*, so will the child. To ask how printing develops under these circumstances yields an uninteresting answer: in the traditional classroom, printing develops as instruction forces it to develop.

Note that there is an implicit assumption motivating the practices of the traditional classroom. The assumption is that printing does not develop—at least not well—if it is not taught. Printing, like reading or mathematics, is an academic subject learned only in school and does not develop "spontaneously" or "naturally." Several considerations suggest, however, that this is not true.

We have already seen, for example, that at the age of 4 or 5 years, Deborah and Rebecca had an interest in reading and counting and pursued these topics at home in an informal and self-directed way. Also, many parents observe that their children become interested in making letters and put considerable effort into this kind of work. It appears that printing can also be learned in an informal way. Here are some of the things children do in their homes:

1. They ask a parent to make individual letters and then attempt to copy them. For a period of several weeks, they work at copying a few letters; then they request different ones.

2. Children copy letters from books, magazines, etc. They sometimes spend a considerable amount of time at this activity. The copying is selective; at a given point in time, they copy certain letters but not others.

3. Once children know the names of the letters, they sometimes ask a parent to spell words and try to write down what was spelled.

4. Children sometimes practice the printing of letters which earlier were copied. They sometimes repeat a letter over and over again on a single sheet of paper.

5. Children do considerable work with printing before learning to read. They are able to make many letters before they can read a single word, except perhaps their name.

6. Sometimes, children seem to correct some errors by themselves. The *A* repeated many times on a page is sometimes better formed at the end than at the beginning. On other occasions, a parent points out errors and tries to show the child how to correct them.

7. At times children show no interest in printing and resist suggestions to engage in it.

Several features of these activities stand out. The child plays an active role in the informal learning process. On a "motivational" level, he usually initiates the activities in question. He decides when he would like to print, just as he determines when he would like to play with a certain toy. If he does not want to print for several weeks or months, he does not do it. Sometimes he practices printing; he drills himself. On a "cognitive" level, the child also determines what he will print: he asks the parent for certain letters but not others. He copies *D* but not *A*. He sometimes corrects his own errors.

SOME QUESTIONS

These then appear to be some features of the natural development of printing. Wheeler, Tulis, and I set out to study the problem in greater detail. Here are some of the questions which we tried to answer through an empirical study:

1. Is the natural development of printing a general phenomenon, characteristic of both middle- and lower-class children? When given the freedom and opportunity to do so, do most or all children engage in printing and other forms of graphic activity?
2. If children do choose to engage in such graphic activity, how much effort do they put into it? Do they work hard at learning to print, or is their activity inconsequential?
3. Do children engage in self-imposed practice or drill when learning to print?
4. Under these circumstances, does the quality of printing improve? Do the printed letters become more legible?
5. What are the major types of graphic activity which children engage in? Do they scribble, make pictures, write sentences, devise symbols?
6. Do the various aspects of graphic activity appear in sequence, for example, first scribbling, then drawing, then printing, etc?
7. When children learn to print a word, do they at the same time learn to read it? Or are writing and reading learned separately, with the result that they must be connected at a later time?

THE METHOD

There seemed to be two alternative methods for obtaining answers to our questions. One possibility was to observe children in poor and middle-class homes. We thought that this was impractical. For one thing, we might not be accepted into certain homes. For another, we might have to wait for months or even years for spontaneous printing to occur. The second alternative was to observe printing in a classroom where it is not taught, and where children have the freedom to choose their own activities. In such classrooms (called "open" classrooms by Kohl, 1967), children work individually or in small groups at a variety of tasks. The children have a major role in deciding what to do and when to do it. Most frequently, their work involves the manipulation of concrete objects rather than the reading of texts. There is little teaching in the traditional sense. (See Featherstone, 1967, for a description of the English "Infant" school, a pioneering effort along these lines.) The observation of printing in such a classroom would be a practical method for obtaining answers to our questions: such observations could involve relatively large numbers of children and could be done in a relatively short period of time. Consequently, we decided to study printing in the open classroom.

The class was a kindergarten in a rural-suburban school. The room was divided into several work areas: blocks; house corner (with toy sink, stove, refrigerator, bureaus, etc.); science (with microscopes, balances, etc.); writing and reading corner (with books, picture dictionaries, etc.); and many other areas as well.

The children arrived at school between 7:30 and 8:00 A.M. and engaged in free play until about 8:15 when the Pledge of Allegiance was recited. After this, the most frequent activity again was free play which lasted until snack time, about 9:30. After snack, there was again free play (restricted this time to its relatively quiet manifestations) and outdoor play. These lasted until 10:30 when the children went home. Occasionally the teacher initiated various activities involving the whole class: story time, movies, play acting, and the like. These activities were infrequent and scheduled at irregular times. The bulk of the children's time—at least 75 percent—was spent in free play, in which the children generally worked alone or in small groups. The teacher or other adults in the room circulated among the children if they requested it. For example, on a given day, the teacher might first read a story to a child in the reading area; she might then help a child in the science area to light a bulb; she might then go to the workshop area to help a group of children build a wagon. As she and other adults circulated about the room in this fashion, one child might read a book with another's help; another child might listen to records alone; a third child might play with three or four others in the doll corner area. In general, there was a great deal of interaction among children, a fair amount of exchange between the teacher and small groups of children; and a minimum of teaching in the classic sense—that is, the teacher lecturing at the whole class.

Before school opened, we removed from the room all printed matter—books, signs, alphabets, plastic letters, labels, etc. During the second week of school, all children were tested on their ability to read and produce letters, numbers, and words; after the test, the printed matter was returned to the room. About three weeks after the start of school, each child was given a bound, hard-cover notebook with lined pages, a folder to store it in, and a narrow-point felt pen. The children were told that they could write anything in their notebooks, more or less whenever they wanted to (except, for example, during snack time). To facilitate notebook work, we set up a writing corner with tables, chairs, and books, as well as a place for storing the notebooks overnight. (Later, alphabet and word charts were added to the writing corner.) When a notebook was filled, the child was given another and was allowed to keep the first.

There were only a few rules relating to children's notebook work. Children were not allowed to write in another child's notebook or to tear out pages, since this would disrupt our data gathering procedures. Children were not allowed to take the notebooks home, since brothers and sisters might write in them and again confuse the data. Aside from these prohibited activities, children were permitted to do anything in the notebooks: make scribbles throughout, write one letter on each page, draw pictures, etc.

The teacher understood the aims of our research, to collect data on the development of graphic activity as it occurred "naturally," in the absence of instruction. Consequently, she limited her activities to an occasional approval of the children's work when they showed it to her, and to helping them when they (infrequently) asked for assistance. Only on three occasions, in January and February, did she feel the need to engage in formal instruction. At these times, she made letters and numbers on the blackboard (10, 9, f, k, w, t, p, and 5) stressing the order and direction of the strokes. The children were required to copy each symbol several times. The teacher stopped formal instruction when she came to the conclusion that it was less effective than spontaneous work in the notebooks.

The classroom contained 20 children. Ten were lower class (6 boys and 4 girls) and 10 were middle class (7 boys and 3 girls). At the outset of the school year, the average age was 5.3 years.

Our methods of study were fairly straightforward. At the beginning of the school year, we gave all of the children simple tests to determine their initial level of reading and writing ability.

Throughout the year, at roughly two week intervals, we made Xerox copies of work in the children's notebooks. This allowed us to determine what any child did at any point during the year.

In April and May (that is, during the eighth and ninth months of school), we gave each child a simple test to determine whether he could read words he had written in his own notebook.

Finally, throughout the year, we made observations of individual children as they worked in their notebooks. We determined, for example, how long they spent in notebook work, whether they said out loud what they had written, and so forth.

RESULTS

Consider each of the questions in turn.

1. *Is the natural development of printing characteristic of both middle- and lower-class children? When given the freedom and opportunity to do so, do most or all children engage in printing and other forms of graphic activity?*

The answer is yes. For example, at one time or another during the course of the year every child in the room engaged in some form of graphic activity (scribbling, pictures, printing, etc.). If one considers printing alone—specifically the production of isolated letters (that is, letters not included in words) —the result is the same. Table 5-10 shows that every child made isolated

TABLE 5-10   Proportion of Children Making Isolated Letters, by Social Class and by Time Period

	1	2	3	4	5	6	7	8	9	10	11	12	13	14	15
Middle Class	0.7	0.3	0.4	0.6	0.4	0.5	0.6	1.0	0.9	0.5	0.7	0.7	0.7	0.5	0.7
Lower Class	0.8	0.5	1.0	0.7	0.6	0.6	1.0	1.0	0.9	1.0	0.8	1.0	0.9	0.6	0.8

Middle-Class Average = 0.61
Lower-Class Average = 0.81
Group Average   = 0.71

Source: Ginsburg, Wheeler, and Tulis, 1971, p. 35.

letters at least once during the year. If we consider the average proportions of children making isolated letters across all of the time periods, we find that .81 of the lower-class children and .61 of the middle-class children make isolated letters. The difference is not statistically significant.

2. *If children engage in graphic activity, how much effort do they put into it?* One measure of this is the amount of time spent at graphic activity. Each time they engaged in graphic activity, middle-class children spent an average of 11.3 minutes, and lower-class children 15.5 minutes. The difference is not statistically significant. This is a substantial amount of time for 5-year-olds to devote to one kind of work. There are no social-class differences in something that might be called persistence or lack of impulsivity.

3. *Do children engage in self-imposed practice or drill when learning to print?* We defined drill as the repetition of a letter, number, word, or sequence of these. Thus, drill is *a a a,* or *abcabc,* or *ball, ball.* To examine the frequency of drill, we simply counted the number of notebook pages on which drill occurred and divided by the total number of pages, for each child separately. Middle-class children drilled themselves on 10.9 percent of the pages, whereas the figure for poor children was 13 percent, a nonsignificant difference.

4. *Does the quality of children's printing improve over time?* Yes. The letters get better, and there are no social-class differences in this.

5. *What are the major types of graphic activity?* We found it necessary to distinguish among the following broad categories of graphic activity: (a) Scribbles; (b) Designs; (c) Pictures; (d) Letters (either alone or in words); (e) Numbers; (f) Words (in isolation or in phrases or sentences); (g)

Phrases; (h) Sentences; (i) Symbols. All children engage to at least a moderate extent in most of these types of graphic activities. The exceptions are the most advanced forms, namely phrases, sentences, and symbols, which are infrequent. There were no significant social-class differences except in the case of scribbles, where poor children made more of them than did middle-class children.

6. *Do the various aspects of graphic activity appear in sequence?* The pretest showed that at the beginning of the year neither middle- nor lower-class children could print or read very much except their own names. Then all children, again regardless of social class, showed a fairly regular sequence in the development of graphic activity. At the beginning of the year, they spent a great deal of time making scribbles, designs, and pictures, and these decreased in frequency thereafter. During the middle of the year, but not at the beginning or end, children made many isolated words. Toward the end of the year, they began to concentrate on phrases, sentences, and symbols. There was no regular pattern in the occurrence of the child's name, numbers, and letters in isolation.

7. *When children print a word, do they at the same time learn to read it?* To examine this issue, each child was asked to read at least five words printed in his notebook. Middle-class children were able to read 18 percent of the words they wrote and lower-class children 22.9 percent. The difference is not significant. Nevertheless, the figures are not high for either group. Children can read only some of what they write. Remember, though, that this class offered no reading instruction.

SOME CONCLUSIONS

Our study shows that under proper environmental conditions poor children, like middle-class children, can engage in self-directed learning, at least when printing is involved. The poor child is active in the sense that he chooses to print when he does not have to. It is a mistake to think that the poor child is necessarily apathetic or lacks curiosity.

He is active, too, in the sense that he puts time and effort into graphic activity. It is a mistake to think that the poor child is necessarily lazy or impulsive, or that he lacks persistence.

The poor child can learn from his own encounters with the world. Printing improved over the course of the year without adult instruction and often without any assistance from adults. It is a mistake to think that the poor child must be taught.

Let us be clear about the role of the environment in all this. The natural development of printing feeds on an appropriate environment. The word "natural" should not be construed to mean "genetic" or "independent of the environment." In the view of Piaget and other cognitive theorists, the process of natural development is a continual interaction between the child and his environment. In the present case, it is clear that for printing to develop the child needs paper, writing implements, letters to copy, and sometimes help from adults. In the absence of these environmental conditions, printing does not develop, at least not well. While obviously necessary for growth, the environment does not simply shape the child and mould his activities according to plan. This is a central tenet of the theory of natural development: the child uses the environment as much as it uses him. The child needs paper, pen, and letters to write; but these do not write without him. It is clear that children chose when and what to write; instruction did not force printing on them.

In sum, we can say that under certain environmental conditions, namely the open classroom, poor children as a group display the same motivational tendencies and cognitive abilities as do middle-class children. This statement must, of course, be qualified by reference to the age of the child and the subject matter involved. Our evidence concerns 5-year-olds learning to print, not 12-year-olds doing mathematics. Within these limits, our study suggests that poor children, as a group, are not unmotivated to learn or intellectually deficient on beginning the early years of school. Under the proper environmental conditions they can learn quite as well as anyone else. And these conditions need not involve "compensatory education" or "remedial training." Poor children do not need a Head Start; they need a decent education. And we do not need large masses of evidence to prove this point: one convincing case suffices to show that poor children *can* be successful in certain types of classrooms. Our own data shows this in the case of 5-year-olds printing in the open classroom; other writers (e.g., Kohl, 1967, whose work we reviewed in chapter 3) make the same point concerning older children's work in a variety of areas.

GENERAL CONCLUSIONS

I began this chapter by asking how poor children's intellect develops as well as it does. Unfortunately, much of the research we have reviewed is not particularly informative: sometimes it is of poor quality; sometimes it does not grapple with the important issues. Nevertheless, I must now make an attempt to summarize what we have learned. And where the available evidence yields few answers to our questions, I will attempt to offer some speculations based on general cognitive theory.

Activity in the Child

My first conclusion is that *poor children's intellect shows healthy development because these children are active learners who play a major role in shaping their own growth.* One source of evidence on this point is my study of the natural development of printing in the open classroom. Another is Kohl's account of black children's interest in and exploration of the written language. A third is Labov's observations of black youth's skill in the spoken language.

This conclusion makes sense in terms of what we know about cognitive development. For example, it is consonant with Piaget's theory which stresses the child's activity in acquiring the cognitive universals and which further proposes that active development is the inevitable result of the child's biological endowment.

Piaget (1952b) postulates that all species inherit two basic tendencies: *organization* and *adaptation.* Organization refers to the tendency for all species to systematize or organize their processes into coherent systems, both physical and psychological. In his interaction with the world, the individual tends to integrate his psychological structures into coherent systems. For example, the infant has available the separate behavioral structures (habits) of either looking at objects or of grasping them. He does not initially combine the two. After a period of development, he organizes these two separate structures into a higher-order structure which enables him to grasp something at the same time he looks at it. Organization, then, is the tendency common to all forms of life to develop coherent forms of behavior and thought. The tendency toward organization is a characteristic of the child's nature and need not be taught.

The second inherited tendency is *adaptation.* All organisms are born with a tendency to adapt to the environment. The ways in which adaptation occurs differ from species to species, from individual to individual within a species, or from stage to stage within any one individual. Nevertheless, the tendency to adapt in some way or another is an inherited and universal feature of life.

Let us be clear on the way in which adaptation and organization are inherited. They are biological factors in the sense that they are tendencies common to all species. But the particular ways in which an organism adapts and organizes its processes depend on its environment, its learning history, and on other factors. In Piaget's view, the human being does not inherit particular intellectual reactions; rather he does inherit a tendency to organize his mental processes and to adapt to the environment in some way.

Piaget feels that it is crucial to appreciate the child's active tendencies: it is the child who organizes his behavior and thought, and who adapts to the environment. Piaget is not an empiricist, stressing the environment's power over the individual. Rather he is an interactionist, emphasizing the contributions of both individual and environment. He stresses that the environment does not mould behavior by imposing itself on a passive subject, evoking the child's response, and rewarding it. Instead, Piaget's central theme is that the child seeks contact with the environment and initiates ways of coping with it. His curiosity does not let him wait for environmental events to happen; rather he searches them out and seeks increased levels of stimulation. When some environmental event occurs, the child does not register it passively; instead he interprets it; he tries to assimilate it into what he knows. And it is this interpretation, not the event itself, which affects his behavior. For example, a child sees an adult rise and put on his coat. He cries because he interprets the event as indicating the adult's departure. Another child sees the same episode but he does not cry because it means nothing to him. "Experience"—seeing the adult's behavior—has affected the two children quite differently since they interpret the event in distinct ways. Thus, it is fair to say that the environment does not exert effects *on* the child but *with* him.

These principles are not mere speculation. Piaget and his colleagues have provided a wealth of empirical evidence documenting this point of view, and their work has produced a revolution in our view of the child.

It is important to note that similar conclusions regarding the child's active nature have recently emerged, quite independently of Piaget, from work on language. For example, Lenneberg (1967) presents a biological theory of language which stresses the role of the child as an active agent. He shows how the capacity for language develops in the course of physical maturation. But maturation alone—or any other purely nativistic factor—does not suffice to produce language. The child obviously needs to hear a body of spoken language, and just as obviously he will speak the language he hears. Nevertheless, language—that most cultural of cognitive acquisitions—is not simply imposed on the child; here, too, a simple empiricist view does not work. Lenneberg writes:

> Primitive stages of language [in the child] are simply too different from adult language to be regarded as a direct mirroring of the input [adult language]. Nor is there any evidence that the adults surrounding the child are the causative or shaping agents that determine language onset or its course of development. . . . Social settings may be required as a trigger that sets off a reaction. . . . In a given state of maturation, exposure to adult language behavior has an excitatory effect upon the actualization process much the way a certain frequency may have an excitatory effect upon a specific resonator. . . . In the case of language onset, the energy required for the resonance is, in a sense, supplied by the individual himself. . . . Thus, the propagation and maintenance of language behavior in the species are not comparable to cultural tradition which is handed down from generation to generation. The individual does not serve as a passive vehicle or channel through which information is transmitted; instead he is an autonomous unit constituted in very much the same way as other units around him. . . . Thus, the individual is seen as functioning by virtue of his own power supply, so to

speak; he constructs language by himself (provided he has the raw material to do it with) . . . (pp. 377–78).

Once again, we see that the child is active, operating under his own "power supply." Given speech to hear, and given a proper level of physical maturation, he will himself construct the spoken language. Biological factors guarantee this learning just as they guarantee that the child will develop the modes of thought which Piaget describes. As we saw in Chapters 3 and 4, his membership in a particular society or social class makes no difference for these aspects of development. Poor children, too, are biologically intact organisms; they are human; and so like the rest of us they will learn language and acquire thought.

The Environment

A second *reason for poor children's healthy intellectual development is the fact that their environment is quite adequate for promoting the basic forms of cognitive activity.*

Most writers do not agree with this and instead propose that poor children's environment is inadequate in one of two (contradictory) ways. One view, again in the empiricist tradition, is that poor children's environment is deprived. It fails to provide adequate stimulation, with the result that intellectual development is retarded. We know that the retardation is largely myth. What about the deprived environment? I have not seen any convincing evidence in support of this view. I do not know of any systematic studies which examine poor children's homes and discover a lack of stimulation. The same is true of the second view, also in the empiricist tradition, which asserts that poor children's environment contains too much stimulation for proper learning to occur. In this connection you will no doubt recall Klaus and Gray's statements to the effect that in poor children's homes there is no one place for any object and that the television set blares all day. Unfortunately, Klaus and Gray do not produce any evidence in support of their position. Also, it seems to me that their first proposition (no one place for any object) could not be true of any human habitation, and that their second (the TV) is unfortunately characteristic of most homes, both middle and lower class.

In any event, there is little systematic evidence concerning the two prominent theories of poor children's environment. I must also admit that there is little evidence in favor of my position. Yet I can point to some case history and anecdotal accounts of poor environments. Oscar Lewis (1966) reports on the lives of Puerto Rican slum dwellers in New York City. In several passages he describes the apartment of one family. The room, about fifteen feet square, was crowded with furniture. There was a metal double bed, an orange curtain fastened to a sprinkler pipe, a steam radiator, tables, a television set, a record stand, a toy duck, cheap decorations (such as black glass panthers, artificial flowers, ceramic animal figurines, and Chinese dolls), a record player, radio, lamp, a bottle of rubbing alcohol, dolls, and many other things.

This is by no means an environment which lacks stimulation. There is much for a child to learn in such a room: there are colors and shapes and sounds; there are things to play with and explore; there is ample raw material for the intellectual processes to work with. Is there perhaps too much stimulation? The room may be noisy and there may be many things happening there, but I cannot believe that the stimulation is overwhelming for the child. I say this for several reasons. One is that if the stimulation were painfully excessive, the adult would probably find it uncomfortable, too, and would try to quiet things down. The second is that children thrive on stimulation. They sometimes enjoy a lot of noise and commotion. Third, when children want to do their own work, they have a remarkable capacity to tune out distractions. I have observed very noisy and rambunctious open classrooms where individual children sit in a corner reading, apparently oblivious to all the commotion in the room.

So if Oscar Lewis's account is at all representative, poor children's homes contain abundant stimulation, and I cannot see why it should be called excessive. But is Lewis's description typical of poor homes in general? As I remarked earlier, there exists no systematic evidence on this issue. Nevertheless, if one reads the novels and autobiographies of writers such as James Baldwin, Malcolm X, Ralph Ellison, and others, one must be convinced that the poor environment is in many respects quite rich. It is often unpleasant and degrading and oppressive, but it does not lack for stimulation and challenge.

After all, what kind of environmental support does a child—any child—need for normal intellectual development? What sort of raw material does he require for the construction of knowledge? The answer depends on the kind of knowledge involved. In the case of language, what a child needs is to hear other people speak, and every poor family does that. In the case of form perception, what the child needs is shapes to see and to explore. Would anyone maintain that the poor child's world is formless? In the case of object permanence, what the child needs is an environment containing things which continue to exist even when unobserved. Surely the poor child's world is no different from ours in this respect. In the case of the "concepts" *up, down, behind, in front of,* and all the rest, what the child needs is again a world of real things, and there can be no doubt that he has it. In the case of memory, he needs a past, and unfortunately everyone has one.

I maintain, in short, that the poor child's environment is in many respects quite adequate for intellectual development. He is active and wants to make sense of the world. He lives in a rich and stimulating environment, not in an institution. And the interaction between the active child and his world inevitably produces knowledge—the cognitive universals.

The Role of the Parents

Third, *poor children do not need a great deal of parental teaching to develop adequately.* As I pointed out earlier, most parents are quite unaware of many aspects of cognitive development and so could not teach it even if they wanted to. I also showed that teaching is not necessarily the typical or desirable mode of cognitive socialization. Often the child initiates and controls the parent's contribution.

The implication is that even if lower-class parents are such poor teachers as Hess and Shipman suggest, this simply does not matter very much for the child's intellectual development. To acquire the cognitive universals, the child does not need teaching. He needs a rich environment (which he has) and a parental assistance which is responsive to his concerns.

In addition, I am by no means convinced that poor adults are such bad parents. Oscar Lewis has this to say about poor families:

> . . . their particular style of communication and the crudeness of their language make them appear less attractive than they really are. When Cruz screams at her three-year-old daughter, "I'll pull your lungs out of your mouth!" and the child continues to disobey without apparent fear, it suggests that perhaps the child is quite secure in her mother's love. . . . And if the children's hurts go unattended, it is equally true that in the long run their mother's lack of concern is not entirely inappropriate in an environment where toughness is necessary for survival. Soledad may seem like a harsh, cruel, inconsistent mother by middle class standards; but one should also note how much time, energy and attention she gives to her children and how hard she tries to live up to her own ideal of a good mother. With much effort she has managed to provide them with a home, food and clothing, even with toys. She has not abandoned them, nor permitted anyone to abuse them, and she is devoted to them when they are ill (p. xxx).

Distinctive Features of Development

Thus far, we have stressed the similarities among children from different social classes. We have seen that all children, middle and lower class, develop the basic features of cognition because they are active and because they live in a stimulating environment. But now consider some distinctive features of poor children's intellect and why they develop.

My fourth general conclusion is that *poor children develop some special intellectual strengths as a result of adaptation to a distinctive environment.*

Unfortunately, there has been little research relevant to this issue. Most investigators in the empiricist tradition begin by assuming that poor children's environment is deprived, not unique, and go on from there to examine possible deficits in intellectual functioning. There are, however, a few exceptions, the most notable of whom is Labov. We discussed earlier his work on black youth's verbal culture—epic poetry, ritual insult, and the rest. These are certainly distinctive. And I think it is fair to call them intellectual strengths or assets, at least within the black community. How do these aspects of verbal culture develop? If you accept the deprivation model, you should be quite astonished that black youths are capable of such elaborate forms of verbal behavior. But from the point of view of developmental theory, their accomplishment is not at all surprising. Children learn what is useful for adapting to the environment. In this case the environment is the gang, and within this context the verbal behavior Labov describes serves many useful purposes. It helps to promote solidarity within the group; it helps to keep outsiders away; and it is a means of preserving and propagating the gang's world-view. Since the verbal culture is so valuable in coping with black youth's distinctive environment, they will *naturally* learn it.

I wish we knew more about this. On the one hand, we have little detailed knowledge of the unique features of lower-class environments. And what we do know derives not so much from systematic research as from informal observation, anecdote, and fiction. On the other hand, we know little about poor children's distinctive intellectual skills. Researchers have generally concentrated either on an examination of the ways in which poor children fall short of middle-class accomplishments, or on the cognitive universals.

But knowledge of the distinctive features of poor children's intellect can be quite crucial, especially for education. Here is an example provided by my wife, Marlene Ginsburg:

> About three years ago I taught junior high art in a small rural town. Two of my five classes were the lowest track kids. They were a strange conglomeration of so called "behavior problems," "slow learners," etc. They were very much aware of their standing in the school and often referred to themselves as the "retards." The other teachers who had some of these kids for English, math, and other courses were always giving me the "scoop" on so and so: "He's culturally deprived and can't be taught." "If he gives you any trouble, send him to the principal." "Be tough . . . let him know who's boss," etc. By and large these two classes were failures by all conventional standards—the teachers and administration believed it and the kids believed it. All these kids had one thing in common—they were poor. I remember my "period of awakening" to poverty at this time. We lived on the outskirts of a rural area where many of my students lived. I would go horse-back riding on the dirt roads which were almost impassable by car and occa-

sionally run across an old abandoned bus or wood shack. I would see smoke from a chimney or clothes on a line and would be horrified to think people lived in such places.

Jim lived in one of these shacks with several other children, no mother, and a father who drank. He was what could be termed anti-social. Even within a classroom that had a great deal of freedom and lack of control, he seemed uninterested and bored. One day a girl brought in some things from nature for a collage. Jim perked up and told me about the kinds of trees and wildlife he had found on the land around his house. He had spent a good part of his life walking in the woods and teaching himself about the world around him. He had an incredible fund of knowledge about birds, wildflowers, fungus, rocks, animals, trees, mushrooms, fish, etc. And more importantly, he seemed transfixed when he talked about it. I suggested that instead of coming to art class for the next few days he take walks around the school for that hour and collect things for me. Then he could "teach me" and perhaps together we could discover some project he could work on. It took him a long time to believe that I trusted him and was actually allowing him to leave the school (freedom!!).

The next three weeks were a period of intellectual excitement for the two of us. Jim would show up breathless at my door at lunch time and take me outside to show me some rare wildflower, or he would bring in a mushroom or a special rock. Most often he was the teacher and I was the awed student—he made an unknown world come alive to me. At other times, I would take out my art books and show him how other people *like him* had felt a communion with nature and a desire to record it. We looked at Fuertes' paintings of birds and works by Constable, Turner, Van Gogh, Cezanne, Grant Wood, etc. We looked at sculpture and talked about how the organic forms are derived from nature. We looked at Weston's photographs of green peppers, pebbles, and the sea. Jim borrowed my books and read them.

We had long discussions and arguments. He began to see art as part of life, part of his life. What had happened to Jim up to this time is, I think, a good example of the madness of our educational system. Here was a boy who had unique knowledge, and yet other teachers never saw this.

Our relationship soon was killed. After three weeks, I was reprimanded for allowing a student to leave the school building alone. There were rules, I was told, that had to be obeyed.

Poor Children's Deficiencies

Poor children develop the cognitive universals, and they develop distinctive skills which are useful for coping with their own environments. Yet what is useful is often relative. This leads to the next proposition: *Poor chil-*

dren's skills are sometimes unsuited to the typical school, and poor children may fail to develop some abilities which it emphasizes.

First, consider skills unsuited to the typical school. Labov's work again offers a constructive example. While toasts are adaptive in the gang culture, the middle-class teacher may not appreciate them. He often considers them obscene; he does not sanction the values they express; and he does not approve of the use of black dialect. So what is an asset in the gang is a liability in school. But schools can operate under different assumptions and can change their values. Kohl appreciated black dialect, and his students' literary work flourished. This is, of course, largely a political matter as is often true in education: whose values shall dominate the schools?

Next, consider poor children's failure to develop skills which the schools stress. The lower-class environment may not adequately prepare its children in at least one academic skill of genuine value. In many middle-class families, there are books around and parents often read to the children. When they first arrive in school, many middle-class children already know how to print a few letters and read a few words, and they may even enjoy it. All this obviously helps middle-class children in adjusting to schools which place a high value on reading and writing.

Probably activities of this sort are less common in lower-class families. A study by Milner (1951) suggests that lower-class parents read less to their children than do middle-class parents. Of course, we need more evidence on this matter, but suppose that lower-class families do not place a great deal of emphasis on reading and writing. If they do not provide the specific experience which is necessary for these skills to develop, then poor children are at a disadvantage from the beginning in the traditional school.

Another way of putting the matter is this. General experience with the world—contact with the universal environment of things and people—provides the poor child with the basic intellectual skills of language, concrete operational thinking, and all the other cognitive universals. And yet general experience is not sufficient for the development of some special skills, namely reading and writing, that the school requires. These special (nonuniversal) skills require a special environment. For reading and writing to develop, the child needs a literate environment. Given it, he will learn the fundamentals of reading and, I think, does not need to be taught in the usual sense. Recall the open classroom which Wheeler, Tulis, and I studied. It was a special environment, containing books, pens, paper, and so on. Without these things, the natural development of printing would not have occurred; with them, printing did develop in a self-directed way, and traditional teaching was not required.

So poor children may enter school with an initial deficiency in reading. In the current educational system, this initial deficiency is often crippling. It often overwhelms the poor child and prevents him from doing capable academic work in a variety of areas. In the current system, if early reading is deficient, then later reading is apt to be weak too. And if this is true, then the child has difficulty in mathematics, in history, indeed in almost all academic subjects.

This situation may be evaluated in several ways. One is to say that in the early grades of school the poor child needs extra help in reading so that he can compete successfully with other children. The poor child's deficiency must be corrected as soon as possible so that he can get on with the job of education. This approach has something to recommend it. Within the current educational system, it certainly makes sense to give any child extra help in reading if he needs it.

Yet there are other ways of looking at the problem. One can criticize traditional schools for placing too much emphasis on reading in the first place. As we shall see in Chapter 6, it is reasonable to suppose that traditional schools, as well as efforts at reform within the traditional framework, exaggerate the importance of reading and that this over-emphasis has damaging effects on education. From this perspective, the chief reading problem is not the poor child's but the schools'.

Further, several writers show that it is not very difficult to learn reading and writing if the educational system is radically changed. Recall Kohl's report. Once his students were motivated by the open classroom, many had little difficulty in learning what they had failed to pick up for the past four or five years, and many students displayed genuine literary accomplishments. Similarly Featherstone (1967) reports that in the English Primary Schools reading is learned in an informal and spontaneous way, and students do not seem to have much trouble with it. Also Furth (1970) has proposed and experimented with a "school for thinking" where reading is not stressed as curriculum content but is slowly introduced as a by-product of other thinking activities. We shall further discuss experiments of this type in Chapter 6.

In sum, poor children may be deficient in reading when they arrive in school. Yet there is reason to believe that the traditional school creates many of its own difficulties by over-emphasizing reading in the first place. Other approaches to education suggest that reading is easily learned and therefore that poor children's initial deficit should not be a serious handicap.

chapter six

Intellect and the Schools

Having reviewed the literature on poor children's intellect and its development, we must now examine the psychological assumptions underlying various attempts to reform education. Do these assumptions make sense in the light of what we know about poor children?

COMPENSATORY EDUCATION

In the course of this book we have had occasion to discuss two programs of compensatory education—Bereiter and Engleman's in chapter 3, and Klaus and Gray's in chapter 4. At the risk of repetition, I will now review the basic philosophy and assumptions of programs like these and then make a few general points about them.

Assumptions

Compensatory education programs are based on a set of interlocking assumptions concerning the environment and its effects on the poor child. The first assumption is that the poor child's environment is inadequate. Most theorists have assumed that it is deprived, that it offers few opportunities for stimulation or excitation. The notion of environment refers not only to the world of things and objects, but also to the social milieu, especially the parents. In this view, the parents provide for the poor child impoverished forms of language, arbitrary modes of discipline, and inadequate models of conceptual activity. Other theorists believe that the poor child's environment is inadequate in that it contains an over-abundance of stimulation. The poor child's world is chaotic, noisy, and disorganized.

I have tried to show that the assumption of an inadequate—deprived or over-stimulating—environment is incorrect. In chapter 5, for example, we saw that there are few social-class differences in many aspects of maternal behavior. In general, the similarities among the social classes are far more striking than the differences. And lower-class parents seldom if ever show the complete absence of a pattern of behavior characteristic of the middle class. We also saw in chapter 5 that there is virtually no evidence showing that the poor environment contains a deficit or surfeit of stimulation. Indeed, anecdotal accounts support the conjecture that the poor environment, while often depressing and degrading, does not lack for stimulation or opportunities to learn. It would appear as if the restraints of a middle-class perspective have prevented many researchers from noticing the richness and challenge of the lower-class world.

A second assumption of the compensatory education movement is that the environment is the major determinant of the child's intellectual growth. The environment shapes the child's language, thought, perception, and behavior. By this analysis, if the environment is inadequate, it exerts deleterious effects on cognition; if the environment is stimulating, it causes cognition to bloom.

In child psychology, this extreme form of empiricism is usually welcomed as a kind of holy deliverance from an equally extreme form of nativism. From the empiricist view, the nativist position is an incorrect theory which leads to regressive and disastrous social policies. The nativists assert that intelligence is pre-determined by heredity and so one can do almost nothing to improve the presumably inadequate intellectual processes of the poor. This, say the empiricists, is untrue: intellect is not predetermined and so one can by various means uplift the poor from their current condition of intellectual disadvantage.

The empiricist position is well intentioned and humane, but at the same time it is wrong. As you have seen, I do not of course argue for old-fashioned nativist theory but for a developmental view which recognizes both the contributions of biology and of the environment. From the developmental perspective, which we reviewed in chapter 5, the child's intellectual processes are not simply shaped by the environment, just as they are not fully or largely determined by heredity. Instead, biological processes guarantee that the child himself takes an active part in the learning process, so that he shapes the environment just as much as it shapes him.

A third assumption of the compensatory education movement is that, as a result of the environment and its power to shape human behavior, the poor child develops deficient intellectual processes. His language, thought, and perception are all inadequate; and these deficiencies in intellect almost guarantee his failure in school. This assumption too is incorrect. We saw in chapter 2 that the poor child's relatively low IQ does not indicate massive deficiencies in mind. We saw in chapter 3 that the poor child's language may be rich and complex. And chapter 4 showed us that the poor child is adept at many forms of intellectual activity. All children, regardless of social class or even culture, possess certain basic and important cognitive skills. In addition, poor children are characterized by some unique intellectual abilities, adaptive in their own environments, and perhaps by some mental activities which are deficient, at least in relation to certain demands of the middle-class environment. While poverty is not a desirable state and while it may not ennoble those who live in it, it also does not produce serious retardation of their thought processes.

The fourth assumption of compensatory education is that schooling should be designed to remove and correct intellectual deficits. Accordingly, Bereiter and Englemann have developed language training programs, and Klaus and Gray have constructed curricula in perception, language, and thinking. Again the basic assumption is incorrect, and there are several reasons for this. The simplest is that poor children do not suffer from the deficiencies which compensatory education attributes to them, and so compensatory education is not necessary for what it was designed to do.

Furthermore, the belief that poor children are deficient is often self-defeating and leads to the kinds of results which compensatory education intends to prevent. Here is an example.

A Cornell graduate student, Greg Lehne, and I interviewed and observed a second grade child who was having considerable difficulty in school. She is from a poor family, as are most of the children in her school. The interviews and observations centered on Terry's work in reading and mathematics and on her general intellectual development. It became clear very quickly that Terry was a lively and alert child who most definitely did not suffer from severe intellectual deficit. She was generally eager to learn, although she could be quite stubborn and noncommunicative, even withdrawn. It became clear, too, that she had a great deal of difficulty in reading. Lehne discovered that she could easily discriminate among the letters but that she had trouble with sounding.

Why did she have this problem? Our hypothesis was that her reading book was very bad. It was a Dick and Jane type which does not make it easy to abstract the letter-sound correspondence rules. The book contains relatively long sentences in which the rules for sounding are not obvious. The result is that if a child does not know how to sound, he can read the book only by doing what Terry did: memorizing passages, remembering single words, guessing from context. It is possible, of course, to construct books along different lines. For example, some of the Dr. Seuss books emphasize in clear and amusing ways the role of sounding. The *Hop on Pop* book contains on one page a sentence constructed around the words *Ed, Ned, Red, Bed, Ted.* Of course, the child can try to remember the sequence or guess it from context. But it is also easy to discover that the initial letter makes a difference in how the word sounds.

We had a conference with the teacher about all this. We told her that Terry was having difficulty because she had not been given a good opportunity to learn to read and that the reading series was not useful, at least for Terry. We advised using books constructed along the lines of the Dr. Seuss books and also involving Terry in creative writing (our assumption being that learning to spell words is a good way of learning to read them).

In the ensuing conversation, which I regret is not tape-recorded, several points emerged. The teacher felt (but, of course, could not prove) that when the children first entered kindergarten, they had a strong interest in learning to read. In the kindergarten, they "learned the letters"—apparently to discriminate among them and to name them. But in the first grade, they were required to spend the whole year on "reading readiness." This consists of exercises in which the child must, for example, learn to discriminate triangles from rectangles, identify which of a set of three members is different from the other two (the "oddity task"), and the like. Reading readiness does not seem useful because it has almost nothing to do with reading. Reading involves discriminating among letters, learning the sounds associated with letters or combinations of letters, and the like. Discriminating among geometric forms or solving oddity problems does not make a significant contribution toward helping the child to do this. The teacher agreed that reading readiness is not beneficial and made the observation that after a year of reading readiness the children are behind on reading and *many no longer want to read.* We asked her, why then bother with reading readiness? She said that the principal did not think that poor children are intellectually prepared for reading in the first grade. Specifically, they cannot perform the requisite "auditory discriminations." The teacher did not seem to know whether to believe this or not. I asked her if her students could understand ordinary speech and she said of course they could.

So you see what is happening. In this case, poor children apparently enter school wanting to read. They make a start at it in kindergarten but then are not allowed to continue because the principal thinks they are intellectually deficient. They must then suffer through a year of reading readiness, with the result that the prophecy is self-fulfilling: they fall behind on reading and some no longer have an interest in learning it. They then enter the second grade, are given a reading series which is very poor, and fall even further behind in reading. The teachers and principal see all this and conclude that poor children *cannot* learn to read very well. It is then easy to blame the reading failure on the children's intellectual deficiencies, on the presumed lack of books in their homes, and on inadequate socialization. The proposed solution is more compensatory education, more reading readiness. And the result is simply more failure which only serves to reinforce the school's misguided assumptions concerning poor children. So a cycle is established: there is failure, and the school attempts to exorcise it by appeal to the faulty assumptions of compensatory education; the failure persists and perversely the compensatory education view is strengthened.

As I pointed out at the end of chapter 3, there is an important difference between the philosophy of the open classroom and that of compensatory education. In the latter view, there are deficits to correct and the adult must control the process of remediation. By contrast, the open classroom approach assumes that the child is a storehouse of potentiality, not defect, and that proper assistance from the teacher will allow the child to develop in a self-directed way. Thus, while both approaches agree that the poor child must learn and grow, they differ radically in their conceptions of the nature of this growth and of the proper means for fostering it.

A fifth assumption, held by at least some proponents of compensatory education, is that early remedial training can have long term effects on the child's education. Giving the child a Head Start should contribute to his success in elementary school several years later. Common sense argues against this. Early education, compensatory or otherwise, may be useful for some 4- and 5-year-old children. But why should its effects persist for many years? Is it not reasonable to assume that the child's performance in the elementary school is mainly the result of the nature of that school and not of some experiences which he had several years earlier? If a poor child attends a very good kindergarten and a very bad fourth grade, he will most likely do well in the former and badly in the latter.

For all these reasons, then, compensatory education makes little sense. It is based on wrong assumptions concerning the nature of the lower-class environment, the developmental process, the intellect of the child, the techniques of education, and the effects of early experiences on later performance. As a result of these faulty assumptions and perhaps other factors, compensatory education does not work. The typical finding (see, for example, the U.S. Commission on Civil Rights, 1967) is that while compensatory education at the ages 4 and 5 may raise the level of poor children's academic achievement in kindergarten or perhaps the first grade, there is no effect on educational performance after that time. My interpretation of these findings is as follows. The initial gain may be due to the fact that compensatory education programs teach many of the same skills which are emphasized in kindergarten and the first grade—for example, activities such as naming colors or discriminating squares from triangles. But after the first few grades, poor children are typically confronted with an inadequate educational system, a system that assumes poor children cannot do well and that is not designed to foster their unique potentialities. It should come as no surprise that poor children do badly in a situation like this, that a few years of early compensatory education cannot prevent later academic failure, and that the only way to improve the situation is to reform the schools at all levels.

Not only is compensatory education a failure, but it also tends to divert attention from the real issue, namely reform of the public schools. Of course, workers in compensatory education do not propose that the schools should not be reformed. Nevertheless, their work tends to nourish the hope that the crisis in education can be significantly lessened by remedial work with young children, and this diverts attention from the more pressing problems of the schools. An example is as follows. When Head Start ran into difficulties, several workers proposed that the situation could be improved by instituting compensatory education with infants and by training lower-class mothers to rear their babies properly. Programs of this type now exist, and my guess is that they will be no more effective than other forms of compensatory education. The money would be better spent on improving public education.

While I maintain that compensatory education is not a reasonable solution to the educational crisis, my position should not be misunderstood. I do not argue that early childhood education—nursery schools, day care centers, etc.—is generally without value. Early education, handled properly, can be useful for children in a variety of ways at the time they experience it. Four-year-olds too can do interesting art or mathematics or literary work. But such experiences cannot innoculate children against the diseases of the schools.

INNOVATION WITHIN THE FRAMEWORK OF TRADITIONAL EDUCATION

Perhaps the most common attempt at improving poor children's education involves innovations within the framework of the traditional school. Before analyzing the psychological assumptions underlying such attempts, I should be careful to specify what I mean by traditional schools and by innovations within their framework.

Traditional education involves the following kinds of practices: a predetermined and structured curriculum; a considerable amount of power in the hands of the teacher, and a relatively small amount of freedom for the student; a requirement for all students in a class to learn approximately the same things at the same times; a lack of free social exchange among students in the classroom; the imposition by the teacher of rules of conduct and other standards; an emphasis on the reading of textbooks; and the heavy utilization of standard tests as the measure of academic achievement. These are some characteristics, and no doubt the reader can think of others. And as we multiply the number of characteristics, it becomes very unlikely that any one school can be considered traditional in all respects. Nevertheless we all know of schools which partake of some of these characteristics to some extent.

There have been several observational studies which attempt to provide useful empirical data on teachers' and students' behavior in traditional schools. The investigators typically begin by classifying a school as traditional or progressive on global, semi-intuitive criteria. Then careful observations are collected on certain aspects of the school.

For example, Minuchin, Biber, Shapiro, and Zimiles (1969) studied four schools, two relatively traditional and two progressive. The investigators collected extensive observations on a fourth grade classroom in each school.

Consider first some aspects of traditional teaching. Table 6-1 presents the results. Traditional teachers tended to stress memorization or drill rather than the understanding of principles. Children had to copy multiplication problems and facts rather than discover the basic relationships. In traditional schools, children had to learn facts rather than search for the principles which they suggest. Teachers from traditional schools tended to decide what problem the children would work at and even how they would solve it.

In these classrooms, the subject matter tended to be distant from the children's experiences. They were not encouraged to relate their personal knowledge to what was being studied. The scope of the content accepted as relevant to the class was defined quite narrowly. In one class, a child was asked to answer a question about Magellan. He did so, but included in his response a good deal of extraneous information on meridians, galaxies, and the like. The teacher made fun of the long words he used and of his "more-than-necessary" knowledge. In traditional classrooms, the teacher expected that the child would keep up with the group; if he did not, she did not often help him. She did not seem to perceive her task as developing the child's ideas but as presenting her own which often interfered with the child's. Similarly, it was the teacher who set the pace. She decided when and how quickly things were to be learned: she tended to hurry the children because she felt it important to cover certain material by a certain date. In the traditional classroom there was considerable emphasis on maintaining law and order. The atmosphere was often discordant.

The investigators point out that other researchers have come to similar conclusions. Anderson (1939) found that over 59 percent of teachers' time was spent in "dominative" acts. Hughes et al. (1959) found that 40 percent of teaching acts were "controlling" and "directive." Perkins (1964) found that 75 percent of the time students had to stay in their seats; there was infrequent use of discussion (5.5 percent) or individual work. There was a low frequency of praise (1 percent), "thinking" questions (1 percent), and using a student's idea (4 percent).

When we turn to the children's behavior, we find (see Table 6-2) that in the traditional classroom children were judged to be restless, uneasy, and passive. To a slight extent a small group of children tended to dominate the work while others were slighted. In traditional classrooms children were often

TABLE 6-1 Differences in the Modern and Traditional School Teachers' Structuring of Children's Learning

Dimension	Classroom Frequencies	
	Traditional	*Modern*
Quality of Thinking Encouraged		
1. Symbolic Skills		
Understanding principles	4	9
versus		
Memorization or drill	19	5
2. Conceptualization		
Emphasis on conceptual development	0	8
versus		
Emphasis on concepts as facts	10	3
3. Problem-Solving Orientation		
Partly child-determined	3	21
versus		
T-determined	15	0
Cognitive Exploration		
1. Relevance of Subject Matter to Children's Experience		
Close	4	17
versus		
Distant	31	6
2. Scope of Content Accepted as Relevant		
Wide	3	7
versus		
Narrow	5	1
3. Assistance Given by Teacher		
Active help	2	15
versus		
Ignoring, not helping	19	1
4. Function of Teacher's Comments		
Develop	1	15
versus		
Interfere with children's ideas	19	0
5. Pace		
Teacher's and children's pace		
Consonant	17	30
versus		
Dissonant	13	0
6. Atmosphere		
Harmonious or task-oriented	12	27
versus		
Discordant or to maintain order	21	1

Source: Minuchin *et al.,* 1969, p. 104.

TABLE 6-2   Differences between the Modern and Traditional School Children's
Cognitive Behavior in the Classroom (Total N=65 records)

Dimension	Classroom Frequencies	
	Traditional	Modern
Involvement in the Work of the Classroom		
Children's Affective Response		
Enjoyment	6	26
versus		
Passivity or restlessness	27	4
Participation		
By few, or core group	20	17
versus		
By most or all	13	11
Task-Relatedness		
Related to task	14	23
versus		
Unrelated to task or mixed	19	8
Quality of Verbalized Thinking		
Opportunity to Express Ideas		
Ample or limited	18	21
versus		
None	15	7

Source: Minuchin *et al.,* 1969, p. 117.

engaged in activities not particularly relevant to their work. For example, if the teacher had to leave the room, work was disrupted; the children did not pursue it on their own. The children did not often have an opportunity to engage in free discussion, to elaborate on their own ideas.

What about the interaction between teacher and child? In traditional schools (see Table 6-3) teachers and children initiated about the same number of contacts with one another. By contrast, in the modern schools, children tended to initiate contacts far more often than teachers. The traditional teachers were often hostile, sarcastic, or derogatory.

Here is an example:

The teacher has asked the children to explain the errors they made in an arithmetic lesson. Jack explains his error, which was merely carelessness. The teacher twists her hands in front of her and says to the group, "What shall we do?" The children respond, "Break his neck" (p. 25).

Despite this, or because of it, the children were neutral or friendly in their behavior toward the teacher.

TABLE 6-3 Analysis of Interpersonal Incidents
in the Classrooms

Classroom Frequencies		
Interpersonal Incidents	*Traditional*	*Modern*
Initiation of Contacts		
Teacher	60	31
Child	57	89
Manifest Affect		
Teacher To Child		
Friendly or neutral	26	23
Hostile	29	2
Child To Teacher		
Friendly or neutral	10	26
Hostile	2	1

Source: Minuchin *et al.,* 1969, p. 126.

This then is a partial description of a few traditional schools. It is hard to tell precisely how typical they are. But that does not really matter: we all know that events like these are fairly common in many schools.

Innovation within the framework of traditional education takes several forms. It often involves the use of new texts, curricular material, and the like. Reading is an area where the traditional school frequently has difficulty and where many innovations have been attempted. Sometimes the innovation may involve the substitution of one series of reading texts for another. (Usually the series covers the entire elementary school reading program, from kindergarten to the sixth grade, so that adoption of a new series is a major decision.) Sometimes the innovation may involve the substitution of one method of teaching reading for another. A school may decide that the whole-word method has not been as effective as desired and that the phonics method might be superior. The teacher then conducts the lessons differently than before and uses new text books, wall charts, and the like. Sometimes, innovations within a traditional school may shade over into the open classroom approach (described below) so that there is no clear distinction between the two. For example, an otherwise traditional school may adopt the procedure of sending children to a "learning center" where they may have the opportunity to work at reading, using certain audio-visual devices, at their own pace.

How effective are such innovations for poor children? There is of course no simple answer. One would have to examine each case to determine the precise benefits or liabilities involved. I think though that there are several considerations which suggest that innovations of this type, while perhaps producing some amount of improvement, nevertheless do not usually result in a significant and dramatic impact upon the education of poor children and are not likely to do so in the future.

One consideration is empirical evidence of various sorts. Chall (1967), in her comprehensive review of research on reading, reports that many studies fail to show large or even significant differences in children's reading scores as a function of various innovations in the teaching of reading. Some studies show the phonics method to be superior, some the whole-word method, and many are inconsistent. Taken as a whole, the evidence supports the view that innovations in reading instruction within traditional schools do not produce a dramatic effect. (I have a colleague who maintains, not entirely flippantly, that about one third of the evaluation studies in any area of education show that method A is slightly better than method B, one third show B slightly better than A, and one third indicate a lack of significant difference between the two.)

The so-called new math is another case in point. While many traditional schools have adopted new math textbooks and other procedures, this does not seem to have broken the cycle of failure in which poor children find themselves. For example, in the City of Ithaca, many more or less traditional schools have for years attempted various innovations in mathematics, as well as other subjects. Yet all this has failed to produce dramatic changes in educational achievement, at least as measured in conventional ways. The schools containing the most poor children still score the lowest on various measures of mathematics achievement.

So innovations within the framework of traditional education have not been too successful. It also seems to be true that those schools or classes which *have* achieved a high degree of success with poor children have not been traditional in orientation. For example, Kohl's class (discussed in chapter 3) produced truly dramatic achievements, and it was very much outside the framework of traditional education. (We will review other cases of this sort below.) Similarly, the kindergarten that I studied with Wheeler and Tulis produced very fine work in its poor children, and it too was an open classroom.

In sum, my first argument is that traditional schools have not done very well at innovation, whereas other kinds of schools have.

Why should this be so? One answer, I think, is that the psychological and philosophical framework of traditional schools tends to prevent innovations in them from being successful. Since the framework of the traditional school is misguided, especially in regard to poor children, this form of education can only attain a limited degree of success.

Success, Failure, and the Standardized Test

One of the faulty assumptions underlying the traditional school is that standard tests measure important aspects of knowledge. I shall argue in the following pages that, on the contrary, in many cases standard tests and classroom examinations fail to capture much that is important about children's cognition. As a result, the teacher has an inadequate understanding of what his students know. This is especially true in the case of poor children, and it has several deleterious effects. For one thing, the widespread use of standard tests makes it difficult to evaluate the effects of various innovations: they may in fact work much better or much worse than the tests indicate. For another, the inadequate portrait of children's knowledge given by standard tests makes it hard for a teacher to help his students. If he does not know what they really have learned or have failed to learn, he cannot be of much help to them. Let us now review the argument in some detail.

THE NATURE OF THE TESTS

The traditional school uses two major kinds of examinations to obtain information about its students' accomplishments. One is the standardized test of achievement, which exerts considerable influence over the entire system of traditional education. Standardized tests, usually constructed by educational psychologists, are typically administered to all of the students in a school system at least once a year for the purpose of assessing their achievement. The test results are used to determine the student's assignment for the following year, to evaluate the current teacher's effectiveness, and so forth. The second major criterion of success and failure is the classroom test constructed by the teacher. This is a less formal and less precise version of the standardized test. The teacher simply prepares a list of questions, gives them in a standard way to the class, and tries to be objective in scoring the results, which determine the students' grades.

In addition, teachers use other, informal methods of assessing students' achievement: casual discussions, inspection of his homework, and the like. The extent to which such informal methods are employed must vary considerably among teachers.

Despite the use of informal assessment procedures, it is fair to say that in traditional education standard tests and classroom examinations are the ultimate criteria and the most important sources of information concerning students' achievement. The tests may determine whether the student is promoted, or influence his chances of getting into college, or form the teacher's opinion concerning his abilities; in these matters, informal procedures usually play a minor role.

Recognizing then that such tests are the keystones of traditional education, we must attempt to evaluate them.[1] There are many different standard

---

[1] The usual method for validating standard tests is to correlate them with other standard tests or with teachers' ratings. If the correlation is high, then the test is considered useful. This is somewhat like requiring that the judge in a criminal trial be a member of the Mafia.

tests, and by various criteria some are better than others. Yet most tests (almost all) share four basic features: they picture the student's knowledge in terms of simple, unidimensional traits; they fail to provide information on the details of his thought processes; they often measure shallow aspects of knowledge; and they are administered in a rigid way.

Consider the Stanford Achievement Test, an examination used in many schools. This test, which is administered to groups of children, is designed "to measure the important knowledges, skills, and understandings commonly accepted as desirable outcomes of the major branches of the elementary curriculum" (Kelley *et al.*, 1964, p. 2). After explaining how to use the test booklet, the examiner first gives the student thirty-five minutes to do arithmetic computation. This involves addition, subtraction, multiplication, and division problems such as:

$$
\begin{array}{r}
6\ 4\ 0 \\
-\ 3\ 7\ 3 \\
\hline
\end{array}
$$

and

$$
\begin{array}{r}
3\ 5\ 9 \\
+\ 4\ 8\ 5 \\
\hline
\end{array}
$$

In each case the student must choose his answer from five alternatives, one of which is always "not given." There are 39 problems in all, and this part of the test is scored separately from the rest. The student receives three different kinds of scores for arithmetic computation: a percentile rank, a stanine score, and a grade score. All of these essentially give his rank relative to his peers.

The second part of the test is arithmetic concepts. The child is given a potpourri of problems whose diversity is hard to describe without giving a full list. There are problems in reading Roman numerals (What does IV mean?); in averaging (What is the average of 4 and 10?); in the ordering of fractions (Which of these fractions is largest? ½, ³⁄₁₀, etc.); in reading numbers (Which is seven thousand and ninety-three?); in remembering certain arithmetic terms (In the example $6 - 4 = 2$, which is the minuend?); and so on. There are 32 such problems, and again the number of correct answers is simply totaled to yield a percentile rank, grade score, or stanine. The third portion of the test, which we shall not discuss at any length, involves word problems.

One feature of this test is its conception of knowledge as a simple, unidimensional trait. The Stanford Test divides mathematics achievement into three gross abilities: calculation, concepts, and applications (word problems). According to the test, the student's knowledge of mathematics may be said to consist of these three traits, each varying along a simple, quantitative dimension. The student is thought to acquire some degree of ability or skill in each area. He may have more computational skill than most of his peers, or in the course of the year he may have acquired a higher degree of conceptual ability than he had at the beginning.

Whether or not the test constructors intend this definition of knowledge, it is implicit in the test: like the IQ, mathematics achievement is a simple trait, or set of such traits, and some students possess more of the traits than do others. And this conception of knowledge influences the thought of many teachers. Over the past several years, I have been working with teachers on the assessment of children's knowledge of mathematics. My usual procedure is to engage teachers in a discussion of a television tape concerning one child's work in mathematics. In most cases, the teachers begin by interpreting the child's behavior in terms of global traits, for example, "his computational ability is high, but his conceptual skill is low." This type of thought seems to pervade traditional schools. At the same time, many teachers are increasingly dissatisfied with achievement testing. They have an intuition that the tests give little useful information and that children's cognition is more complex than the tests suppose it to be.

Postponing for a moment a discussion of the validity of the standard test conception of knowledge, let us examine a second feature of tests, namely their failure to provide information on details of the thought processes. Suppose a student receives a percentile rank of 60 on computational skills. What does this mean? The score does tell us something about his performance: He is successful on more problems than 59 percent of his peers. While such information may be of some minimal value, it tells us little about how the child does computation and even less of what he understands of it. For example, if the student fails the problem

$$\begin{array}{r} 6\ 2\ 2 \\ -\ 5\ 3\ 7 \\ \hline \end{array}$$

he may have done so because he does not know how to "borrow," because he has forgotten some simple subtraction facts (e.g., that $12 - 7 = 5$), because he is a little sloppy even though he does know how to borrow and does remember the simple subtraction facts, because he did not have enough time to do the problem, and so on. The test does not give information of this sort. Instead, it ignores the methods of solution and simply combines correct answers (regardless of how they were achieved) into a total score.

The concepts portion of the test is even more ambiguous than the calculational. The concepts problems are widely diverse, requiring many different cognitive operations for their solution. Similarly, errors are bound to occur as a result of many different sorts of techniques. For example, one set of operations is required to read Roman numerals and another set to average two numbers. It is incorrect to think that a mysterious "conceptual ability" permits the student to solve both problems or that a lack of this trait prevents him from doing so. Combining the responses to diverse questions like these simply obscures a complex set of cognitive processes. It is obvious that the test does this; the only remaining question is how harmful the practice is.

Moreover, it is not at all clear that the test measures "concepts" in the first place. Is the ability to read Roman numerals a concept? And what about being able to average two numbers or to remember what the minuend is? In most cases, what the test measures are not concepts but low-level computational or similar skills: reading numbers, remembering obscure terms, and the like. So not only does the test fail to give useful information on the processes which children use in working the problems, it also gives a misleading definition of what it measures.

A third feature of the tests is their shallowness. Much of the Stanford Test deals with calculation in a rigid way. The child is given a series of problems to compute, and solving them mainly requires the routine application of the calculational techniques he has been taught in school. Standard tests do not seem to capture much of the child's "deep understanding" of the subject matter. I shall try to justify this assertion with several extended examples to be presented below.

A fourth feature of the tests is their standard administration. Everyone is familiar with this, and it requires no extended discussion.

It appears then that standard tests conceive of knowledge in terms of simple, quantitative traits; that the scores which the tests yield obscure the mental operations used in dealing with the various problems; that the tests measure rather superficial aspects of knowledge; and that they are administered in a rigid way. These features require further discussion.

ACHIEVEMENT AS QUANTITATIVE TRAITS

Is it useful to think of students' knowledge in terms of simple, quantitative traits, such as computational ability? Various cognitive theories suggest that the answer is no. These theories generally show that knowledge is far more complex than standard tests imagine it to be. In reviewing the IQ test we saw that it is a mistake to think of "intelligence" as a simple, unitary trait or as a quantitative entity. People do not have more or less of this mysterious entity "intelligence"; rather they employ complex sets of mental operations to solve various problems. Similarly, in reviewing research on language, we saw that it is not useful to think of speech as a unitary and quantitative trait of verbal ability. To understand language, one must conceive of it as a complex system of rules and operations on elements. For example, Labov's work on black dialect showed that a complicated set of rules governed the use of the copula and many other aspects of speech. Understanding children's language requires the description of these rules and of the relations among them. In reviewing material on intellectual processes, we saw that Piaget's theory conceptualizes knowledge in several ways: in terms of sensorimotor activities, imagery, mental operations, and the like. Thus the child's conception of *number* at different developmental levels is comprised by a set of interrelated mental operations on certain elements. If a child fails the conservation of number problem, he does so because he centers on certain aspects of the available information but not others, because his imagery is static rather than dynamic, because his reasoning fails to employ the techniques of reversibility or compensation. It is not useful to posit that he fails the problem because he is low on numerical ability.

In brief, modern cognitive theory has found it necessary to conceptualize knowledge in complex terms. It finds little value in notions of simple, quantitative traits. The conception of knowledge which underlies standard tests is outmoded and should have been abandoned somewhere about 1920 (the date of Piaget's initial work); the standard test conception of knowledge gives very little insight into what children know.

METHOD OF ADMINISTRATION

Is it useful to give achievement tests in a standardized fashion? Again, cognitive theories suggest that the answer is no. Because of their conception of knowledge, modern cognitive theories have developed new methods for assessing it. Piaget began his studies of children's knowledge by administering standard tests. He soon discovered, however, that this method was of little value. The number of correct responses gave scanty information concerning children's methods of reasoning, concerning the mental processes which lay behind their right or wrong answers. He found that it was necessary to question the children in a flexible manner concerning the reasons for their responses. This type of clinical interview can provide a wealth of information about a child's thought processes.

In a similar fashion, Labov found that the administration of standard tests in school shed little light on poor children's linguistic abilities. To get relevant information, he found it necessary to use unorthodox methods such as recording black youths' speech during a bus ride or on the streets. Earlier I quoted Chomsky to the effect that if one wants to obtain useful information about language one must use a variety of devious techniques.

In reviewing the literature on the IQ we saw that at least some groups of poor children do not perform at their best in a standard testing situation. I also tried to show that by its very logic the standard testing approach cannot be effective in establishing the intellectual competence of poor children.

In sum, several branches of cognitive theory do not find standard testing a useful technique for determining cognitive competence in any children, lower- or middle-class. And other studies show that standard testing is particularly inappropriate for poor children. These considerations suggest that standard tests are apt to yield superficial results and that they are likely to underestimate the competence of poor children.

THE SUPERFICIALITY OF TESTS
AND THE RICHNESS OF CHILDREN'S KNOWLEDGE

I have maintained that test scores reflect superficial aspects of knowledge and fail to capture the richness of children's intellectual activities. Several examples support these interlocking propositions and give further reasons for supposing that the standard test notion of knowledge as a quantitative trait is incorrect.

Consider first the case of Jane, a 9-year-old, the daughter of professional parents. Jane was having difficulty in school, and her teacher was at a loss to know what to do. The Stanford Achievement Test showed that Jane was in the 14th percentile in arithmetic computation and in the 68th percentile in arithmetic concepts. She was interviewed on television tape by my colleague Ezra Heitowit. In the first interview, Jane was given the problem

$$
\begin{array}{r}
8\ 7 \\
+\ 3\ 9 \\
\hline
\end{array}
$$

She wrote

$$
\begin{array}{r}
8\ 7 \\
+\ 3\ 9 \\
\hline
1\ 5 \\
1\ 1 \\
\hline
2\ 6 \\
\end{array}
$$

The interviewer (I) said: "Maybe you can explain what's going on here. If I'm not mistaken, you've added 7 and 9. And you get?"

Jane (J) answered: Fifteen.
I: And then you add 8 and 3 and get?
J: Eleven.
I: Eleven and put it right underneath and add these two together.
J: Yes.
I: And get what?
J: Add these two together and get 26.

So this was the first problem Heitowit uncovered in Jane's work. How did she develop such a strange strategy? Since we do not know her learning history, we can only speculate. Perhaps a teacher once used a method like this to teach the relation between place value and addition. If we have 87 + 39 we can first add the units column, getting 16. Thus

$$
\begin{array}{r}
8\ 7 \\
+\ 3\ 9 \\
\hline
1\ 6
\end{array}
$$

Then we add the tens column to get 11 tens or 110. Thus:

$$
\begin{array}{r}
8\ 7 \\
+\ 3\ 9 \\
\hline
1\ 6 \\
1\ 1 \\
\hline
1\ 2\ 6
\end{array}
$$

Jane may have partially learned the teacher's method (with a crucial error in lining up the numbers), failed to understand its rationale, and then simply repeated it in a blind fashion thereafter.

Jane's second problem was this:

I: Let me give you two other numbers, 132 and 14. And I ask you to add them up. (Heitowit wrote 132 + 14.)

Jane: I don't know if I can do them that way. I can only do them on top of each other.

Jane wrote:

$$
\begin{array}{r}
1\ 3\ 2 \\
1\ 4 \\
\hline
2\ 7\ 2
\end{array}
$$

So here she shows a new error, namely lining up the numbers from left to right. But at other times Jane did problems of this type quite well; in general, her work was quite inconsistent.

After viewing the tapes of these interviews, we developed several hypotheses concerning Jane's difficulties. Perhaps she does not know that the sum of two positive whole numbers must be larger than either alone. (That is, if you add two numbers together, the sum must be bigger than either of the numbers added.) We wondered about this because she added 87 + 39 to get 26. On the other hand, maybe she does not realize that 26 is smaller than either 87 or 39. In other words, perhaps Jane knows nothing about the ordering of the numbers. For her it is *not* true that $1 < 2 < 3 < 4 \ldots$.

So our first thoughts were that Jane does not understand addition in some deep sense. She does not know what happens when you add two numbers and/or she does not appreciate the ordering of the numbers.

There is, however, an alternate hypothesis: Jane "really understands" addition but just cannot do simple computations on paper. She comprehends the basic ideas but cannot calculate, either because she is not trying or does not know how to. What do I mean by "really understands"? Consider what happened next.

We prepared some special problems to test our hypotheses.

I: Well, here's what I'd like you to do. I'm going to give you a string of numbers to write. (He dictated.) 2,342; 79; 163; 15,700; 6; 940. Now what I would like you to do is to write these numbers out in increasing order, the smallest one first, the next largest one, and so on.

Jane wrote: 6; 79; 163; 940; 2,342; 15,700.

So we ruled out one hypothesis, namely, that Jane did not know the ordering of the numbers.

I: Good. Now I'd like you to—suppose I tell you now to add these up.
J: (Sighed. Such big numbers!) She wrote:

$$
\begin{array}{l}
6 \\
7\ 9 \\
1\ 6\ 3 \\
9\ 4\ 0 \\
2\ 3\ 4\ 2 \\
1\ 5\ 7\ 0\ 0 \\
\hline
\end{array}
$$

I: Now without doing it, tell me what would you do to add them up?
J: I'd probably add that [the first column on the left] and carry to that [the second column from the left] and carry to that and carry to that.

Now we see that Jane has another problem with addition. Not only does she line the numbers up wrong, she also adds and carries from left to right!

I: I see. Before you do that, I'd like you to look at the numbers we have here and estimate—or guess, sort of an educated guess—as to what the sum should be when you add them all together.
J: (Appeared to be thinking.)
I: What seems like a reasonable number to get?
J: Seventeen thousand and . . . uh . . . eighteen thousand, and . . . eighteen thousand, three hundred, and ninety-two.

I: (Quite surprised.) That's a pretty good guess. I mean you were pretty precise all the way out to the last unit. How did you estimate that?

J: I know that it would probably be more than 1700.

I: Seventeen hundred? 17,000 I think you mean.

J: Yes, 17,000, and then I just decided, I said, and just *guessed* the rest.

After all, the interviewer had asked her to guess.

I: How did you know that it would be more than 17,000?

J: Well, that's 2,000 [pointing to the 2,342] and that's 15,000 [the 15,700] which is 17,000 and all of this [the rest] adds up to probably more than 1,000, and I know it would probably be 18,000 and I just guessed the rest.

Note how much understanding of addition is implicit in Jane's estimation procedure. Her behavior is based on the assumption that the two numbers which contribute the most to the sum are the two largest numbers. By comparison the other numbers are insignificant and can almost be ignored. She knows, too, on an implicit level that the sum must be larger than the parts. She knows that rounding is a useful technique in estimation problems. And she has a good feel for the problem: she realizes that all of the other numbers (besides 15,000 and 2,000) add up to about 1,000 although it's not very important.

This example is instructive on a number of counts. It shows first that Jane's knowledge of mathematics is extraordinarily complex. Sometimes she does computations properly; sometimes she does not. When incorrect, she uses a variety of calculational routines. At the same time, when she is given an estimation problem which requires for its solution some procedures not usually taught in school, Jane does remarkably well. In fact, her estimation procedures seem to be based on at least an implicit understanding of certain basic principles of addition. Another way of looking at this is to say that when Jane must use the teacher's methods (the standard computational routines), she does poorly; when she is allowed to use a method of her own invention (the estimation procedure), Jane does well.

The example also shows how valuable are informal testing procedures. The interviewer followed up Jane's responses, based his questions on what she had just done and not entirely on some pre-determined plan, and devised new problems to pursue ambiguities in Jane's previous response. All this yields a rich collection of data concerning Jane's knowledge of mathematics. The interview shows what Jane can and cannot do in some detail. From a record like this one can begin to develop a cognitive theory of Jane—that is, a portrait describing the mental operations comprising her knowledge of mathematics.

By contrast, the information yielded by standard tests is sparse indeed. You will recall that the Stanford Achievement Test showed that Jane was in the 14th percentile in arithmetic computation and in the 68th percentile in arithmetic concepts. There is some accuracy to this; indeed, Jane's concepts are better than her calculations. But the picture given by the standard tests is too vague; it presents only the blurred outlines and fails to describe her knowledge in rich detail, that is to say, in a way that would be of use to a teacher attempting to help Jane. Also the tests are superficial. They fail to show what aspects of addition she does understand, and they fail to describe the interesting work she can do on problems of estimation.

Here is another example. I twice interviewed a boy whom I shall call Peter concerning his knowledge of mathematics. At the initial interview, I knew nothing about him, except that he was 13 years old and had difficulty with mathematics in school. I found out later that his grades were poor, that his IQ was 87, and that he was in the lowest track of the seventh grade. The Iowa test of Basic Skills showed that his vocabulary grade level was 4.3 (it should have been close to 8.0 since the test was given at the end of the seventh grade); reading was 5.8; arithmetic concepts 7.7; arithmetic problems 4.1; total arithmetic 5.9.

On a standard form concerning mathematics achievement, the teacher commented:

> *Classwork—satisfactory when done.*
> *Attitude—poor.*
> *Attention—poor.*
> *Conduct—fair.*
> *Does he come in for help?—no.*
> *Does he get his work done on time?—no.*
> *Does he hand in neat work?—fairly.*
> *Want to see parents?—yes.*

The teacher added a few comments:

> *Immature.*
> *The boy that he hangs around with is less mature than Peter himself.*
> *He doesn't take responsibility for anything.*
> *Craves attention.*
> *Paces himself with his friends.*
> *Quite grave in appearance.*
> *Probably capable.*

Peter came from a working-class black neighborhood in a medium-size city. His father worked the night shift (midnight to 8 A.M.) in a large factory, and his mother worked the evening shift (3 P.M. *to* 11 P.M.) at the same place.

The conditions for the first interview were far from ideal. Peter did not know me at all and probably wondered what I wanted from him. Children who often get into trouble at school do not take such encounters lightly. Nevertheless, I tried to put Peter at ease not by idle chit-chat, but by having him help me set up the video recording equipment. He knew that he was to be on television and seemed to enjoy the prospect.

I began by asking Peter what kind of work he was doing in school, and he told me long division.

I: Can you give me an example of a hard division problem that you work with?

Peter wrote: $10 \overline{\smash{\big)}\ 1701}$

That is not a very difficult problem for a seventh grader.

I: How do you say that problem?

P: Ten divided by one thousand, seven hundred, and one.

So Peter said it backward. But could he do the divison?

He wrote: $10 \overline{\smash{\big)}\ 1701}$ with 0170 above

I: How did you get that? You did that pretty quick. . . . Which number did you write first? (Peter pointed to the zero.)

I: Why did you put a zero there?

P: I usually do that so no number goes there.

I was moderately surprised at this. I thought at first that the writing of the zero might be an entirely blind procedure whose purpose he did not understand. But his remark indicated that he knew quite well that the zero's function was merely to fill up space.

Peter went on to indicate that he solved the problem by doing the conventional "short division" algorithm: 10 goes into 17 once with 7 left over, etc. He did all this in his head.

I: Let's try another one. Let's do $23 \overline{\smash{\big)}\ 4281}$. How do you say it?

P: Twenty-three divided by four thousand, two hundred and eighty-one. (Again he said it backwards, although in the previous case this did not affect his ability to solve the problem.)

I: Tell me what you are doing as you go along.

P: I'm saying, how many 23s goes into 4? Zero. Then I go to the second place. How many 23s in 42?

He wrote: 23 $\overline{)\,42^{19}81}^{\displaystyle 01}$

I: What are you writing down now?

P: (Pointing to the small 19.) That's how many are left over from 42.

Peter had subtracted 23 from 42 in his head and had got the correct answer, 19. He was using the short division method, so far correctly, on a problem for which long division should have been easier.

Now Peter needed to divide 23 into 198.

P: How many 23s in 198? Eleven. [Note that he said the problem more or less correctly this time.]

I: Eleven. How do you know there are 11?

Peter started to check. He did:

$$\begin{array}{r} 23 \\ \times\ 11 \\ \hline 23 \\ 23 \\ \hline 253 \end{array}$$

Then:

$$\begin{array}{r} 23 \\ \times\ 10 \\ \hline 00 \\ 23 \\ \hline 230 \end{array}$$

These guesses show that Peter lacks knowledge of a simple calculational fact: the missing number must always be less than 10.

After seeing that 11 and 10 did not work, he tried:

$$\begin{array}{r} 23 \\ \times\ \ 5 \\ \hline 115 \\ 23 \\ \hline 148 \end{array}$$

I: What did you do there? You got 115, right?

P: And I added 23 more to it, and it came out 148.

I: Why did you add 23?

P: To see how close I would get if I added another 23.

I: Why did you add? You were multiplying before.

P: Then I added 23 and it came out 148.

I: What is another way of getting 148?

P: By adding 23 times 6.

My interpretation of all this is that Peter knew the equivalence between multiplication and addition. He realized that adding 23 to 5 × 23 is the same as getting 6 × 23. He did the addition incorrectly, and he did not state his method very well (as when he said "by adding 23 times 6" when he meant "by multiplying 23 times 6"); yet he was able to see that multiplication is repeated addition.

The previous example was no fluke. He did:

$$
\begin{array}{r}
23 \\
\times\ \ 5 \\
\hline
115 \\
23 \\
\hline
148 \\
23 \\
\hline
171 \\
23 \\
\hline
184
\end{array}
$$

Also he checked his work by pointing to each of the successive sums and saying "six, seven, eight." In other words, he identified the sums for what they were, the equivalents of 6 × 23, 7 × 23, and 8 × 23.

Peter then completed the problem.

His solution seems rather interesting. On the one hand, he did so much of it in his head and was fairly successful. This is a lot of mental work to do, however unnecessary it may have been. On the other hand, his solution contains elements of inventiveness. When searching for the answer to 198 divided by 23, he converted the usual multiplication check into an addition check. Moreover, this was not simply a calculational routine: his counting of the sums indicated that he realized on a very explicit level that repeated addition can be interpreted as multiplication. Is this really so inventive? I am assuming of course that he was not taught to do this, and yet I have no evidence to support my assumption. However, I have shown this tape to many teachers and they were impressed too. At school children are usually taught to do things "by the book" so that any amount of inventiveness may be considered remarkable.

Next I gave Peter a series of problems involving divisors and dividends increasing by factors of 10. I encouraged him to guess, not to calculate the answers.

I: Let's start with this one; we're just guessing now.

$$1 \overline{\smash{\big)}\ 15}$$

(Peter wrote the correct answer immediately.)
I: Why is it 15?
P: Because there's 15 ones that go into 15.

Then I gave him 150 divided by 10, which he did correctly.

I asked him to guess again and wrote $10 \overline{\smash{\big)}\ 1{,}500}$. I was interested in finding out whether he understood the role of factors of 10.

But that was not Peter's concern. He wrote down

$$
\begin{array}{r}
100 \\
\times 10 \\
\hline
000 \\
100 \\
\hline
1{,}000
\end{array}
$$

then

$$
\begin{array}{r}
50 \\
\times 10 \\
\hline
00 \\
50 \\
\hline
500
\end{array}
$$

I did not realize why he was doing the two multiplications (10 × 100 and 10 × 50). In the hope that he would tell me why, I simply pointed out that he did them.

I: So you multiply here 100 times 10, and you get 1,000. And here you multiply 50 by 10 and you get 500. Right?
P: Yes.
I: But what do you think the answer will be up here [that is, what is the answer to the original problem, 1,500 divided by 10]?

$$
\begin{array}{r}
150 \\
10 \overline{\smash{\big)}\ 1{,}500}
\end{array}
$$

Peter wrote:
I: How do you know that?

P: Because there's a hundred tens in 1,000 and 50 tens in 500, so they make 150 altogether.

Again Peter had surprised me by inventing his own method of solution. The original problem was 1,500 divided by 10. But Peter transformed this into a new problem. He saw that 1,500 ÷ 10 is the same as the sum of 1,000 ÷ 10 and 50 ÷ 10. In other words:

$$\frac{1,500}{10} = \frac{1,000}{10} + \frac{500}{10}$$

This, of course, is a manifestation of the distributive law for division.

$$\frac{a + b}{c} = \frac{a}{c} + \frac{b}{c}$$

What Peter had done once again was to solve a routine computational problem by devising an idiosyncratic method based on sound mathematical principles. For him, computation was not simply a mechanical sequence of calculations; it was instead a problem to be solved by rational methods.

Peter had difficulty with estimation problems. I wrote down

$$5 \overline{\smash{\big)}\, 1242}$$

and said that I would give him a list of possible answers. His job was to guess—not calculate—which of the answers was most likely to be correct. The possibilities I gave him were 1,300; 1,000; 500; 200; and 100, in that order.

This could have been done by first rounding 1242 into 1200 and then dividing 5 into 1,200 or even 1,000. (Recall Jane's rounding procedure for addition.) But Peter simply could not do anything sensible with this problem. His first guess was 1,300—a number bigger than the dividend—and he never got the problem right.

That was the end of my first interview with Peter. He had worked hard for about forty minutes altogether (after a full day at school).

In the second interview, a week later, I gave Peter many problems of different types. One was a word problem:

I: Suppose you're the manager of the A & P [a food store]. Suppose there are five A & Ps in the city.

P: I'm the manager of all those A & Ps?

I: Yes. Suppose you get 210 bags of oranges in your warehouse and each bag of oranges has 20 oranges. And you want to give each store the same number of oranges—the same number of bags of oranges. OK? How many bags would you give to each store?

He wrote:

$$
\begin{array}{r}
042 \\
5\,\overline{)\,210\,}
\end{array}
$$

then:

$$
\begin{array}{r}
42 \\
\times\ \ 5 \\
\hline
210
\end{array}
$$

But he was not sure and asked me to repeat the problem again. I did, and finally asked, "How many bags would each store get?"

P: Forty-two.
I: Forty-two. What about the 20? You didn't do anything with the 20, the 20 oranges in a bag. How come you didn't do anything with that?

Of course his answer was correct and I knew it. I was deliberately misleading him to see if he could ignore an irrelevant part of the problem and resist an adult's suggestion. Piaget often uses such counter-suggestions to test the firmness of a child's conviction.

P: You didn't need to. You said there were 210 bags. The five stores are already to divide. Five stores into 210 bags.
I: What about the 20?
P: There's 20 oranges in a. . . . You want to know how many oranges, too?
I: No. just how many bags.

At this point Peter almost did some silly things. He wrote:

$$
\begin{array}{r}
42 \\
20 \\
\hline
62
\end{array}
$$

I asked, "What are you doing now? What would that give you, 62 bags? But he crossed it out and wrote instead:

$$
\begin{array}{r}
42 \\
20 \\
\hline
00 \\
84 \\
\hline
840
\end{array}
$$

He answered, "No. Eight hundred and forty oranges."

So Peter resisted the irrelevancy and me quite well. In fact, he converted the irrelevancy into a sensible problem and solved it.

What can we conclude from these examples of Peter's work? My claim is that Peter knows more mathematics than his teacher or the educational tests or the school system give him credit for. I do not maintain that Peter is brilliant or that he has learned as much mathematics as other seventh graders (many of whom begin algebra at this time) or as much as he himself could have learned under other conditions. I do claim, however, that Peter can do some interesting and even inventive mathematical work. His mathematical thought is basically sound, and he even has the courage to resist arbitrary adult authority. Moreover, Peter gives the impression of overall intelligence. Despite his low IQ score, he can be alert, bright, interested, and hard-working; he does not appear to be intellectually deficient.

As in the case of Jane, the test scores give very little insight into Peter's abilities. For example, the test shows him to have low computational ability. To some extent this is true. Peter makes many computational errors and often does not produce the correct answer. At the same time, the test is uninformative and superficial. It is uninformative because it fails to give detailed information on the strategies Peter uses for the solution of computational problems. It is superficial because it fails to reflect his genuine computational skills (for example, his use of repeated addition to do multiplication).

CONCLUSIONS

We have seen that the traditional school is incorrect in its vital assumption that standard tests provide an accurate assessment of children's knowledge. The tests fail to do this for several reasons. One is that their conception of knowledge—in terms of simple, quantitative traits—is incorrect. Cognitive theory shows that knowledge is complex and cannot be conceptualized in the manner of standard tests. Case studies of individual children demonstrate this complexity. A second reason for standard tests' failure is their use of rigid methods of administration. Cognitive theory shows that this is not a sound method in general, and several studies demonstrate that it is especially inappropriate for poor children in particular. A third reason is the standard tests' failure to provide information on those mental operations which result in correct or incorrect responses. A glance at standard tests shows that their level of description is very global. And case studies confirm that children in fact use complex forms of reasoning to do mathematics. Fourth, standard tests fail because they are superficial. Case studies show that standard tests give a poor impression of what children can do and ignore some of their most interesting intellectual activities.

It would appear then that traditional forms of testing do not give an accurate indication of children's knowledge. Traditional education's basic criteria for success and failure are seriously deficient, so that it is hard to know where illusion leaves off and reality begins.

Such a situation makes it very difficult to institute effective innovations in traditional schools. How can you know whether a new text or a new curriculum is superior to another if you have poor ways of conceptualizing and measuring what children learn and understand? Similarly, how can you help a child—middle or lower class—if you have a poor appreciation of his difficulties? One example of this difficulty is Peter's experience. On the basis of standard tests he was placed in the lowest track in school; the teacher thought that his work was at best "satisfactory"; he was forced to repeat a grade because of his low achievement; and no one in his school had any real idea of how to help him. Such occurrences are far from atypical, and standard tests must assume a large part of the blame for them.

In short, successful education requires a sound conception of children's knowledge. Lacking that conception, traditional schools or innovations within them can achieve only a limited degree of success.

Children's Learning

Traditional schools cannot be extremely successful because their practices are based, at least implicitly, on faulty conceptions of the ways in which children learn.

Here are some of the conceptions and the related practices.

The first assumption refers to the passivity of the child's learning. In the traditional classroom, the teacher is clearly the dominating force. He determines the content of the curriculum, the order in which various topics are to be studied, the manner in which problems are to be solved, the time at which various matters are to be dealt with, and so forth. All of these practices imply certain beliefs—overt or covert—about the child and the ways in which he learns. The teacher's determination of the curriculum content implies that the child is not motivated to study important subjects. The teacher imposes an order in which topics are to be considered; this is based on a belief that learning must be orderly and that the child cannot organize his own learning in a coherent fashion. The teacher's determination of methods for solving problems suggests that there are proper solutions and that the child could not himself devise them or develop reasonable alternatives. The teacher even decides when learning is to take place; the assumptions must be that the child ordinarily wastes time or cannot organize his learning efficiently. In sum, traditional practices see the child as a passive being who cannot take a major part in organizing his own learning; he must be directed, organized, controlled, motivated, and managed in order for learning to occur.

The second assumption refers to the media for learning. In traditional classrooms, the chief devices for learning are the textbook and the lecture. From the earliest days of school, children are given texts to read, and from them must learn mathematics, history, geography, and all the rest. School is largely a place to read, and when the child is not reading, he is listening to the teacher talk. This of course implies a belief that children's learning proceeds best through books and similar verbal activities. In this view, the aim of education is to impart adult, verbal knowledge. The practice implies a disbelief in the proposition that children learn through exploration of objects, through manipulation of things, and through other concrete activities.

The third assumption refers to learning in the group. In the traditional classroom, all children proceed through the curriculum at roughly the same pace. In a group, they read the text together, do the problems together, and listen to the teacher's lectures together. The assumption underlying these practices must be that all of the children at a given age level can be motivated to learn the same things at the same times and in the same ways.

The fourth assumption refers to social interaction. In the traditional classroom, children are usually required to sit in a specified place and are not allowed to engage in free interaction with their peers. The teacher dominates the social process, and it is only by his permission that interaction among children can take place. Silence is good and talking is bad. The assumption behind these practices is that learning is facilitated by silence and that spontaneous conversation disrupts intellectual activity. Further, if children were allowed to interact normally with their peers, the main result would be play or chaos, not serious academic work.

These then are some traditional practices and assumptions underlying them. In discussing the assumptions, there are at least two dangers. One is to exaggerate the extent to which traditional schools partake of these characteristics. As I mentioned earlier, there is no such thing as the traditional school; instead schools employ many different practices, each of which may be traditional in some degree. Consequently, it would be unusual to find a school whose practices fully embody all of the assumptions described. A few such caricatures of traditional education may exist, but most schools do not employ techniques which are so clear-cut.

The second danger is the reverse of the first: it is the tendency to underestimate the pervasiveness of traditional practices and assumptions. While few schools are traditional in all respects, the assumptions of traditional education are nevertheless highly influential. This is sometimes true even when the school's or teacher's official rhetoric is nontraditional. For example, Dianne Gwynne, a Cornell undergraduate, reports that in one local school the teacher maintained that her class was modeled after the British Infant School system. The children were allowed to work at tables scattered about the room instead of desks all facing the teacher; there were periods of free activity, and so on. While the expressed ideology was nontraditional, classroom practice was in fact based on traditional principles. The teacher continued to lecture at the blackboard and the students were required to listen (sitting of course at tables, not desks). The students were assigned seats at the tables and were not allowed to initiate their own work. The "free activity" comprised only the last 10 minutes of the day, and the children used it only to line up at the door so that they could leave as soon as the bell rang. In my experience, situations like these are not at all uncommon: the correlation between a school's stated beliefs and its actual practices is rather low.

In brief, we must attempt to avoid two misleading interpretations of the schools: one is that they are caricatures of traditional education; the other is that they are as nontraditional as they say they are. Granted all this, we shall now examine the various assumptions.

THE CHILD AS PASSIVE LEARNER

Is the child a passive learner, as the traditional system assumes? Of course, I grant from the outset that the poor child—indeed, every child—does learn in a passive manner in the traditional school. There he is apathetic, shows little interest or initiative, cannot organize his own learning, and so forth. The assumption of passivity seems to be an accurate description of children in traditional schools. But the real question is not how children ordinarily behave in traditional schools; it is whether they are *necessarily* passive. Do poor children learn in a passive way outside the context of the traditional school?

Several lines of evidence are relevant to this issue. First, we have seen, particularly in Chapter 5, that all children, regardless of social class, display considerable activity, curiosity, and initiative in acquiring the cognitive universals. All children take an active role in learning language, in acquiring the sensorimotor schemes, and the like. These cognitive activities are not taught by parents or otherwise imposed by the environment; the child controls much of this learning himself. So in the natural environment, the poor child can be an active learner.

Second, informal observation suggests that in poor children this type of learning is not limited to the cognitive universals. The poor child develops in a distinctive environment which poses unique difficulties and demands, and he somehow learns to meet these challenges, again largely without the benefit of adult instruction. For example, part of Labov's work describes the gang culture to which some youths in Harlem must learn to adapt. Youths in this situation must learn the gang's style of speech, its verbal culture, and its values. They must also learn to steal, to fight, and to survive in a hostile environment. To suppose that a passive, apathetic child can master all of these difficulties is incredible. If he behaved on the streets as he does in the traditional school, the poor child's chances of surviving his environment would be very minute indeed. Adaptation to his natural environment requires the poor child to be active, curious, energetic, cunning, and all the rest.

Third, there is evidence that in poor children active learning need not be limited to nonacademic subjects (the cognitive universals or the requirements of the lower-class environment). Several educational experiments show that in nontraditional classrooms poor chidren can be genuine intellectuals. As we have seen, Kohl's work demonstrates that under certain conditions poor children can manifest an active interest in literature, in art, in writing, in science, and in all the other activities which schools typically emphasize. It is worth noting that Kohl's experience is not the only one. Koch (1970) has shown that poor children can create interesting and expressive forms of poetry. Ashton-Warner (1963) has found that "primitive" Maori children in New Zealand can take the initiative in learning to read. Dennison (1969) has found that poor children with extreme emotional difficulties can nevertheless learn in active and impressive ways. Robert Davis, director of the Madison Project, has documented on film ghetto children's learning and invention of interesting and complex mathematics. It is certain, then, that poor children can be active learners in school.

EDUCATION AS READING AND LISTENING

Does the poor child learn best through reading and listening to lectures, as the traditional school believes? Again, several lines of evidence are relevant to the issue, and the first concerns children in general. We have seen in Chapter 4 that young children's thought is often nonverbal, depending little on language for its work. The linguistic determinism of Bernstein receives little support from theorists like Piaget or Lenneberg. In many respects, young children seem to learn best from interaction with the world of objects and events. Children develop nonverbal intellectual processes to cope with the environment and often cannot put into words a good portion of their knowledge. This is not to deny, of course, that young children talk and that they can express themselves quite well in a number of areas. The proposition is, rather, that one major form of learning in young children involves the exploration of objects and events and that much of young children's thought is nonverbal. In Piaget's view, it is not until adolescence that verbal processes come to have a major role in learning and thought. In any event, it is clear that in the natural environment the child does not learn primarily through reading and listening.

Second, it seems to be the case that a strong emphasis on reading and lecturing is particularly unsuited to poor children. We saw in Chapter 3 that poor children may speak a dialect that, while not deficient, is often different from the teacher's. Under these circumstances, it seems unwise to base a good part of the educational process on the teacher's language. Even though poor children have an adequate understanding of Standard English, they must find it somewhat unfamiliar, and perhaps its extensive use makes them feel uncomfortable or out of their element. Perhaps too the emphasis on lectures in an unfamiliar dialect makes poor children feel that school is a place where one does strange things in a strange form of speech; school does not really belong to them.

GROUP LEARNING

Can children at the same age level be interested in the same topics and learn them at the same time? The answer is no, and almost every theory in psychology agrees that it is no. For example, Piaget has shown that while all children acquire the cognitive universals, the rate of learning differs from child to child and from culture to culture. The Skinnerians emphasize that children's learning histories differ from one another, so that what is reinforcing for one child may not be for another, and so that what interests one child may not interest another. The most superficial observation should suffice to show that children of the same age have widely divergent interests, learn at different rates, and can resist learning when not interested. The results of both ordinary observation and scientific evidence point to the obvious conclusion that children must receive some form of individualized learning experiences.

This proposition seems to hold with special force in the case of poor children. They are in some respects different from middle-class children. To some extent, they come from different backgrounds, have different interests, hold different values, and even possess different intellectual abilities. Given all this, it makes no sense to force poor children to study the same topics in the same ways and at the same times as middle-class children. Like anyone else, the poor child is unique, so that group learning cannot adequately serve his needs.

SOCIAL INTERACTION

The traditional classroom attempts to restrain spontaneous social interaction among students. Is this conducive to genuine learning? There is no doubt that such practices are necessary within the context of traditional schools. In this setting children do not know how to make use of free time and indeed increasingly display propensities toward violence. Yet this is all irrelevant to the real issue. In the natural environment, or in nontraditional schools, does spontaneous social interaction promote learning?

Some of Piaget's observations, which we have not reviewed in this book, suggest that children may learn a good deal from spontaneous discussion, argument, and conflict (see Ginsburg and Opper, 1969, chapter 3). The young child acquires some of his beliefs and values from the narrow confines of the family. His natural egocentrism endows these beliefs and values with an authority and certainty that they do not deserve. As the child enters school and expands his contacts with peers, his narrow beliefs are challenged and subjected to the criticisms of other points of view. Conflict of this type helps the child to abandon his egocentrism and to appreciate alternative perspectives.

Labov has found that the peer group can foster and propagate a rich verbal culture. The gang is a miniature society, governed by its own laws, traditions, and culture. One of the functions of the society is to preserve and strengthen the verbal culture. Labov shows that through spontaneous interaction gang members teach each other the values and content of the culture, practice its main forms, and stimulate the creation of new cultural products. It appears then that spontaneous social interaction among peers can have beneficial effects on cognitive development in general and on the maintenance of a viable lower-class peer culture in particular.

Other observations show that peer interaction has an important place in the nontraditional classroom as well. Many of Kohl's observations show that significant intellectual activity originated in the peer group. For example, an argument about the meaning of certain words led to excursions into etymology and later into literary activity of many types. In Kohl's class children often debated and argued and disagreed, and these conflicts contributed in no small way to the stimulation of the class. Kohl's students were often noisy and sometimes disruptive and hostile. But behavior of this type did not put an end to learning. Children can do significant work in what may appear to the adult to be chaotic conditions.

Conclusions

Traditional schools are based on wrong assumptions concerning children's knowledge and learning. As a result, such schools can achieve little success, especially with poor children. As a result, too, innovations within the framework of traditional education are apt to produce only minor improvements when a revolution is called for.

Furthermore, there are signs that the traditional system, even when apparently successful by conventional criteria, involves severe costs that are usually not considered by its advocates. It is increasingly evident that a large portion of students who have achieved success in the system is nevertheless alienated by its practices and values. Miriam Wasserman (1970), in a superb book on the New York schools, presents a teen-ager's feelings about her education, and they seem typical:

. . . The whole purpose of education it sounds like to me is, in elementary school to get into a good junior high school, and then from high school . . . the whole big ultimate thing is for college. And why you are going to college nobody really knows, except the implication is it's probably to get a good job, but everybody is ashamed to say that, so they vaguely pretend it's because you want to become an educated person. But very few people believe that. . . . School prepares you to go into a society and to expect to dislike most of the things that you are going to be doing in your life. . . . It seems as if the whole thing is just one big preparation for nothing (p. 427).

The problem, then, is not just reforming poor children's education. We must be concerned about the spirit and values and intellectual life of children who make it in the system.

We need a fresh start. We require a system of education based on assumptions and values more valid than those held by traditional education. Fortunately, many teachers are beginning to see the need for fundamental change. They use the rhetoric of the open school, sense its validity, and are looking for ways to embody it.

OPEN SCHOOLS

A third approach toward educational reform is the open classroom. In this section I show that it is not a fixed set of practices, but a collection of principles whose aim is to make education responsive to children's needs. The open classroom, which is not a new idea, is constantly in a process of formation. It is not a final solution to the problems of poor children or anyone else: the open classroom is always changing, always attempting to assume a form relevant to the situation of the moment. The open classroom offers hope because it attempts to be guided by principles that psychology shows are basically sound. Moreover, it is an extremely flexible and experimental form of education which can even assimilate the best that traditional schools have to offer. Nevertheless, the open classroom suffers from several weaknesses which must be overcome. For example, it has not yet found satisfactory methods for assessing children's knowledge. Despite this, the open school represents an experiment worth pursuing; it may be able to provide a humane education for all children.

What Is the Open Classroom?

The open classroom is not a new idea. In Great Britain, open classrooms have been in operation for some twenty or thirty years. Their inspiration is perhaps derived from the work of John Dewey.[2] But even before Dewey there were open classrooms in the United States. Cremins (1961) reports that in the 1870s Francis Parker operated a school which seems to have been quite similar to what is currently being attempted in Great Britain.

THE ATMOSPHERE OF THE OPEN CLASSROOM

On my visit to Ithaca's East Hill School, most of whose students are middle class, I went first to the Block Room, a class mainly for first and second graders. It is an old room, with hardwood floor, high ceiling, even a brick fireplace. There are only a few moveable desks, usually unused and stored on the sides. In one quadrant of the room is the reading area with an old rug on the floor and a few easy chairs. On another side is a fairly large table with books scattered on it and children's chairs lining the sides. On other tables, large and small, there are books for reading (no primers, but Dr. Seuss and others), papers, workbooks, a phonograph and records, textbooks, crayons, and other odds and ends. On the walls are collages, paintings, the letters in upper and lower case, pictures of snakes and lizards, and a large sign saying "The bug club." Although the room is old, it is not dismal, decrepit, or forbidding. The overall impression is of warmth, a very homelike atmosphere.

When I arrived, there were only eight children in the room. One of the teachers was doing reading with two children. They pointed to words in a book, read what they could, and she helped, emphasizing the patterns of letter-sound correspondence. In one corner a boy was listening to the phonograph through earphones: he swayed a little and moved his arms apparently in rhythm with the music. At the largest table five girls were engaged in various kinds of work. Three were coloring on dittoed worksheets which specified particular areas for certain colors. One girl was watching, and another worked at addition problems in a textbook. She was trying to add three digit numbers and was making a consistent error:

$$483$$
$$232$$
$$\overline{6115}$$

As the girls colored at the table, they talked about what they were doing. They said that brown goes here and yes this one really is brown and that one really isn't even if it does look a little like brown and look how the

---

[2] Summerhill plays a minor role in the British Infant School movement. Neill, its founder, seems to have experimented mainly with the social side of education, not with the intellectual. Summerhill's classrooms are in fact dull and traditional. By contrast, the Infant Schools are not preoccupied with social development, but with intellectual ability.

different worksheets look the same except for Jenny's who scribbled. The girl doing addition ignored all the talk and continued doing her problems, occasionally muttering to herself.

The boy at the phonograph looked up and asked the teacher if she had brought in the Beatles record and she said she hadn't.

Children came in and out. One girl left to go to the library. She did not bother to ask or inform the teacher. A boy returned from the shop; he was carrying a wooden construction that looked something like a cart. Another child went to the art room. A boy came back from visiting his sister in the third grade.

The "principal"—really the head teacher—came in to get a book; several children trailed him, and they left in a minute or so.

There are no intercoms.

Everyone dresses quite casually. The children sometimes take their shoes off. The teachers wear jeans or whatever is comfortable.

The children publish a newspaper at East Hill School. Some of it is typed, some hand-written. Here are a few things from Volume I, No. 24, June 12, 1970. The second page has articles describing some experiments. "Everyone knows that you can burn paper with a magnifying glass. Does it take more light to burn black or white or yellow or red paper? This is how we found out. . . ."

Another article is titled "What color of light do plants like best?" At the bottom of the page is this message: "I LIKE FORTS BECAUSE THERE KIND'A PRIVATE AND SOMETIMES YE' HAFTA SAY SOMETHING YE' CAN'T SAY OUT IN THE ROOM."

Page 4 contains a short article and some photographs describing a plane trip some children and their teacher took over Ithaca. The city looks different from up there.

There are short stories and advertisements from local businesses. The little children write very short accounts: "We went fishing at six mile creek."

Page 8 gives a report of a trip to the Paleontological Research Institute which, we are informed, has "dinosaur bones, sharks' teeth, fossils, mammoth teeth, and a trilobite."

If you want to know Don Buford's (outfielder, Baltimore Orioles?) batting average, it is on page 12.

There is a map of the United States showing where everyone is going to visit during the summer.

My favorite page is 17. It describes some trips:

"15 of us went to City Court from 9:00 to 11:00. We sat like pigeons in a tar pit. It was very boring. 5 people tickets, 1 stealing bread roll bread and so on."

Another trip was to a local elementary school:

"They have a system like ours only more structured. . . . They had a Learning Center with many things in it. It was very well equipped. But some of the grades had teachers who preferred the traditional school, and so they had regular classrooms. But most of it was real nice."

The second classroom I visited that day was also for first and second graders (roughly, of course). The room was somewhat small and about 12 or 13 children were in it at the time. In one corner of the room two children and a teacher—a male college student—were engaged in building a large toy house, about 4 feet high, from wood, heavy cardboard, and the like. At the time, they were installing the light fixtures, with real wire and sockets, so that house building had naturally become an exercise in electricity. At one large table, a girl was doing problems in a mathematics book. In another corner of the room, there was a rug, a large couch, and small tables with books. Two girls, sitting on the couch, were playing with balls of yarn. Another teacher, a young woman, was lying on the rug and two girls were massaging her back.

At a second large table were six or seven children. One boy, sitting on the middle of the table, constructed an intricate pattern with large triangular blocks. Another boy, seated on a chair, was involved in much the same sort of activity. A girl was completing exercises in a reading and writing workbook. She neatly printed the missing word in sentences like "This is a _____."

A child put a record on the phonograph.

Another teacher sat at a large table and worked with two children on their reading. She pointed at words, asked the children to say them, showed how to sound certain letters. Another child ran around the room looking through a large tube.

When the male teacher finished the house, he came over to the table and worked with the girl for a few minutes on her mathematics. He tried to explain what the textbook exercises involved—for example, circling the objects which belonged in one set but not another.

The children call some teachers by their first name but not others.

The fireplace in this room is bricked up. The children painted grafitti on it—names, slogans, pictures, peace signs.

LEARNING IN THE OPEN CLASSROOM

On first glance, the open classroom may seem somewhat chaotic. The children move in and out of rooms; there is a fair amount of noise; and one wonders whether the children are involved in serious intellectual work of any type. The apparent disorganization of the open classroom is in stark contrast to the orderliness of the traditional school where children looking at books or listening to the teacher at least seem to be attempting to learn something. There is certainly a difference in style between the two types of education. Yet in evaluating each, one must look beneath the surface.

Does serious learning take place in the atmosphere of the open school? Here are a few examples:

In East Hill School, a group of first and second graders became interested in bugs. With the teacher's assistance, they formed the bug club, and for months they pursued the topic on an irregular basis. They read about bugs, collected them, examined them, and so forth.

One young girl became interested in songs played on the phonograph. The teacher suggested that she copy the songs in a notebook. The girl spent many days doing this, and the songbook became her chief method for learning to read.

In the open classroom, children pursue reading in many ways. Some children do workbook exercises over a long period of time. Some ask adults or older children to read to them. Some attempt to escape the commotion— for example, by hiding under a table or in the fireplace—in order to read books of various types. Some children spend a good part of each day reading, and others may ignore it for a long stretch of time.

In the area of mathematics, some children regularly work with a teacher on the Cuisenaire rods. Others use a conventional workbook.

A group of older children, led by a Cornell mathematician, Robert Speiser, spent many hours constructing a two-dimensional model of a city.

East Hill students can study Chinese, Russian, and other foreign languages.

In many open schools, writing is a major activity. Children keep diaries, write stories, novels, poetry, and reports of scientific experiments.

In brief, the open school seems to foster a good deal of serious and creative work. But it is done in an informal manner, not according to a rigid schedule. This should not appear at all unusual or unorthodox. The open classroom is to some extent similar to children's natural environment. While neither is extensively programmed or managed, both promote genuine learning.

ADDITIONAL FEATURES OF OPEN CLASSROOMS

The open school is a complex system, sometimes misunderstood. Several of its features are worth emphasizing.

Open schools are not monolithic. There is no fixed set of practices which define the open school. The open school takes many forms, and its advocates sometimes disagree among themselves as to what these should be.

Moreover, schools may be said to be governed by open classroom principles in varying degrees and in different areas. Some schools attempt to follow the principles in some practices but not others; some schools embody the principles more fully than do others.

Open schools are in a constant state of flux and are always groping for new forms. An activity that is successful one year may be abandoned the next because it does not seem to meet the needs of a new group of children. The open school is as unpredictable as the children in it, and it does not represent a final solution.

The open school is a community. Children do not just attend a classroom, or series of classrooms, but a school. They visit friends in other rooms, ask other teachers to help, decide some issues as a school. The school as a whole belongs to them: they go where they want to go and use what they need to use. I think that there is probably an optimal size for open schools. East Hill has about 175 students. It is possible to get to know almost everyone there. I find it hard to believe that this kind of community can be maintained in a school of, say, 500 children.

The open school operates under an informal and relaxed social code. Children can talk without permission, can go places when they wish, do not raise their hands, are not artificially polite to teachers. Under these circumstances, there prevails an atmosphere in which children can work. The level of "noise" is higher than in traditional schools, but it does not prevent children from concentrating on what they are doing. In this atmosphere, children impose discipline on themselves. The lack of arbitrary adult authority helps to foster self-discipline and does not have as its inevitable result the burning of desks and slitting of throats.

The open school is "free" and "structured" at the same time. Take the case of reading in the early grades. The teacher has in mind some general "goals"—he would like the children to accomplish something in reading or writing. The teacher tries out certain techniques for attaining these goals. He may have observed in the past that several activities foster reading—having books around the room and reading to children and allowing them to write and putting them in contact with older children who already read, and so on. All this is a "structure" which the teacher provides. Yet at the same time the child is "free." If for some reason he has no interest in reading, even for a few years, many teachers in open schools will let him be. They may attempt to provide new structures, but they will seldom if ever sit him down and force him to read every day from 9 to 10.

Open school teachers are quite eclectic in their use of methods and materials. The open classroom may contain standard textbooks, workbooks, scientific apparatus, mathematical games, live animals, and anything else that may help children learn. It may contain apparently contradictory materials:

phonics reading texts along with traditional primers; mathematical games along with new math textbooks. There is no orthodox set of materials for the open classroom, and the teacher will use anything that he thinks can help. At times this may result in expropriating some traditional materials and techniques. For example, a child studying a foreign language may require some drill in vocabulary. One efficient way of doing this is to use a workbook or a programmed learning machine, or the like. Some aspects of learning are necessarily tedious and mechanical, and the traditional approach may help since it seems to specialize in activities of this type.

The open classroom approach makes some use of educational technology but is not dominated by it. The guiding assumption is that teaching machines, computer-assisted instruction, audio-visual materials, television, and other forms of technology may serve a useful purpose but should not comprise the entirety of educational practice. Generally speaking these devices are highly structured techniques. For example, a learning machine presents the material in one order and in one order only, defines some answers as correct and others as incorrect, and can respond in only limited ways to the unique requirements of each student. This is a narrow and rigid form of education. At the same time such devices can be valuable for at least two reasons. One is that they make tedious learning a little more efficient and a little less dull. The other is that they permit some degree of individualization; the child can work at the teaching machine by himself when he wants to. So educational technology may be useful for some aspects of learning. Nevertheless, it is usually unable to foster the more creative and spontaneous forms of intellectual work and therefore has only a limited role in the open school.

The open school is concerned with some of the basic content of the traditional curriculum, but in addition it does a great deal more. It is absurd to think of a rigid curriculum in connection with the open school. It does not operate under a plan such that in the fourth week of school children at the fifth grade level must be studying Chapter 4 of some textbook. At the same time teachers in open schools have general goals. They want children to learn something of reading, writing, and arithmetic. And in open schools children work hard at these activities. But there is a good deal of time left over for other things as well. Children in open schools often have the opportunity to read interesting novels, to explore various topics in mathematics, to develop their abilities in art and music, and to pursue a variety of unconventional topics which usually do not have a home in school.

Open school techniques are most highly developed for the early grades of school. In Great Britain, for example, open classrooms were first implemented on a large scale in the Infant Schools (equivalent to approximately the first three grades of American elementary schools) and were only later extended to higher grades. No doubt, at the older age levels open schools must take different forms, but what these are is as yet quite uncertain.

Psychological Principles

At the most general level, open schools attempt to make education responsive to the child's cognitive abilities, spontaneous interests, and natural style of learning. To do this, it is necessary to have a psychology of the child. This psychology is sometimes implicit, sometimes crudely formulated, and sometimes eloquently described. Open schools picture the child as a natural intellectual who in his ordinary environment is engaged in an active search for meaning, sense, and beauty.

ADULTS AND CHILDREN

In the open school view, one must begin with a very simple proposition: children are different from adults; the former are not simply miniature, but less wise, versions of the latter. Children are individuals who have distinctive interests, cognitive abilities, and approaches to learning. They are qualitatively different from adults and require unique learning experiences.

This proposition is in agreement with the findings of modern cognitive theory, particularly Piaget's. As we saw in Chapter 4, Piaget's theory shows that the child progresses through a series of cognitive stages, each different from and more complex than the one preceding. At each point in cognitive development, the child's mental structure is qualitatively different from the adult's, and he views the world from a unique perspective. For example in the case of number, the young child, although able to count to 20 or more, has no conception of certain fundamental mathematical ideas: he does not conceive of number in the same way as does an adult. He may believe that a set of five elements contains more than a set of nine, if only the physical arrangement takes a certain form.

If the child's thought is different from the adult's, the educator must make a special effort to understand the unique properties of the child's experiences and to adapt education to them. This the open school tries to do. It tries to develop sensitivity—a willingness to learn from the child, to look closely at his actions, and to avoid the assumption that what is appropriate for the adult is necessarily so for the child. The open school tries to discover the perspective of the child and to construct education around it. For these purposes, an informal interaction with the child is required; in general, standard tests are not sensitive to these matters.

CONCRETE ACTIVITY

The open school assumes that the child is active and that in the early years this activity takes a predominantly concrete form. The child is intrinsically motivated to learn; he is a source of energy in initiating many activities; he seeks contact with and understanding of the world; and he is deeply involved in the self-directed exploration of objects and the development of new modes of thinking.

For all these reasons, a good open school should encourage the child's activity, his manipulation and exploration of objects. When the teacher tries to bypass this process by imparting adult knowledge in a verbal manner, the result is often superficial learning. But by promoting activity in the classroom —by providing for the child a wide variety of potentially interesting materials on which he may act—the teacher can exploit the child's potential for learning and permit him to evolve an understanding of the world.

Again the open school view is consonant with the findings of cognitive psychology. As we saw in Chapters 4 and 5, Piaget's theory proposes that the child is an active organism who initiates contact with the environment. From self-directed interaction with his world—interaction that is at first concrete—he develops a succession of cognitive structures. Similarly, in Lenneberg's view, the child is the source of energy for his own development. He is not simply moulded by environmental forces, but uses available stimulation to form his own adaptation to reality.

INDIVIDUAL DIFFERENCES

The open school assumes that children at the same age level often differ from one another in many ways and therefore require correspondingly different learning experiences. Even though young children generally learn best through concrete interaction with the world, this kind of activity must take different particular forms with different children. Even though children share many of the same cognitive abilities—the universals—they also vary in their interests, in their pace of learning, and in the times at which they become involved in various activities.

As a result, the classroom must be oriented more toward the individual than the group. Since there are individual differences in almost all areas of cognitive development, it is unlikely that any one task or lesson will arouse the interest of or promote learning in all members of the class. Further, children must be given considerable control over their own learning. Some may need more time than others to deal with the same material; some may approach the same problem differently from others.

Again, this proposition is in agreement with almost all psychological theories. For example, even though Piaget's main emphasis is on the similarities among children (at a given point in development), he frequently points out the fact of individual differences in the rate of cognitive development and in its concrete manifestations.

SOCIAL INTERACTION

The open school assumes that spontaneous social interaction is useful for children's intellectual growth. Physical experience and concrete manipulation are not the only ways in which the child learns. Another type of experience leading to understanding of the world is social—the interaction with peers and adults. Children stimulate each other's interests, argue, learn from one another, and learn about one another.

For these reasons, social interaction should play a major role in the classroom. Children should converse, share experience, and in general feel free to act as children with one another. As some noted authorities have maintained, "Let us restrict the vow of silence to selected orders of monks and nuns."

The relation between social interaction and learning has not been extensively investigated in psychology. As I mentioned earlier, Piaget's theory has devoted some attention to this issue. He has proposed that social interaction promotes healthy conflict which in turn leads to the abandonment of egocentrism. Spontaneous social contact, especially with peers, leads the child to realize that his view of the world may not be generally accepted; others do not necessarily share his opinions and are not as tolerant of his inconsistencies as he is himself. Experiences like these may force the child to clarify his opinions and thought.

THE DELICATE MANEUVER

Given these views—views that are obviously in radical opposition to those of traditional education—the open school attempts to make the educational process responsive to the nature of the child. The open school is a delicate maneuver in designing educational experiences relevant to the lives of individual children. This approach attempts to identify the child's interests and abilities, to stimulate them, and to provide opportunities for their expansion. Since children have diverse interests, these must be nourished in diverse ways. The open school therefore assumes many forms—forms that are hopefully responsive to children's needs—and continually experiments with new ones. It attempts to provide for children the experiences that are appropriate to their current needs.

This requires a teacher with the utmost sensitivity and skill. He must first achieve an accurate perception of the child's interests and abilities and must then have the wit, often on the spur of the moment, to provide the necessary experiences, materials, and opportunities. To accomplish this, the teacher must be open to almost any form of method or device. Sometimes the child needs the opportunity to engage in an independent exploration of objects; at other times, he needs to study highly structured materials; at other times still, he needs to work in close collaboration with his teacher. The open school does not rule out any forms of educational experience; instead it seeks to make their use contingent on the requirements of the child.

In the open school, there is a sharing of power between teacher and student. There is a mutual influence, a reciprocity of responsiveness. The teacher "controls" the child by providing an environment responsive to his needs; the teacher is "controlled" by the child since the former attempts to adapt to the latter; the child "controls" his own learning when he makes use of an opportunity provided by the teacher. Teaching in the open school is one of the most difficult jobs imaginable.

The Deficiencies of Open Schools

Open schools are an experiment which is still in progress. They have many difficulties yet to overcome, and I do not wish to minimize them.

One is the problem of assessing the child's knowledge. The open school needs accurate methods for determining what children know; without them, it is difficult to devise educational experiences relevant for individual children's needs, and it is also difficult to evaluate a teacher's or a school's general level of accomplishment. Unfortunately the major form of assessment—standardized testing—used in many schools is severely deficient on many counts which I have already described and do not therefore need to repeat here. But what forms of assessment shall replace standard tests? In the open school, teachers rely a good deal on informal interaction with children to get an idea of their current level of intellectual functioning. This is highly desirable, but not sufficient. For one thing, some teachers may not be as sensitive in such situations as they should and therefore need assistance of some type. I think myself that teachers can benefit from training in the clinical interview technique of Piaget and in naturalistic observation. But both these possibilities need to be worked out.

A second difficulty is that it is hard for a teacher to keep track of everything that is happening in an open school. In this environment, children are engaged in many different activities, often in different rooms. The teacher obviously needs to know what his students are up to so that he can gauge what needs to be done in the future. Yet the activities are so varied and numerous that it is hard to be aware of all of them.

A third difficulty is that many of the open school's techniques are too private and hard to communicate. Teachers in open schools use many complex methods for stimulating and satisfying students' interests. Yet there is sometimes a mystery as to what these methods are or how they work. While open schools have developed an often effective "practitioner's knowledge" of education, it is often implicit, nonverbal, idiosyncratic, and difficult to describe. But if open schools are to acquire wide-spread influence, they must attempt to rationalize their techniques, to make them more public.

A fourth difficulty involves developing open schools appropriate for older children. In general open schools have been most effective for children up to the age of about 12. In Great Britain, for example, the open school movement has achieved considerable success in the case of children from about 5 to 8 years of age, and is beginning to be effective for children from about 9 to 12 years. But after this point, it is not clear what forms open schools should take. A good deal of education still requires reform, from junior high school through the universities.

A fifth difficulty is in a way not the open school's, but the larger community's. The open school is a way of life based on values of freedom. In some instances there develops a clash between the values of the community and those of the open school. Some individuals resent, for example, the open school's lack of emphasis on adult authority and the traditional virtues of obedience. These people see the open school as a threat to their way of life. I think that there is some truth to their fears. But they must decide which they cherish more—some abstract and perhaps outmoded principles or humane education for children.

In conclusion, the open school is imperfect and has many difficulties to overcome. Fortunately, many educators and psychologists have begun to acquire an interest in this form of education, so that over a period of time, the open school's shortcomings may be remedied.

Open Schools for Poor Children

We need to experiment with open schools for poor children. There are several reasons.

First, open schools are based on sound psychological assumptions whereas other approaches to reform—compensatory and traditional education —are not. Open schools recognize that the child is an active and natural intellectual and can, therefore, attempt the delicate maneuver of accommodating education to his interests and needs. Compensatory education incorrectly assumes massive intellectual deficit in the poor child and is therefore engaged in a futile attempt to remedy a deficiency that is more imaginary than real. Traditional education misunderstands the nature of knowledge and the ways in which children learn and consequently is bound to achieve only a limited degree of success.

Second, open schools maintain an optimistic view of the poor child. On the one hand, they recognize his intellectual strengths and potentialities, and this very recognition helps to foster them. On the other hand, open schools do not fall into the trap of creating intellectual deficiencies by assuming them in the first place.

Third, open schools attempt to assist the poor child in developing his own potentialities. They recognize that he has much to draw on and much to contribute[3] and that he must develop in a way that is distinctive. Open schools do not attempt to impose on the poor child middle-class styles, standards, and values. This is as self-defeating as the assumption of intellectual deficit.

Fourth, open schools are innovative and flexible. They value the attempt to explore all the possibilities, however unorthodox they may be. Open schools are not limited by narrow conceptions of education and by conventional restraints on experimentation.

Finally, we know that open schools can work quite brilliantly. There is now a considerable amount of informal evidence to this effect. One cannot help but be impressed by reports like those of Kohl (1967), Herndon (1968), and others who have had intimate contact with poor children in open classrooms. Moreover, there is now beginning to emerge some more formal evidence concerning the effectiveness of the open classroom in educating poor children. In chapter 5, I cited the results of the Ginsburg, Wheeler, and Tulis study. Silberman (1970) documents several cases of highly successful open schools: Chicago's CAM academy (pp. 95–96); Harlem Prep (pp. 96–97); Public Schools 129, 192, and 146 in Harlem (pp. 99–100, 112); Public School 123 in Harlem (pp. 298–306); several Tucson, Arizona schools (pp. 311–18); and many others. Silberman shows that when standard test scores are available, they usually demonstrate that children in schools like these perform at least at the national average (whereas poor children in traditional schools typically score much lower than the average). For example, at P. S. 146, one of the schools in Harlem, the fourth grade read at three months above the national median, and more than a year above the median of 15 other East Harlem schools. Thus open schools achieve some measure of success even when traditional criteria are employed. And of course open schools achieve considerable success in nontraditional areas as well: Silberman presents many examples of the excitement, spontaneity, and serious intellectual work that characterize these schools.

Open schools make sense, and they can work. They are what we need for all children.

---

[3] It is interesting to note that in the 1960s poor blacks played no small role in educating the rest of America, including social scientists, about the nature of social and political reality in the country. This was a time when compensatory education was trying to help the blacks!

WHAT PSYCHOLOGISTS CAN DO

What can psychologists do to promote the necessary revolution in education? First, they can continue to pursue basic research into the development of the child. Education should in part be based on an accurate view of children's intellectual development, their modes of learning, their social interaction, their personalities. Insofar as basic research contributes to the general understanding of children, it will be valuable for educators. And obviously, the better the research, the more valuable it will be.

All this may be a truism, but there are nevertheless several points worth emphasizing. One is that basic research of the most unlikely kinds can be valuable for education. For example, who would have thought that an esoteric and technical study of children's use of the copula and other grammatical forms would have important implications for educational practice? Yet Labov's work is indeed important, indeed revolutionary. Some students of psychology are too quick to consider some types of research as "irrelevant" because they seem to have no immediate application or because they are conducted in the laboratory or because they are too technical. This is a mistake. It does not matter whether research has immediate application or whether it is conducted in the laboratory or whether it is technical. All that matters is whether the research is good—whether it contributes to an understanding of children.

Another point is that psychologists doing basic research or teaching it can make a greater effort to communicate their discipline to educators, particularly teachers. Of course teachers usually take courses in child psychology while they are in college, and that is desirable. But after that point, teachers typically work in isolation and are forced to discontinue their own education in child psychology just when they need it the most. Psychologists should accept the responsibility of providing for the continuing education of teachers. This is most effective, I think, when it takes place in an informal manner in the teacher's classroom. The teacher wants to interpret his own students' behavior in psychological terms, and the psychologist may be able to help him do this. Such a situation may be of as great a benefit to the psychologist as to the teacher. Teachers often have something to teach psychologists, and so does the observation of children in classrooms. At the same time, teachers should not expect psychologists to solve their problems. Psychologists may know something about children, but they know little about the details of educational practice. That is the teacher's business.

Second, psychologists can contribute to educational reform by conducting basic research into educational problems. While it is hard to define this type of research in any rigorous way, we may consider a few examples, the first being the case of reading. In recent years, Eleanor Gibson, Harry Levin, and several other psychologists (for a review, see Levin and Williams, 1970) have performed basic investigations into the psychology of reading. Their research focuses on such issues as the basic perceptual skills involved in the act of reading, the manner in which grammatical information affects reading, and the like. In general, the research attempts to provide a thorough analysis of the cognitive operations which underlie reading. This is a most difficult task which presents many challenging problems for experimental psychologists. The research is basic in that it contributes to the understanding of a fundamental issue: What exactly does the child learn when he learns to read? This approach is clearly different from most educational research which generally attempts to determine whether one method for teaching reading is more effective than another.

A second example is provided by recent research into children's mathematical thinking. Earlier in this chapter we discussed Jane's and Peter's performance on a variety of mathematical problems. We saw that their performance was remarkably complex and that any theory of their understanding of mathematics must be correspondingly complex. Again, research of this sort presents an interesting challenge for cognitive psychologists. The basic question is this: What is the nature of the child's mathematical understanding?

Basic research of this type is not only scientifically intriguing, but may eventually have important practical applications as well. For one thing, if we have a sound idea of what reading or mathematical understanding involves, we may then be able to develop useful procedures for testing the child's achievement in these areas. As I have tried to demonstrate, current standard tests are not generally based on an accurate conception of what children learn and as a result are not very useful. If an accurate conception were available, then it should be possible to construct useful assessment procedures. In other words, educational measurement must be based on a sound theory of children's academic knowledge, and to arrive at this theory we need basic research into educational problems.

Whatever the reasons, research of this type has not attracted the interest of many child psychologists. We may hope that in the future the situation will change.

Third, it is useful for psychologists to conduct new kinds of applied research into educational issues. The problem of evaluation has naturally received much attention in educational psychology. The typical procedure has been to compare several classrooms on a variety of standard tests, taking care to use the proper control groups, statistical procedures, and the like. Evaluational research usually concentrates on "outcome" or "outputs"—the final results as assessed by standard tests. If one class has a higher average score on some outcome measure than does another, the first is considered superior. Thus, evaluational research typically shares many of the assumptions of traditional education—especially the assumption that what is crucial for education is the final "product" or "output."

This approach to evaluation is not suitable for the open classroom. A focus on "outcomes" may be of some value, but it slights many important aspects of education in open schools. It slights such vital intellectual matters as the processes of children's thought and such crucial motivational factors as children's spontaneity, enthusiasm, their performance under conditions of free choice. In brief, evaluational research usually concentrates on what the traditional school considers to be of importance and not on what the open school values.

Psychologists can help to remedy this situation by developing new and more flexible procedures for evaluation. Again this is no simple task. Some of the most interesting features of education—for example, a child's delight—are the hardest to conceptualize and measure. But the enterprise of open schools requires our best efforts.

Although potentially important, psychology's contribution should be kept in proper perspective. It should be clear that education is far more strongly influenced by political, moral, and economic factors than by psychological research. Innovations will not be accepted and implemented if they run counter to current beliefs, threaten social institutions, and require more financial support than the public is willing to give. Genuine reform in education thus requires a major transformation of the public consciousness. We can only hope that psychology will contribute in some small way to this transformation.

references

Anderson, H. H., "Domination and Social Integration in the Behavior of Kindergarten Children and Teachers," *Genetic Psychology Monographs*, 1939, *21*, 287–385. Cited in P. Minuchin, B. Biber, E. Shapiro, and H. Zimiles. *The Psychological Impact of School Experience*. New York: Basic Books, 1969. P. 129.

Ashton-Warner, S., *Teacher*. New York: Simon and Schuster, 1963.

Baughman, E. E., and G. W. Dahlstrom, *Negro and White Children*. New York: Academic, 1968.

Bayley, N., "Comparisons of Mental and Motor Test Scores for Ages 1–15 Months by Sex, Birth Order, Race, Geographical Location, and Education of Parents," *Child Development*, 1965, *36*, 379–411.

———, "Consistency and Variability in the Growth of Intelligence from Birth to Eighteen Years," *Journal of Genetic Psychology*, 1949, *75*, 165–96.

Bee, H. L., F. V. Van Egeren, A. P. Streissguth, B. A. Nyman, and M. S. Leckie, "Social Class Differences in Maternal Teaching Strategies and Speech Patterns," *Developmental Psychology*, 1969, *1*, 726–34.

Beilin, H., "Perceptual-Cognitive Conflict in the Development of an Invariant Area Concept," *Journal of Experimental Child Psychology*, 1964, *1*, 208–26.

———, J. Kagan, and R. Rabinowitz, "Effects of Verbal and Perceptual Training on Water Level Representation," *Child Development*, 1966, *37*, 317–29.

Bereiter, C., and S. Englemann, *Teaching Disadvantaged Children in the Preschool*. Englewood Cliffs, N.J.: Prentice-Hall, 1966.

Bernstein, B., "Social Class and Linguistic Development: A Theory of Social Learning," in A. H. Halsey, J. Floud, and C. A. Anderson, eds.,

Education, Economy, and Society. New York: Free Press, 1961. Pp. 288–314.

——, "A Sociolinguistic Approach to Socialization: With Some Reference to Educability," in F. Williams, ed., *Language and Poverty.* Chicago: Markham Publishing Co., 1970. Pp. 25–61.

BINET, A., and T. SIMON, *The Development of Intelligence in Children.* (E. S. Kite, trans.) Vineland, N.J.: Publication of the Training School, 1916.

BOWER, T. G. R., "Discrimination of Depth in Pre-Motor Infants," *Psychonomic Science,* 1964, *1,* 368.

BROPHY, J. E., "Mothers as Teachers of Their Own Preschool Children: The Influence of Socioeconomic Status and Task Structure on Teaching Specificity," *Child Development,* 1970, *41,* 79–94.

BROTTMAN, M. A., "Language Remediation for the Disadvantaged Preschool Child," *Monographs of the Society for Research in Child Development,* 1968, *33,* 8 (Ser. No. 124).

BROWN, R., *Social Psychology.* New York: Free Press, 1965.

CAZDEN, C. B., "The Neglected Situation in Child Language Research and Education," in F. Williams, ed., *Language and Poverty.* Chicago: Markham Publishing Co., 1970. Pp. 81–101.

CHALL, J., *Learning to Read: The Great Debate.* New York: McGraw-Hill, 1967.

CHOMSKY, N., "Discussion of Miller and Ervin's Paper," in U. Bellugi, and R. Brown, eds., "The Acquisition of Language," *Monographs of the Society for Research in Child Development,* 1964, *29* (Ser. No. 92), 35–39.

COLEMAN, J. S., et al., *Equality of Educational Opportunity.* Washington, D.C.: U.S. Government Printing Office, 1966.

CONRAD, H. S., and H. E. JONES, "A Second Study of Familial Resemblance in Intelligence. Environmental and Genetic Implications of Parent-Child and Sibling Correlations in the Total Sample," *39th Yearbook, National Society for Student Education,* 1940, Part II, 97–141.

CRANDALL, V. J., and A. PRESTON, "Patterns and Levels of Maternal Behavior," *Child Development,* 1955, *31,* 243–51.

CREMINS, L., *Transformation of the American School.* New York: Vintage, 1961.

CRONBACH, L. J., *Essentials of Psychological Testing* (2nd ed.). New York: Harper and Row, 1960.

DENNISON, G., *The Lives of Children.* New York: Random House, 1969.

DEUTSCH, M., et al., eds., *The Disadvantaged Child.* New York: Basic Books, 1967.

DEUTSCH, M., and B. BROWN, "Social Influences in Negro-White Intelligence Differences," *Journal of Social Issues,* 1964, *20,* 24–35.

DIXON, T., and D. HORTON, eds., *Verbal Behavior and General Behavior Theory.* Englewood Cliffs, N.J.: Prentice-Hall, 1968.

FEATHERSTONE, J., "The Primary School Revolution in Britain," *New Republic* (reprint). First published in the *New Republics* of August 10, September 2, and September 9, 1967.

FREEBERG, N. E., and D. T. PAYNE, "Parental Influence on Cognitive Development in Early Childhood: A Review," *Child Development,* 1967, 38, 65–87.

FRIEDRICHS, A. G., T. W. HERTZ, E. D. MOYNAHAN, W. E. SIMPSON, M. R. ARNOLD, M. D. CHRISTY, C. R. COOPER, and H. W. STEVENSON, "Interrelations among Learning and Performance Tasks at the Preschool Level," *Developmental Psychology,* 1970, in press.

FURTH, H. G., *Piaget for Teachers.* Englewood Cliffs, N.J.: Prentice-Hall, 1970.

————, *Thinking Without Language: Psychological Implications of Deafness.* New York: Free Press, 1966.

GETZELS, J. W., and P. W. JACKSON, *Creativity and Intelligence.* New York: John Wiley, 1962.

GIBSON, E. J., *Principles of Perceptual Learning and Development.* New York: Appleton-Century-Crofts, 1969.

GINSBURG, H., and S. OPPER, *Piaget's Theory of Intellectual Development.* Englewood Cliffs, N.J.: Prentice-Hall, 1969.

GINSBURG, H., M. E. WHEELER, and E. A. TULIS, "The Natural Development of Academic Knowledge: The Case of Printing and Related Graphic Activities." Final report to the Office of Education, 1971.

GLADWIN, T., and W. STURTEVANT, eds., *Anthropology and Human Behavior.* Washington, D.C.: Anthropological Society, 1962.

GLASMAN, L. D., "A Social-Class Comparison of Conceptual Process in Children's Free Recall." Unpublished doctoral dissertation, University of California, 1968. Cited in A. R. Jensen, "How Much Can We Boost I. Q. and Scholastic Achievement?" *Harvard Educational Review,* 1969, 39, 113.

GOLDEN, M., and B. BIRNS, "Social Class and Cognitive Development in Infancy," *Merrill-Palmer Quarterly,* 1968, 14, 139–50.

GOLDSCHMID, M. L., "The Relation of Conservation to Emotional and Environmental Aspects of Development," *Child Development,* 1968, 39, 579–90.

GOODNOW, J. J., "A Test of Milieu Effects with Some of Piaget's Tasks," *Psychological Monographs,* 1962, 76 (No. 555), 1–22.

GREENFIELD, P. M., "On Culture and Conservation," in J. S. Bruner, R. Olver, and P. M. Greenfield, *et al., Studies in Cognitive Growth.* New York: John Wiley, 1966. Pp. 225–56.

HALSEY, A. H., J. FLOUD, and C. A. ANDERSON, eds., *Education, Economy, and Society.* New York: Free Press, 1961.

HERNDON, J., *The Way It Spozed to Be.* New York: Simon and Schuster, 1968.

HERSHENSON, M., "Visual Discrimination in the Human New Born," *Journal of Comparative and Physiological Psychology,* 1964, 58, 270–76.

HERTZIG, M. E., H. G. BIRCH, A. THOMAS, and O. A. MENDEZ, "Class and Ethnic Differences in the Responsiveness of Preschool Children to Cognitive Demands," *Monographs of the Society for Research in Child Development,* 1968, 33 (Ser. No. 117).

HESS, R. D., and V. SHIPMAN, "Cognitive Elements in Maternal Behavior," in J. P. Hill, ed., *Minnesota Symposia on Child Psychology,* Vol. 1. Minneapolis: University of Minnesota Press, 1967, 57–81.

————, "Early Experience and Socialization of Cognitive Modes in Children," *Child Development,* 1965, 36, 869–86.

HOLT, J., *How Children Fail.* New York: Pitman, 1964.

HONZICK, M. P., J. W. MACFARLANE, and L. ALLEN, "The Stability of Mental Test Performance between Two and Eighteen Years," *Journal of Experimental Education,* 1948, 18, 309–24.

HUGHES, M., *et al.,* "Development of the Means for the Assessment of the Quality of Teaching in the Elementary Schools," Office of Education, Cooperative Research Project No. 353. Salt Lake City: University of Utah, 1959. Cited in P. Minuchin, B. Biber, E. Shapiro, and H. Zimiles, *The Psychological Impact of School Experience.* New York: Basic Books, 1969, P. 129.

HUNT, J. McV., *Intelligence and Experience.* New York: Ronald Press, 1961.

INHELDER, B., and J. PIAGET, *The Growth of Logical Thinking: From Childhood to Adolescence.* New York: Basic Books, 1958.

JENSEN, A. R., "How Much Can We Boost I. Q. and Scholastic Achievement?" *Harvard Educational Review,* 1969, 39, 1–123.

JONES, L. V., "A Factor Analysis of the Stanford-Binet at Four Age Levels," *Psychometrika,* 1949, 14, 299–331.

KELLEY, T. L., R. MADDEN, E. F. GARDNER, and H. C. RUDMAN, *Stanford Achievement Test, Directions for Administering, Intermediate I Arithmetic Tests.* New York: Harcourt Brace Jovanovich, 1964.

KLAUS, R., and S. GRAY, "The Early Training Project for Disadvantaged Children: A Report after Five Years," *Monographs of the Society for Research in Child Development,* 1968, 33 (Ser. No. 120).

KOCH, K., *Wishes, Lies and Dreams.* New York: Chelsea House Publishers, 1970.

KOHL, H., *36 children.* New York: New American Library, 1967.

KOZOL, J., *Death at an Early Age: The Destruction of the Hearts and Minds of Negro Children in the Boston Public Schools.* Boston: Houghton Mifflin, 1967.

KUHN, T. S., *The Structure of Scientific Revolutions.* Chicago: University of Chicago Press, 1962.

LABOV, W., P. COHEN, C. ROBINS, and J. LEWIS, "A Study of the Nonstandard English of Negro and Puerto Rican Speakers in New York City," Final Report, U.S. Office of Education Cooperative Research Project No. 3288. New York: Columbia University, 1968. Mimeographed, 2 volumes.

LEE, E. S., "Negro Intelligence and Selective Migration: A Philadelphia Test of the Klineberg Hypothesis." *American Sociological Review,* 1951, 16, 227–33.

LENNEBERG, E. H., *Biological Foundations of Language.* New York: John Wiley, 1967.

LESSER, G. S., G. FIFER, and D. H. CLARK, "Mental Abilities of Children from Different Social-Class and Cultural Groups," *Monographs of the Society for Research in Child Development,* 1965, 30 (Ser. No. 102).

LEVIN, H., and J. P. WILLIAMS, eds., *Basic Studies in Reading.* New York: Basic Books, 1970.

LEWIS, O., *La Vida.* New York: Random House, 1966.

LOBAN, W. D., *The Language of Elementary School Children.* Champaign, Illinois: National Council of Teachers of English, 1963.

———, *Problems in Oral English.* Champaign, Illinois: National Council of Teachers of English, 1966.

McNEILL, D., "The Development of Language," in P. H. Mussen, ed., *Carmichael's Manual of Child Psychology,* Vol. 1. New York: John Wiley, 1970, 1061–1152.

McNEMAR, Q., *The Revision of the Stanford-Binet Scale.* Boston: Houghton Mifflin, 1942.

MERMELSTEIN, E., and L. S. SCHULMAN, "Lack of Formal Schooling and the Acquisition of Conservation," *Child Development,* 1967, 38, 39–52.

MILNER, E., "A Study of the Relationship between Reading Readiness in Grade One School Children and Patterns of Parent-Child Interactions," *Child Development,* 1951, 22, 95–112.

MINUCHIN, P., B. BIBER, E. SHAPIRO, and H. ZIMILES, *The Psychological Impact of School Experience.* New York: Basic Books, 1969.

MUSSEN, P. H., ed., *Carmichael's Manual of Child Psychology,* Vol. 1. New York: John Wiley, 1970.

NEWMAN, H. H., F. N. FREEMAN, and K. J. HOLZINGER, *Twins: A Study of Heredity and Environment.* Chicago: University of Chicago Press, 1937.

OPPER, S., "Intellectual Development in Thai Children." Doctoral dissertation, Cornell University, 1971.

PALMER, F. H., "Early Intellective Training and School Performance. Summary of NIH Grant HD-02253." Unpublished manuscript, 1969.

————, "Socioeconomic Status and Intellective Performance among Negro Preschool Boys," *Developmental Psychology,* 1970, 3, 1–9.

PERKINS, H., "A Procedure for Assessing the Classroom Behavior of Students and Teachers," *American Educational Research Journal,* 1964, 1, 249–60. Cited in P. Minuchin, B. Biber, E. Shapiro, and H. Zimiles, *The Psychological Impact of School Experience.* New York: Basic Books, 1969.

PIAGET, J., *The Child's Conception of Number.* (C. Cattegno, and F. M. Hodgson, trans.) London: Routledge & Kegan Paul, 1952a.

————, *The Moral Judgment of the Child.* (M. Gabain, trans.) New York: Harcourt Brace Jovanovich, 1932.

————, *The Origins of Intelligence in Children.* (M. Cook, trans.) New York: International Universities Press, Inc., 1952b.

————, *Play, Dreams, and Imitation in Childhood.* (C. Cattegno, and F. M. Hodgson, trans.) New York: Norton, 1951.

PRICE-WILLIAMS, D. R., "A Study Concerning Concepts of Conservation of Qualities among Primitive Children," *Acta Psychologica,* 1961, 18, 297–305.

RICCIUTI, H. N., "Object Grouping and Selective Ordering Behavior in Infants 12 to 24 Months Old," *Merrill-Palmer Quarterly,* 1965, 11, 129–48.

RIST, R. D., "Student Social Class and Teacher Expectations: The Self-Fulfilling Prophecy in Ghetto Education," *Harvard Educational Review,* 1970, 10, 411–51.

ROBINSON, W. P., "The Elaborated Code in Working Class Language," *Language and Speech,* 1965, 8, 243–52.

ROSENTHAL, R., and L. JACOBSON, *Pygmalion in the Classroom.* New York: Holt, Rinehart and Winston, 1966.

ROTHENBERG, B. B., and R. G. COURTNEY, "Conservation of Number in Very Young Children," *Developmental Psychology,* 1969, 1, 493–502.

SAAYMAN, G., E. W. AMES, and A. MOFFETT, "Response to Novelty as an Indicator of Visual Discrimination in the Human Infant," *Journal of Experimental Child Psychology,* 1964, 1, 189–98.

SCHOLNICK, E. K., S. OSLER, and R. KATZENELLENBOGEN, "Discrimination Learning and Concept Identification in Disadvantaged and Middle-Class Children," *Child Development,* 1968, 39, 15–26.

SEASHORE, H., A. WESMAN, and J. DOPPELT, "The Standardization of the Wechsler Intelligence Scale for Children," *Journal of Consulting Psychology,* 1950, 14, 99–110.

Silberman, C. E., *Crisis in the Classroom.* New York: Random House, 1970.

Sitkei, G. E., and E. C. Meyers, "Comparative Structure of Intellect in Middle- and Lower-Class Four-Year-Olds of Two Ethnic Groups," *Developmental Psychology*, 1969, *1*, 592–604.

Spence, J. T., and M. C. Dunton, "The Influence of Verbal and Non-Verbal Reinforcement Combinations in the Discrimination Learning of Middle and Lower Class Children," *Child Development*, 1967, 38, 1177–86.

"State Reports on Ithaca Schools," *Ithaca Journal*, Ithaca, New York, May 29, 1970, P. 11.

Stevenson, H. W., A. M. Williams, and E. Coleman, "Interrelations among Learning and Performance Tasks in Disadvantaged Children," *Journal of Educational Psychology*, 1971, 62 (in press).

Stodolsky, S. S., and G. Lesser, "Learning Patterns in the Disadvantaged," *Harvard Educational Review*, 1967, 37, 546–93.

Templin, M. C., *Certain Language Skills in Children: Their Development and Interrelationships.* Minneapolis: University of Minnesota Press, 1957.

Terman, L. M., and M. A. Merrill, *Revised Stanford-Binet Intelligence Scale: Third Edition.* Boston: Houghton Mifflin, 1960.

Terrell, G., K. Durkin, and M. Wiesley, "Social Class and the Nature of the Incentive in Discrimination Learning," *Journal of Abnormal and Social Psychology*, 1959, 59, 270–72.

Tuddenham, R. D., "The Nature and Measurement of Intelligence," in L. Postman, ed., *Psychology in the Making.* New York: Knopf, 1962. Pp. 469–525.

Tulving, E., "Theoretical Issues in Free Recall," in T. Dixon, and D. Horton, eds., *Verbal Behavior and General Behavior Theory.* Englewood Cliffs, N.J.: Prentice-Hall, 1968. Pp. 2–36.

Unikel, I. P., G. S. Strain, and H. E. Adams, "Learning of Lower Socioeconomic Status Children as a Function of Social and Tangible Reward," *Developmental Psychology*, 1969, *1*, 553–55.

U.S. Commission on Civil Rights, *Racial Isolation in the Public Schools,* Vol. I. Washington, D.C.: U.S. Government Printing Office, 1967.

Vernon, P. E., "Environmental Handicaps and Intellectual Development: Part I," *British Journal of Educational Psychology*, 1965a, 35, 9–20.

———, "Environmental Handicaps and Intellectual Development: Part II," *British Journal of Educational Psychology*, 1965b, 35, 117–26.

Wachs, T. D., I. E. Uzgiris, and J. McV. Hunt, "Cognitive Development in Infants of Different Age Levels and from Different Environmental

Backgrounds: An Exploratory Investigation," *Merrill-Palmer Quarterly,* 1971 (in press).

WALK, R. D., and E. J. GIBSON, "A Comparative and Analytical Study of Visual Depth Perception," *Psychological Monographs,* 1961, 75 (15).

WASSERMAN, M., *The School Fix, NYC, USA.* New York: Outerbridge and Dienstfrey, 1970.

WILLIAMS, F., ed., *Language and Poverty.* Chicago: Markham Publishing Co., 1970.

ZIGLER, E., and E. C. BUTTERFIELD, "Motivational Aspects of Changes in I. Q. Test Performance of Culturally Deprived Nursery School Children," *Child Development,* 1968, 39, 1–14.

ZIGLER, E., and J. DeLABRY, "Concept Switching in Middle-Class, Lower-Class, and Retarded Children," *Journal of Abnormal and Social Psychology,* 1962, 65, 267–73.

ZUNICH, M., "Relationship between Maternal Behavior and Attitudes Toward Children," *Journal of Genetic Psychology,* 1962, 100, 155–65.

index